Toxic

Our stress response system is magnificent – it operates beneath our awareness, like an orchestra of organs playing a hidden symphony. When we are healthy, the orchestra plays effortlessly, but what happens when our bodies face chronic stress, and the music slips out of tune? The alarming rise of stress-related conditions, such as heart disease, diabetes, and depression, show the price we're paying for our high-pressure living, while global warming, pandemics, and technology have brought new kinds of stress into all our lives. But what can we do about it?

Explore the fascinating mysteries of our hidden stress response system with Dr. Wulsin, who uses his decades of experience to show how toxic stress impacts our bodies; he gives us the expert advice and tools needed to prevent toxic stress from taking over. Chapter by chapter, learn to help your body and mind recover from toxic stress.

Dr. Lawson R. Wulsin is a Professor of Psychiatry and Family Medicine at the University of Cincinnati, specializing in the care and study of the mind and body (psychosomatic medicine). He provides psychiatric care in medical and psychiatric settings, training physicians to combine family medicine and psychiatry. His passion is translating the science of stress into terms that help people to understand and treat their stress-related conditions.

"In this brilliant and eminently readable book, Lawson Wulsin highlights the role of chronic stress and trauma as the most burdensome (and neglected) public health issue in our society, affecting multiple organ systems in the body that have a profound impact on our social, financial, and medical well-being. Illustrated with vivid case histories, Wulsin presents the complex and multidimensional impact of toxic stress, while providing us with exciting and life-altering evidence-based solutions."

"Wulsin's *Toxic Stress* is a *tour de force*. His writing style is refreshing and vivid, and his understanding of contemporary research is encyclopedic and up to date. This is a terrific book."

"Dr. Lawson Wulsin's new book is authentic in its timeliness. The nation and indeed the world are going through a so-called *syndemic* of toxic stress. We are struggling to adapt to synergistically interacting epidemics – viral pandemics; climate change disasters; refugee displacement; nativistic political movements; racial, ethnic, and sexual orientation animus; adverse childhood experiences; opioid addiction; suicide; the widening gulf between rich and poor; religious scandals; the assault of social media on truth and trust; and of course the seemingly endless wars – to name but a few. The resulting toxic stress, which Dr. Wulsin discusses so effectively in his fine book, is at work in stealth, like fashion planting the poisonous seeds of metabolic syndrome that will result in the plethora of stress-related diseases that comprise the bulk of human suffering and morbidity and mortality around the globe. Dr. Wulsin impressively analyzes the burgeoning science of mind, body, and lifestyle medicine that has emerged to fight this syndemic. We do have evidence-based practices and practice-based evidence in medicine that can help our neighbors and our communities build their resilience and robustness. Dr. Wulsin's book provides us with a pro-active prescription that can help us promote health and, in some cases, prevent the stress-related illnesses described in this book. In this way, this book is both timely and hopeful."

"*Toxic Stress* towers over other books that offer help for stressed-out readers. This insightful and compassionate guide by a renowned medical scientist and practicing physician examines the myriad toxic stressors to which all of us are being exposed in the twenty-first century, and the many ways in which toxic stress can affect our health and well-being. It goes on to explain how we can build resilience to prevent stress-related illnesses and how to find help for stress-related problems. And it leaves us with good reasons to believe that we can find ways to thrive, even when we're swimming in a sea of troubles."

Kenneth Freedland, PhD, Editor-in-Chief of *Health Psychology*

"We know we are stressed. Thank goodness, we now have a valuable, easy-to-read, practical book that helps us figure out what to do about it! Lawson Wulsin, MD is a highly experienced and knowledgeable psychiatrist who writes with humor and great insight. Using interesting clinical vignettes and understandable explanations and solutions, this book is a must-read for those who want to improve the connections between stress–behavior–illness ... and get healthier!!"

Michelle B. Riba, MD MS, author of *College Psychiatry: Strategies to Improve Access to Mental Health*

"An easy-to-read and very catchy book which is, to many doctors, opening the black box of the complex bodily stress system and the risk factors for toxic stress. Healthcare professionals tend to ignore the problem of toxic stress despite it causing a range of diseases and also premature death. This book should be mandatory reading for doctors across the world."

Per Fink, PhD DMSc, Aarhus University Hospital and Aarhus University

"This is an erudite, informative, and engaging book written by a master physician. Dr. Wulsin draws on both his own experience as a clinician and his thoughtful reading of the research literature to tell a story that we all need to hear: the story of stress. He explains how, whilst stress is an integral and inescapable part of all our lives, it can become toxic and make us ill. He also gives us sound advice about what we, and the healthcare system, should do about it. This is a sound and thought-provoking read for anyone interested in health, whether as patient, physician, or healthcare planner."

Michael Sharpe, MA MD, University of Oxford

"In this fabulous book, it becomes clear *How Stress Is Making Us Ill and What We Can Do About It*. Dr. Wulsin outlines the adverse health consequences of toxic stress, but also the various advantages of resilience when coping with adverse life situations. Readers will find helpful information about how mind and body influence each other, which is especially important when stress levels are high. You will also find useful examples of how to talk about stress with your doctor, family, and friends. This inspiring book makes stress understandable for a broad range of readers and also for healthcare professionals."

Willem J. Kop, PhD, Emeritus Editor-in-Chief of *Psychosomatic Medicine*

TOXIC STRESS

How Stress Is Making Us Ill
and What We Can Do About It

Lawson R. Wulsin, MD

CAMBRIDGE
UNIVERSITY PRESS

CAMBRIDGE
UNIVERSITY PRESS

Shaftesbury Road, Cambridge CB2 8EA, United Kingdom

One Liberty Plaza, 20th Floor, New York, NY 10006, USA

477 Williamstown Road, Port Melbourne, VIC 3207, Australia

314–321, 3rd Floor, Plot 3, Splendor Forum, Jasola District Centre, New Delhi – 110025, India

103 Penang Road, #05–06/07, Visioncrest Commercial, Singapore 238467

Cambridge University Press is part of Cambridge University Press & Assessment, a department of the University of Cambridge.

We share the University's mission to contribute to society through the pursuit of education, learning and research at the highest international levels of excellence.

www.cambridge.org
Information on this title: www.cambridge.org/9781009306584

DOI: 10.1017/9781009306577

First published 2024

Printed in the United Kingdom by TJ Books Limited, Padstow Cornwall

A catalogue record for this publication is available from the British Library

A Cataloging-in-Publication data record for this book is available from the Library of Congress

ISBN 978-1-009-30658-4 Paperback

Contents

Part IV   Treatment

Part V   Our Next Frontier

Introduction: Your Body's Hidden Symphony

Ashaki is the thirty-three-year-old daughter of a wealthy Black CEO of an IT consulting firm in Los Angeles. She doesn't like to admit it, but she lives at home with her parents. Ten years earlier, just shy of graduating from USC, she was hospitalized and diagnosed with bipolar disorder, for which she's been taking three medications a day for ten years.

What does Ashaki have in common with Luke, the twenty-eight-year-old former coal miner in West Virginia, a White guy, who has been on food stamps and unemployment for two years since being laid off from the mine? He dropped out of high school in tenth grade, and neither of his parents made it past eighth grade.

And what does this former coal miner have in common with Yoko, the forty-five-year-old tenure-track East Asian languages professor who is a happily married (most of the time) mother of two? A woman of Asian heritage. As a child she was repeatedly beaten by her drunk stepfather during third and fourth grades and was raped three times by her first cousin during eighth grade, while her parents lived in Singapore for a year doing mission work. Recently her panic attacks have been well controlled with therapy and medications.

And what does this professor have in common with Arnold, the fifty-year-old White male British civil service accountant who worked for twenty years in London at Whitehall as an administrative officer, never advancing above a lower-level position? Three times he tried for promotions but never made it.

In spite of their differences in age, race, gender, geography, health, and social status, each of these people stands a high risk of dying young.

What sets them on a fast track to dying young? Each of them represents a common group of people who live with persistent or periodically high levels of toxic stress.

Severe mental illness, even among the wealthy and well educated, such as the daughter of the Los Angeles businessman, takes a decade or two off life expectancy.[1] As a Black woman, her exposure to racial discrimination may also add to her burden of chronic stress and risk for early death.[2]

Poverty, both rural and urban, shortens life. Poverty exerts its relentless demands early in the lives of children and persists during their formative years, day after day.

Childhood trauma raises the risks for heart disease, diabetes, severe mental illness, suicide, and early death.[3] These health effects appear early in adult life for people of all races, classes, and nationalities.

And *low social rank* in a tight social order such as the British civil service predicts more chronic illness and early death.[4] This health effect of low social rank has also been observed in animals with complex social hierarchies.

Each of these risks for a shortened life comes to us from sound population studies since the turn of the century. These studies of the social and psychological determinants of physical health present us with alarming associations between events that took place over many years and the later development of physical illnesses severe enough to cause early death.

How can such different challenges for these people lead to a common pathway toward early death?

Severe mental illness, the threat of discrimination of any kind, poverty across generations, the lingering costs of childhood trauma, and the oppressive pressure on the lower ranks of any tight social order provide us with just a few examples of the persistently demanding stressors that may take a sizable chunk of years off our lives. Unlike a traffic accident, an argument, or winning a gold medal, these stressors don't strike and then fade. They hang on with a grip that won't let go.

The list of potential long-lasting stressors is lengthy: incarceration, homelessness, threatening relationships at work or at home, caretaking for a family member with a debilitating condition, job mismatches, sleep deprivation, exposure to pollution, high-crime neighborhoods, substance abuse, culture clashes for immigrants, worry habits and ruminations, loneliness, living alone, chronic pain, and any chronic physical or mental illness.[5]

Any one of these relentless stressors can strain our body's resources over the years, especially if it hits during critical periods of development, such as early childhood or during the frailty of the elder years. The trouble accelerates when these chronic stressors come in bunches, as they often do. Illness leads to poverty, immigration leads to compulsive worrying, job mismatches lead to sleep deprivation, which leads to substance abuse, which leads to threatening relationships at home. One burden becomes many, a train of troubles. No wonder our train of troubles sometimes seems impossible to stop once it gets rolling.

Why do acute stressors generally not cause illness, but chronic stressors can make us sick and hasten death? Why do the sections of the orchestra (our organ systems) continue to play out of tune during chronic stress?

The key paradox here is that acute stressors, if brief, tolerable, and infrequent or predictably regular, help keep our stress response systems fit, tuned up to handle the demands of daily life – a flat tire on the way to work or the babysitter is late. This is good stress because it helps regulate the stress response system, just as regular gentle exercise strengthens and regulates specific muscle groups.

On the other hand, any pattern of stressors that interferes over many months or years (caregiving long term for a loved one, a bad boss and you're stuck in a job you can't leave, childhood trauma and abuse, for example) without allowing the marvelous capacity of our stress response system to recover and self-regulate – any pattern that reduces our resilience – tends to lead eventually to illness.

The Mystery of Toxic Stress

Toxic stress is a black box – a mystery how we end up trapped in it and a mystery how to work our way out. Our COVID-19 pandemic brought the experience of toxic stress into every home, school, and workplace, raising questions once again about the seemingly random ways that stress strikes our bodies and minds, and the ways that resilience often rescues us.

And toxic stress is a mystery not only to those who struggle with stress-related conditions, but all too often toxic stress mystifies the doctors who help them manage these conditions.

What determines who falls ill and who survives or thrives? Why have minorities, the obese, and people with preexisting conditions been among the most vulnerable to severe and lethal COVID-19 infections?

For some this pandemic has delivered the very definition of toxic stress – persistent demands that appear to exceed our resources – and death for millions, more rapidly than any war. For others more lucky or resilient, the coronavirus threat has meant no more than a mild illness or the inconvenience of a miraculous vaccine. For all of us, novel uncertainties about jobs, school, and healthcare ruled our daily lives during this pandemic.

On the other hand, when what threatens us is a predator, a storm, or an argument between siblings about who gets the popsicle, we usually fare well enough. Most of us most of the time face these threats; we manage them, the threats pass, and we recover to face the next hurdle. In fact, clearing these hurdles teaches us, makes us stronger, and builds our resilience. What would we be without them? Managing these kinds of acute stressors grows our resilience by fine-tuning our stress response systems.

But other patterns of stress can cripple us with illness, crush our souls, or kill us young.

Like global warming, the alarming rise in rates of stress-related conditions over the past half-century around the world may be the price we are paying for our high-energy living in the form of these diseases: obesity, diabetes, heart disease, depression, addictions, and autoimmune disorders. What is this trick of nature that turns years of toxic stress into Crohn's disease for one person, multiple sclerosis for another, a heart attack for another? Can a pattern of toxic stress exhaust a pancreas, plug a coronary artery, or inflame an intestinal wall? And what makes some lucky survivors of toxic stress resilient to diseases of any kind?

If you prefer living well to the alternative, it helps to understand the difference between the kinds of stressors that make us grow and the kind that cripple or kill us young. It helps to understand how our stress response systems work and how they fail. Here we are, creators of space shots to Mars, the Internet, and iPhones, yet most of us are still in the dark about the mysteries of our stress response system and the kinds of toxic stress that make us ill.

The hero of this book is our magnificent stress response system, which operates beneath our awareness, like an orchestra of organs playing a hidden symphony, seemingly without effort when we are healthy. What is this hidden symphony, and how does it work, and how does it slip out of tune?

The neuroscience of stress is comparatively young – some say fifty years – and has not yet seeped into the clinical practice of medicine or into our popular culture. In this book, I define the neuroscience of stress as the study of the ways the nervous system coordinates with the other major organ systems to respond to the stressors of daily life.

The Stresses of High-Energy Living

Life is tough, always has been. Evolution has given us a stress response system that is remarkably adapted to coping with many kinds of stressors. And relative to our ancestors, most of us live longer and healthier lives than they did. But in the last century's blink in evolutionary time, our sudden escalation in energy consumption around the world has created stressors that evolution could not anticipate.

- Our sleep can now ignore the day–night cycle.
- We travel enormous distances at great speeds with unlimited frequency.
- Many of us organize our social lives now without villages or extended families to contain us.
- Our volume of communications has risen exponentially, yet many of us cope with loneliness that was unimaginable a century ago, when it was harder to lose touch with those who cared about us.
- Our options for addictive stimulations have never been greater.

These are just some of the novel forces that have conspired to create modern forms of toxic stress despite our having access at the same time to more resources than ever before. We are both blessed and cursed by our high-energy living.

In this book, I focus on the central but often overlooked role of our stress response systems in our most common and costly illnesses, such as diabetes, heart disease, depression, and obesity. Stress is a hot topic in our culture, but a blind spot in most branches of medicine. Most doctors ignore stress or pay it only lip service. Standards of treatment for diabetes and heart disease promoted by our leading medical organizations hardly offer a whisper about stress as a risk factor or a target for treatment.

Yet we know from decades of good neuroscience that severe or persistent stress raises the risks for these common long-lasting illnesses, and toxic stress makes most illnesses harder to treat. We also know that exposure to a lot of adverse experiences in childhood is among the strongest predictors of physical and mental illness in adulthood.

What chance do we have to prevent and manage these illnesses if we don't learn to "see" toxic stress, measure it, and treat it?

Long after persuasive mountains of scientific data have made the case for changing our views about stress, many of us persist with our traditional views of how our bodies work. The culture of modern medicine is built around specialty areas (cardiologists look at the heart, orthopedists fix knees, oncologists treat cancer, for example) with economic investments and turf to protect. The stress response system, as we shall see, respects none of these turf boundaries, and it rules at every level of organization from genes to cells to tissues to organs to individuals to social groups.

And the Big System Is Not Well

Surrounding our individual stress response systems, there is the bigger system of healthcare where we get help. How does the healthcare system determine the ways we treat stress-related conditions? This is a simpler question to answer in countries where healthcare is delivered through a single national health service. In the US, by contrast, where many of the healthcare systems are run as businesses, it is difficult to understand the many ways the many big systems affect our individual stress responses.

The US has consistently ranked in the mediocre range on most international studies of effective population healthcare.[6] The US healthcare culture has, in general, also given low priority to primary care doctors who potentially have the greatest influence on the long-term health of their patients, resulting in low pay and high burnout rates for primary care.

And the US government safety net has picked up the costly pieces neglected by the for-profit and not-for-profit parts of the system, such as the uninsured, the underinsured, those bankrupted by healthcare bills, those denied coverage due to preexisting conditions, and those with chronic mental illnesses. The US healthcare system's problem list is long and expensive, and unique among developed countries.

Paul Starr, professor of sociology and public affairs at Princeton University and former senior healthcare advisor for the Clinton administration, reminds us that the US spends 17.6 percent of its gross domestic product on healthcare, about double the average of 9 percent across other economically advanced societies.[7] The US spends more to get less in terms of good results, and it is the only major advanced society without a national healthcare system. The only partial advance in healthcare reform on a federal level in the US has been the Affordable Care Act of 2010, the target of over fifty efforts to repeal it, all of them unsuccessful (as of 2023).

As we will see in more detail in later chapters, this system of silo-minded, specialty-driven, procedure-focused healthcare for commercial gains tends to ignore improving outcomes for the stress-related disorders that require collaborations across disciplines to achieve incremental gains that prevent and mitigate our most costly common conditions. The US healthcare system reminds us that big systems can present barriers to effective care for stress-related disorders.

Narrowing the Gap

This book tells the stories of people who eventually triumphed over multiple illnesses, beating the odds at a considerable cost by developing a resilience regimen that reversed or slowed the course of these conditions.

I have spent my career providing psychiatric care in medical settings, and I have watched with wonder over the past forty years as the gap between psychiatry and medicine narrowed – a narrowing that has been both painfully slow and promisingly persistent. I have focused my career on this narrowing interface, trying on a daily basis to translate advances in neuroscience into treatment plans that work for patients and their healthcare providers, which in this book means doctors, nurses, and other allied health professionals.

This book profiles the clinicians, the scientists, and the programs that have helped people along the path from toxic stress and illness to health. I explain how the science of the stress response system emerged in fits and starts over the last half-century, building the case for clinical relevance while the practice of medicine often looked the other way.

Fortunately, the tide is changing. In recent years key voices in the reform of healthcare in the US and around the globe have spoken up about the central role of toxic stress in our current epidemics. And in some places the practice of medicine is changing to meet this challenge.

I explore the key dilemmas we face as patients, as providers of healthcare, and as healthcare systems – in the US, quirky like no other system in the world – in our approaches to stress and illness.

Many dilemmas are shared by all nations and cultures, and some pertain to particular nations. Why is the US so peculiarly behind the rest of developed nations when it comes to managing stress-related conditions and saving lives?

My purpose in this book is to sharpen our focus on this mysterious and often invisible thing we call stress, and to clarify how we can think about stress in ways that lead to more effective approaches to common illnesses. Like volcanoes in the ocean, most of the troubles that erupt in our stress response systems lie deep beneath our awareness and go undetected until they take the form of major illnesses.

This book calls for nothing less than a frame-shift, a clearer way of seeing the workings of our stress response system and seeing how dysregulations of that system lead to illness. No book can make this shift in thinking alone, but a good book can guide us to change the way we look for toxic stress and change the way we practice caring for these illnesses.

The overlooking of stress in medicine is a phenomenon of cultural blindness that is similar to our culture's overlooking of global warming. Just as we are waking up to the environmental costs of our high-energy living, we are waking up to the physical and psychological costs as well. There are good reasons why we have not understood our stress response systems as well as we need to, and good reasons why now more than ever we urgently need to face this challenge of toxic stress, both on a personal and on a public health level.

This book aims to show us how we can begin to meet that challenge on an individual level, how we can develop the resilience we need to identify and treat or prevent stress-related conditions. For anyone who is curious about the culture of medicine and healthcare and for anyone fascinated or troubled by the enigma of toxic stress, this book will open that black box and show us the process that transforms distress into a failing heart, brain, or pancreas. And it will show how we can participate in a journey that can move us from reluctant victim to informed expert in our own conditions.

What You Will Learn from This Book

Chapter 1 orients you to the key dilemmas we face in the way we approach stress in our stimulating and consuming culture, in the US and around the world. Recognizing that stress comes in many forms – good, tolerable, and toxic – this chapter describes the size of the problem of toxic stress in a variety of settings and our difficulties identifying the stressors that hurt us.

Chapter 2 spells out why toxic stress remains invisible to most of us, including your healthcare providers. This blind spot is all the more fascinating in the context of the magnitude of the problem of toxic stress, which contributes substantially to poor performance on the major indicators of public health, including death rates.

One complicated and inconvenient truth for modern medicine around much of the world is that we have developed an epidemic of stress-related conditions. This epidemic has been building for decades and will be around when COVID is gone or at least under better control.

Think of the mysterious rise in rates of suicide, depression, and PTSD (posttraumatic stress disorder) over the last three or four decades, beginning in the 1980s. Then think about the rises during the same period of rates of obesity, substance abuse disorders, and ADHD (attention deficit disorder). Then think about the sharp rise in rates of diabetes – now 37 million or one in ten US citizens have diabetes, and a third of our population is on that path with prediabetes. Over half of us are obese. That's never happened before. And it's happening in developing countries now too.

While much of our population is living longer and healthier, too many of us are dying younger. The health gap is widening around the globe.

Another complicated truth – the one that requires this book – is that the stress response system, especially the human kind, is a complex system of systems. Ours is so complex that most doctors avoid thinking about it. We're more comfortable focusing on one organ system or one set of problems.

Medical specialists like me prefer a turf we can know. Trying to understand the stress response system poses the same difficulties as trying to understand global warming or global economics, two other examples of complex systems of systems. If you find this hard to believe, try asking your doctor on your next visit to talk to you about how your stress response system is doing.

Chapter 3 may help with that conversation. It spells out some of the difficulties that stress neuroscientists have faced when studying the stress response system, and it alerts you to some of the difficulties we all run into as we talk about stress in our everyday lives. This chapter cautions us against oversimplifying the story.

No single factor – and certainly not toxic stress – "causes" our most common chronic illnesses. Instead, multiple factors, including toxic stress, drive these processes over long periods. This chapter establishes some terms and frames the journey for exploring how toxic stress drives illness over the lifespan and helps us understand what it takes to develop resilience and keep it.

Our stress response system works well under the best of health, when we're most resilient. As we grow from infancy through adulthood, this complex system of at least nine organ systems develops resilience through redundancy, with plenty of overlap, so one system can support another under strain. In chapter 4, we see what happens from head to toe, whether you're an office worker navigating the demands of daily life or a tipsy lush hearing a scuffling noise in a dark alley.

And in chapter 5 we take a fanciful look at the hidden symphony and see what happens in Usain Bolt's stress response system during his ten-second sprint as the world's fastest human. He is one of the master conductors of the stress response system, with his speed as proof of his prowess. An appreciation of the orchestration required to mount this everyday miracle provides the background for understanding the way persistent and severe stressors disturb this process.

Chapter 6 spells out the features of the dysregulated stress response system that distinguish it from the healthy system. Here, most of all, is where it pays to appreciate the current state of what stress neuroscience can tell us, and what we still need to know. Like oceanographers aware of the enormity of our uncharted waters, we know we have just a few good maps of a few aspects of the stress response system. By focusing on some of the better-studied pathways by which your experience of toxic stress transforms into an illness or disease, we can appreciate the need to think about multiple organ systems over long periods of time, often a lifetime, and to understand the biological, psychological, and social aspects of stress.

Once we appreciate the complexities of the dysregulated stress response system, we can begin to understand how toxic stress turns into illness. Chapter 7 describes six pathways: genes and epigenetics, adverse childhood experiences, high-risk health behaviors, autonomic imbalance, hormonal turmoil, and low-grade inflammation. And each one of these pathways may weave through the others, eventually creating a Gordian knot of dysregulations that may be experienced by you as fibromyalgia, depression after a heart attack, or a perplexing and debilitating tremor in your hands and legs.

Toxic stress, like global warming, is a state of imbalance and impairment in a system that has lost its ability to reset itself. It's brittle now, instead of flexible and resilient and self-regulating. This is just one reason why it makes sense, when evaluating one medical problem in one organ system, to look for related problems in other organ systems or other aspects of a person's psychological or social life.

How fast or slow does this process of dysregulating the stress response system go until a disease emerges? Chapter 8 builds a model for how this process works over the lifespan. One of the lessons is that the apparently sudden onset of diabetes or heart disease in our fifties or sixties can often be traced to subtle dysregulations that began years before, even decades before, invisible to the unsuspecting and asymptomatic (no apparent symptoms). And the pace with which we develop many common disease processes is accelerated by persistent stressors.

Toxic stress accelerates illness and speeds up aging. Are you on a fast track to future illness and early death? And when is the best time to intervene? The answers are not simple, but they begin with knowing the questions to ask.

And answering those tough questions begins with measurement. Good management in all branches of medicine begins with good measurement. One of the biggest barriers to recognition, prevention, and treatment of stress-related disorders has been the troubled waters of stress measurement.

Chapter 9 describes the dilemmas faced by anyone who tries to carefully measure the stress process to guide clinical care. Some of these dilemmas are rooted in the complexities of the stress response system itself. And this chapter describes the options for simple stress measurements available to you and your doctor right now.

More than ever before, most of us now have access to devices that can measure aspects of our stress response systems (you may already have a Fitbit or Apple Watch on your wrist or a smartphone in your pocket) – processes that are otherwise invisible to us – and we now have apps to help us make sense of these new data.

More important than any single measurement of stress is the stress profile, as we see in chapter 10. Modern medical practice depends heavily on profiles, but so far we have no standard stress profile. This chapter presents a few of the options for creating a stress profile that can guide your decisions about risks and treatment planning. It then distills the complexities of stress measurement to three types of assessments: subjective distress, lifetime exposures and responses, and physiologic measures of toxic stress responses.

This chapter discusses the need for psychological consulting services that provide stress profiles, similar to the services that currently provide neuropsychological profiles for people with learning disabilities, head trauma, or early dementia, for example, to guide their treatment plans. For the one in five of us who has been exposed to toxic stress, this stress profile could provide the starting point for a personalized approach to reducing our risks for stress-related illnesses.

Of course, there's no point in creating a stress profile unless we believe we can do something about it. Can you do anything about your specific collection of financial, social, and physical troubles? Many of the most oppressive sources of stress, such as poverty, crime, pollution, childhood trauma, and abusive family members, appear beyond our control. Is it possible to retrain a dysregulated stress response system and regain some sense of resilience after being sick with a severe condition? How long does that process take?

Chapter 11 describes five programs that have been well studied and widely used in some medical settings. Each of these programs exemplifies the effective retraining of specific aspects of the stress response system and the slowing or reversing of the course of an illness. All of them, as well as the emerging trend toward what we now call Lifestyle Medicine, depend on mastering the puzzling process of changing entrenched high-risk health behaviors, sometimes in the context of treatment with medications or surgery. These examples teach us what we can expect to invest in these approaches and what we can expect to reap as health benefits.

Where should people with stress-related health conditions go for help? What might you do differently now if you and your doctors can add up the multiple toxic stressors in your life? Most often the best place to begin and end is with your primary care doctor. Depending on your stress profile and the conditions you're managing, you may see a number of specialists along the way, but if you suspect that stress plays a guiding role in your health, start with your primary care doctor.

You don't have to imagine how that conversation might go. In chapter 13 I present ways you can have that conversation with your doctor. The more you understand the stress lingo, how the stress response system works, and how stress-related illnesses develop, the better these conversations will go.

In the final chapter I take a look forward at what we can do next to improve how we manage toxic stress. As individuals we can create more effective conversations about stress and illness and we can practice habits that help retrain our stress response systems after periods of dysregulation. As nations debate public health priorities, I argue that the time has come to put toxic stress at the top of the list. We can no longer ignore the size and the health impact of our current burden of toxic stress and stress-related conditions.

In the appendix of this book, I imagine what the ideal Resilience Center would look like and how it would function. With such centers, we can relieve the public health burden of toxic stress and common stress-related conditions. Such treatment centers could play a role in a larger public health initiative targeting toxic stress. Imagine that!

Let's begin this journey with a day in the life of Ted Daley, just a regular guy who is unselfishly helping scientists understand toxic stress.

Part I

The Problem

Part I

The Promise

Toxic Stress – You Won't See It Coming (Neither Will Your Doctor)

Ted Daley awoke one August morning to air that felt oddly tropical – both warm and cool, a whisper of a moist breeze – so convincingly tropical that he thought for a second that he was back in the Rift Valley, in Kenya, facing another day of teaching in his Peace Corps assignment. Then the hum and the gentle vibration of the blood pressure cuff tightening around his upper left arm awoke him further to the reality that what he was facing was another August morning in Pittsburgh.

Eight years before, he had risen every day to that tropical air and the racket of birds and the challenges of teaching in that village classroom dimly lit with one lightbulb. His Peace Corps project had shown him he had the grit to maybe even make teaching in impoverished countries a calling.

Instead, he tuned in to his wife's job worries at PNC Bank and the rush of getting Josh off to daycare and the productivity metrics awaiting him at his office in Carnegie Mellon University's PR and marketing department. Waking to this comparatively "corporate" life, he felt a long way from that Rift Valley classroom.

Alice had not yet stirred, and Josh was quiet too, so Ted released his CPAP mask strap and flipped the machine switch off. As he hoisted himself from bed, he felt heavy, the heaviness of unfinished sleep and the possibility of another drag through the day on six, maybe seven broken hours. He tapped the PDA digital device and answered the same routine of questions: Mood level? Stress level? Fatigue level? Who did you talk with in the last hour? Nobody.

This was day two of four (Tuesday and Wednesday, Saturday and Sunday) during which Ted would help a team of stress researchers at the University of Pittsburgh, under the direction of Tom Kamarck, PhD. As a volunteer in the SHINE study, Ted would collect data on how he responded to daily stressors.[1] Just a day in the life of Ted Daley, actually four days as a test subject in a vital research study.

At thirty-eight, Ted felt pretty good. He knew he was a bit overweight, but he carried it well. He wished he slept better. Last year his doc had diagnosed him with sleep apnea (thus the CPAP machine), but other than that, he'd never had medical problems and didn't take any meds. Ted felt reassured to know he was participating in one of the best stress response studies in the country, yet what did they know about how he handled hearing his brother had died? How high was his heart rate while sleeping last night? Is his blood pressure up because this study is more of a hassle than he expected?

Stress Runs the Show

Although we're usually unaware of it, most of what we do minute to minute in our daily lives is motivated by our instincts for stress relief. Rest and sleep relieve fatigue. Dressing relieves the insecurity of nakedness. Eating relieves hunger. Fighting is an effort to appease fear. Overeating, a shot of whiskey, or a deep drag on a joint take the edge off our anxiety, we hope. Talking cuts down on doubt, or disconnection, or loneliness. Learning reduces the uncertainty of not knowing. Evenings, weekends, and vacations ease the toll of work.

Under the surface actions of doing our jobs, going on a date, or taking care of chores, we are also toiling daily in the nether regions of our minds to avoid the troubles we expect from our past experiences and from the wilds of our imaginations – the universal troubles that come with rejection, failure, ignorance, poverty, fatigue, hunger, misery, pain, and illness.

When our efforts at stress relief fall short, we try something else – such as trying again, praying, cursing, slapping a dashboard, slapping the nearest cheek, or bingeing on a bag of Doritos or drinking a six-pack. We do this not because we're clever, but because, like all animals, we've evolved to seek stress relief, fast. We seek relief intuitively with our animal brains, deep beneath the cortex of consciousness, because that capacity to attend reflexively to stress relief has meant the difference between survival and death for our species, and for most others.

Stress, and how we manage our stress, runs the show, day and night. This chapter looks at how coping with stress is such a fundamental part of our lives that we forget it is so.

And Madison Avenue knows this about us. The advertising industry learned early to appeal to our appetites for stress relief. We buy stress relief every time we buy groceries, cigarettes, life insurance, a semester of college, a new pair of shoes, and most things we carry out of our corner drugstore, including pills, sunglasses, and M&M's.

Hollywood knows this about us too. Our appetites for the struggles of others, and our cravings for vicarious resolution, feed the bank accounts of the movie industry, the book industry, and theaters around the world. Storytelling exercises our appetites for the challenges of life and for stress relief. We willingly spend much of our time and money seeking these safe experiences of controlled stress exposures. Stress is a social experience. Stress is a mental challenge. And stress is often a physical exertion.

Stress in our culture, now that we have perhaps more choices than ever in the history of the human race, is both universal to all of us and increasingly particular to each of us. In spite of our modern comforts and buffers, we're all still threatened by pain, fatigue, isolation, illness, violence, and death. Yet we vary widely in how we respond to these universal threats.

The same crying baby that invites solace for the doting grandmother may bring rage to its overwhelmed teenage mother. The repeated updates in yet another weather report on a distant hurricane far out in the South Pacific may bore the wife of the man who obsesses over storm reports for several hours a day in his desperate efforts to protect his family in Cincinnati from storms in the South Pacific.

The Big Four Sources of Stress in America

Every year since 2007 the American Psychological Association has conducted a population-based survey of adults with the help of the Harris Poll called *Stress in America*, tapping current perceptions of stress and its consequences. Consistently the four sources of stress that we have worried most about have been work, money or the economy, family responsibilities, and health. These have not changed during the COVID pandemic.

The good news from the 2021 report was that three-quarters of us continued to fare well in spite of the pandemic. Overall self-reported stress levels held steady for most of the population – a testament to resilience among the majority. That's good news unless you're one of nearly a quarter of us who have been struggling so much we've had trouble making basic decisions, like eating and working. That's good news unless you earn less than $50,000, unless you're a Millennial or Gen Xer or Gen Zer, unless you check your devices constantly, or unless you happen to be a woman or a parent or a caretaker, all of whom consistently report disproportionately high stress levels.[2]

Among those who earn under $50,000, worrying a lot about money roughly doubles our chances of "sedentary or unhealthy behaviors" such as watching more than two hours of TV a day (thank you, Netflix and Hulu), surfing the Internet, napping or sleeping more, eating more, drinking alcohol, and smoking. Unhealthy means these behaviors in high enough doses for long enough substantially raise our chances for serious illness, such as obesity, diabetes, and heart disease.

Note that worse than poverty is worrying about poverty. Not making much money may be about half as toxic as worrying a lot about not making much money. The stress of poverty is tough on health, and worrying makes it tougher. Perceptions count as much as reality.

Gen Zers, Millennials, and Gen Xers report higher stress levels than their parents or grandparents. Does that suggest that life is more stressful now than in previous generations, or is the experience of aging a good teacher of stress management? Maybe we learn to worry less, or we worry more effectively as we age.

Some recent studies of ratings of stress across the life cycle show trends toward higher stress in the first half of life (ages one to forty) than in the second half,[3] but it's difficult to compare the stresses of child-rearing, for example, to the stresses of retirement, illness, and aging.

Life has always been stressful, and always will be, every day. And the demands shift throughout life. Negotiating family conflict may get easier as negotiating three flights of stairs gets tougher. Technically, getting out of bed is stressful: it requires overcoming gravity, whether you're a Manhattan princess or a Kalahari bushman.

At its easiest, daily life presents us with a series of small and manageable challenges, most of which we take care of without a thought or fret: dressing, eating, walking, completing routine tasks at work, cleaning, settling into bed at night. Our modern American culture has made more resources available to us for managing stress than ever before in the history of the human race. Is that reassuring? Probably not.

Stress around the Globe

At various times in my career I've worked in clinics in Cameroon, Honduras, and Kenya. I've taught the principles of mental health care in low-resource countries as part of the Global Health Curriculum of our family medicine residency at the University of Cincinnati. And I've conducted research on maternal depression in the aftermath of the 1998 Hurricane Mitch in Honduras.

Working across these language and culture barriers has reminded me in every setting that, in spite of our apparent differences, we struggle alike around the globe. We struggle to survive, to work, to play, to love and be loved, to avoid being left out or alone.

I've spent the bulk of my life in the US, and this is where I've practiced medicine the most, so this book focuses on examples from the US. But the range of variation around the globe is often instructive. For example, many of the best health outcomes on a national level are found in countries with established national healthcare systems (for example, in all the northern European nations, Spain, Canada, Taiwan, and New Zealand). Countries with poor human rights records, such as North Korea, Syria, Turkey, and Pakistan, have relatively poor health indicators. The US, by contrast, has good human rights records but no national healthcare system, and our health indicators are pretty mediocre.[4]

Cultures influence the experience of stress. In 1994 when Rwanda erupted into civil war, the national language Kinyarwanda had no word for traumatic stress, and no tradition for how to talk about the effects of watching your neighbor hack your mother and your child to death with his farm machete. They soon invented a vocabulary for talking about this process of recovering from these local and national traumas. How we experience stress depends in part on the linguistic as well as clinical resources of our cultures.

In South Africa in the late 1990s President Nelson Mandela asked Archbishop Desmond Tutu to create a procedure for reconciliation to set a national example for the repair of the atrocities of apartheid. This example established a deliberate alternative to the Nuremburg Trial approach and sowed the seeds for the later creation of The Forgiveness Project, a worldwide collection of accounts about how victims and perpetrators of all stripes have found ways to reconcile their differences in daily life.[5] This is global learning at its best about the management of the stresses of toxic relationships.

Until the 1990s brought us the Global Burden of Disease Study, we had no sound way of knowing how much illnesses varied around the world. As we will see in the next chapter, one of the lessons we've learned since then in studying global cultures is that stress-related disorders are not limited to highly developed countries, but rather are common and universal around the world, contributing substantially to the global burden of disease.[6]

Toxic Stress Is Bigger Than You Think

How big a problem is toxic stress, the kind of stress that makes us ill? This is not a simple question to answer. It varies with time and definitions of stress and points of view. As we'll see in more detail later, we begin by focusing on those people who live with a pattern of severe and persistent stress. They are the people most likely to suffer stress-related illnesses. These are your friends and neighbors, coworkers, parishioners, the checker at the grocery store, your daughter's husband, the Uber driver, maybe you.

One lens on this question comes to us from the Centers for Disease Control and Prevention's program on the Behavioral Risk Factor Surveillance System, which has been collecting data on adverse childhood experiences since 2009. People who reported four or more adverse experiences in childhood were at highest risk for adult illnesses. I'll introduce you to someone who fits this category.

But how many people fit this category? More recent data from the same program found that about one in six men and women reported four or more adverse events in childhood.[7] They carry a high risk of illness into adulthood. That's one good estimate of how big our problem of toxic stress might be: one in six.

Another angle on the size of the toxic stress problem comes from the number of adults who live with multiple chronic conditions. What is more stressful than living with a chronic illness? Multiple chronic illnesses. Surprisingly, 19 percent of adults in the US live with four chronic conditions, and 12 percent live with five or more.[8] Again, this group is about one in every six adults, most of them elderly. Many of them live with severe and persistent stress. And the rates of chronic illnesses around the world have been the focus of recent public health reports and initiatives.[9]

A third way to guess about how many people live with toxic stress comes from the data on poverty. Daily life in poverty is the living definition of stress – namely, demands that exceed the resources available, day after day. Officially, the US poverty rate in 2021 was 11.6 percent. Globally it was closer to 9 percent.[10]

These three sets of stressors or stressful exposures – childhood adversity experiences, multiple chronic conditions, and poverty – each capture a segment of our population exposed to extremes of persistent stress, likely with lots of overlap. It seems reasonable to assume that about one in five adults in the US have been or are currently exposed to the kinds of toxic stress that will lead to illness and early death, and this estimate is likely to be true for many other countries.

Meet Teresa

Teresa Langford grew up scrappy in Gurley, Alabama, a small country town near Huntsville, the third of four children. Her parents worked as dairy farmhands. Unlike her two sisters, Teresa spent most of her early years keeping up with her older brother, "Buggy," and playing his games.

When she was eight, her parents separated. Her father took Buggy to live with him, and her mother took the three girls to Florida, looking for work. Within months her mother landed in prison for writing bad checks for food, so the girls were moved back to Gurley with Teresa's grandparents for the four months of the prison sentence. How does a nine-year-old girl manage losing touch with her father, her brother, and then her mother in less than a year?

After her mother got out of prison, Teresa and her sisters were taken back to Florida to find a woman named Winnie had moved in with them. And Winnie slept in her mother's bed. This was rural Florida in the 1970s. Eventually Teresa understood that her mother's sleeping with Winnie was part of what made it hard for her mom to keep steady work.

They moved around a lot. "Between second and sixth grade I went to more schools than I can count. Sometimes we slept in the car," she remembers. Teresa learned young how to run and win and scramble for safety whenever and wherever she could. She was tough and scrappy and proud of it.

At the age of thirty-four, after two tours in the Army, Teresa's routine checkup at the Cincinnati VA primary care clinic showed she had high blood pressure, high cholesterol, and obesity, a condition called metabolic syndrome – alarming at that age. Other than chronic pain in her left knee, Teresa had no complaints. She was tough and upbeat, an example of resilience against adversity – at what cost she had no idea.

So far in her life, she had coped with several major life stressors, only one of which was noted in her health record. Though her father had died at fifty of a stroke and her brother, Buggy, had died at twenty-nine from a heart attack and her mother had had three heart attacks by age fifty-three, it would take a near-death experience with necrotizing pancreatitis at age forty-six before Teresa would seek help for stress. To both patient and doctor, stress as a source of trouble was invisible.

Teresa Langford grew up with more than her share of childhood adversity. By the time she showed up for a routine physical exam at age thirty-four, she already had multiple risk factors for what would become within her next decade six chronic conditions. She and her doctors never saw it coming.

Teresa's story unfolds as this book progresses. You will come to know how life's adversities showed up as toxic stress in Teresa's health and how she and her doctors (I am one of them) helped her tap into her natural resilience to overcome several types of adversity. Teresa has asked me to share her story with you.

The Lightbulb Changed Our Sleep–Wake Cycle

The caveman and my grandfather had their worries. And they died younger than we do today. One torrential rainstorm in the night could drown the sleeping caveman, and one streptococcal infection to a wound from a car accident could take my grandfather's life at thirty-five, leaving five kids and a wife with no life insurance.

I, in my modern life and house, sleep on the second floor where floods can't drown me, and I have health insurance to buy any antibiotic or vaccine that will save me and my family from streptococcus, AIDS, COVID, and the other bugs that might shorten my life.

Does my safe living save me from big worrying? I wish. I know too much. I know that bugs like staphylococcus can develop drug resistance, and instead of floods I can worry about thieves – they have ladders now and they pick locks and shoot fast and drive getaway cars.

In my lifetime what has changed are the types and patterns of stress we're exposed to, our society's awareness and capacity to talk about stress, our widespread access to electric and fossil fuel power, and the big money that industry has learned to make from our growing capacity to spend money on our worries.

Until my grandfather's generation in the early 1900s, humans all over the world rose and fell asleep by the light of the sun. Today in the rural villages of most developing countries where power is scarce or unreliable, the sun still rules, forcing most people to sleep most of the night.

So consider for a moment what the advent of the lightbulb and all that came with it in the early 1900s has done to our day–night rhythms. In developed countries insomnia is now as common as the common cold, sleep medications bring billions of dollars to big pharma, and every academic medical center has a sleep lab.

Add to the lightbulb the exciting and sometimes enraging eleven o'clock news ritual, bedtime Kindle reading, cell phones beeping at the bedside with every incoming tweet and Instagram, and Netflix bingeing – it's a wonder and a testament to our resilience that we sleep at all.

Add all the hours we spend sitting in chairs – the opportunities to ruminate on our troubles have mushroomed in the past century. Evolution did not prepare us for this level of stimulation and rumination, day and night.

These daily challenges to our circadian rhythms take their toll. After months of insomnia, my grouchiness or yours eventually drifts into patterns of work errors and inefficiencies and insecurities that could lead to anxiety or depression that then lead to demotions and job loss. Like alcohol, sleep deprivation in heavy enough doses can make us untrustworthy, erratic, or even mildly dangerous.

Yet most of us will continue to cheat on our sleep as a way of life. We choose to pay the price. It's part of our culture. Everyone does it.

That's a new type and pattern of stress that didn't dog our species until the last century brought us bright lights and urban living. The more recent arrival of screens and devices has jacked up that all-hours stimulation load, day after day, night after night.

Evolution has equipped us well enough for managing acute stress. We instinctively rise to the threat of a brush fire or the attack by a rival band or a car accident. We run or fight or gather our families, and then we recover. We bear a child in labor and then recover. With the help of our tribe, usually, we recover more fully and faster than if we try to cope alone.

Recovering – our ability to return to our resting state – is the key to resilience, the key to preventing the series of acute stressors of daily life from becoming the crushing load of unremitting toxic stress.

According to Eric Nestler, MD, PhD, Director of the Friedman Brain Institute at the Icahn School of Medicine at Mount Sinai, and one of the leading researchers on the genetics of stress, "Through evolution we were only really exposed to acute stresses. Either you survived predator stress or famine or drought, or you didn't. The kind of chronic social stress that we've created for ourselves is very different and not subjected to evolutionary pressure.... All these things that happen to us in response to acute stress are good for us.... With repeated chronic sustained stress, that's when these systems begin to go awry."

By "these systems" he means the many organ systems that make up the stress response system. It's repeated, sustained stress without recovery that kills us young – the relentless toll of daily life in a dangerous neighborhood, the barking hallucinations of schizophrenia over many years, or the persistent toll of caring for a disabled family member while managing our own multiple chronic conditions – anything that accelerates the progression to and through hypertension, diabetes, heart disease, and obesity-related conditions to early death.[11]

Yet where do we draw the lines between good stress, tolerable stress, and toxic stress? Where I draw those lines will be different from where you draw them, and neither of us will benefit from treatment unless our doctors draw those lines with us.

Frame Shot Measurements

That morning, our study participant Ted removed the blood pressure cuff but showered and shaved with the Actiwatch wristband and Sensewear armband on his right arm. Then he slipped the cuff onto his left arm and pulled on yesterday's pants, clipping the cuff pump onto his belt at his right hip. It had become a stretch to get his belt buckle into the third hole, and today, with that extra clip for the cuff pump and the PDA in his back pocket, his pants felt tight.

He hitched the tube from the cuff on his upper left arm around his back and across his waist, plugging it into the pump on his belt over his right hip. Then he pulled his T-shirt on over the cuff and tube, put on a fresh dress shirt and the tie Alice had made from that Tanzanian kikoi. With his watch on his left wrist and the cuff on his left arm and the Actiwatch band on his right wrist and the Sensewear band on his right arm, all of them with their Velcro straps pulled snug, Ted was strapped and ready to go.

Today he had a couple of meetings and two minor deadlines, a lighter day than usual, dull compared to his peak times of year. Maybe the most stressful thing today, he thought, was going to be reporting to the stress researchers every hour. Like the day before, at random times he'd have to tell the app how good or bad he was feeling, and what he was doing, and who he'd been talking with, and what he was thinking or worrying about.

The process, called ecological momentary assessment, collects data beamed to a central website through the PDA and the Body Media Sensewear armband and the Actiwatch wristband. Together these devices record his heart rate and blood pressure and physical activity and sleep patterns and daily events or hassles.

Five times today he would be prompted to pop a dry white pellet into his mouth and suck on it for a minute until it swells with enough of his spit to collect his salivary cortisol, a measure of variations in his stress hormone level. He would drop the swollen pellet into a labeled tube, write the time and date on the label, cap it, and later set it into its slot in the study box in his fridge at home.

Twice today, once in the morning and once in the evening, he would prick his finger and drip five drops of blood onto five circles on a piece of blotter paper and bag that paper and store it in the study box in his freezer, this one to check on IL-6 levels, a measure of variations in his inflammatory responses to daily stress.

Effective treatment of chronic conditions requires measurement. As sophisticated as measurement in medicine has become in the past hundred years – think of MRIs of the brain and genetic profiles for personalized cancer treatments – we still base many of our treatment decisions on the slightest slices of life. What does a single fasting glucose tell us about the range of blood sugars over the past month? A hemoglobin A1C gives a better summary of the average glucose levels. What has your blood pressure been like during your sleep, your jogging, your sexual encounter with your mistress during last Thursday's lunch hour?

Your doctor will only know what your pressure is in her office, and she will use those numbers to decide about your next dose adjustment. Most of what we know about our stress response systems comes from a few isolated measures, which is like trying to guess the content of a movie from a few frame shots. Modern medicine has a lot to learn from more sophisticated measurement of the stress response system over the course of our days and nights. When we can see the whole movie, we're likely to change our definitions of stress, illness, and our treatments. Until then the measures we have are better than no measures at all.

Ted Daley hopes to get more of a window into his stress response system than most of us get. If he's lucky, he will see a four-day slice of his life, months later, when the data have been analyzed and interpreted and presented to him. He's not sure what it will tell him, but it's bound to reveal something useful, he hopes.

Stress to Straitjacket

The slow march of civilization over the centuries has brought most of us a safer, kinder, less violent, and more predictable way of life.[12] Yet we worry because a certain dose of anxiety is necessary for survival. If we're not worrying, we may not be alert enough to dodge the next fist or insult or bus.

Some experts propose that nature has evolved us to expect the worst, to be always on alert, ready to react to the next challenge. We only rest when we're reassured of our safety, something we subconsciously check on many times each day. No wonder we all feel so insecure. We procreate and live longer if we live that vigilant way, and the practice of effective and efficient worry is an acquired skill.[13] If some kinds of worry save us, then what kinds of worry slowly kill us?

Ian is a meticulous man with an accounting job and a pregnant wife. She forced him to come see me as her due date approached because she was alarmed at the hours he was spending on the Weather Channel and on his weather apps.

As he faced fatherhood for the first time, his lifelong fear of storms escalated, and he now spent many hours a day and night (five or six, sometimes more, at the expense of his job as a CPA) ruminating over the weather stories and data, trapped in the unspoken conviction that vigilant worry could protect his new and fragile family. His wife and his boss had tried to snap him out of it with threats of losing his job and divorce, but Ian couldn't – he was stuck and scared.

A hundred years ago Ian would have had a harder time tapping into this endless well of alarming information about distant disasters. He would have studied the sky more than others, maybe prayed harder and more often, but he would have been forced to attend to his physical labors for many hours of the day, usually in the company of his fellow tribesmen, and the dark quiet of long nights bedded close to his family would have imposed many hours of sleep and recovery time.

Disrupted sleep and information overload – two modern sources of chronic stress responses – are unlikely by themselves to derail Ian onto a path of chronic illness in his early thirties. But play it forward. If he toughs it out, or if he skips seeking help, or if he loses his job and his wife, he soon could face the added burdens of unemployment, poverty, and housing insecurity (she said, "You choose the tube, you move!"). That's fertile ground for fast-food by day, fast beer by night to put him to sleep, and no one to soothe his worrying.

Let that combination of stressors play out for a few years, and Ian may then find himself talking with his primary care doc, if he can afford one, about pills for high blood pressure or heartburn pills or WeightWatchers or antidepressants.

Is this how it started for his father, who dropped dead on his riding mower one Saturday when Ian was ten and Dad was forty-five? Who knows? The family never talked about it. Ian told me, "Right as he was rounding the jungle gym, I watched him fall off the mower like a clown and never get up again." Ian, stuck in his straitjacket of anxieties, was caught in a vicious cycle of managing stress in unhealthy ways.

Spotting the Blind Spot

So Ian went to see his primary care doctor about all this stress. Ian's chief complaint was insomnia. His doctor, who was in her late thirties, with special interests in diabetes care and developmental disabilities, gave him a fifteen-minute appointment that included a history of his recent insomnia, a physical exam, routine lab work, suggestion for an over-the-counter drug for the associated heartburn, counseling about diet and exercise and sleep hygiene, a referral to a therapist for his concerns about his job and marriage, and a follow-up appointment with her in three months.

(Ian explained he had had trouble with sexual side effects on an antianxiety pill a few years ago, so he didn't want to risk taking an anxiety or sleeping pill if he didn't have to.) He avoided mentioning the embarrassing flap with his wife about his time on the Weather Channel, since that happened mostly during the day.

For a first visit about a stress-related condition, this sounds pretty good, right? Why is it not good enough?

Ian walked out of this appointment with no measure of the severity of his insomnia or his anxiety with which to gauge progress or worsening in the coming interval between appointments. He had no grasp of his condition, other than the general term *insomnia* or *anxiety*, which is like saying heart disease without saying what kind. And neither he nor his doctor understood whether he needed low- or high-intensity mental health treatment based on his other risk factors for stress-related conditions. Neither of them mentioned his father's death by heart attack at forty-five.

Is Ian's anxiety a self-limiting simple problem or an urgent, complex, and chronic problem? Is three months soon enough to reevaluate? Compared to most people his doctor sees, Ian has just one condition, takes no medications, and is not likely to need precious medical resources. Watchful waiting seemed good enough.

Seasoned primary care doctors see a lot of stress-related conditions and become adept at sorting out the self-limited acute stress conditions from the more chronic and toxic ones. Reassurance, watchful waiting, and brief treatment of symptoms take good care of most acute stress. These clinical encounters generally go well.

But ask a group of seasoned primary care doctors how confident they are about changing persistent stress-related health behaviors such as long-term insomnia, binge eating, smoking, or physical inactivity. Most clinicians will groan or change the subject. They don't do well, and they know it.

Primary care clinicians are lucky if they get 20 percent of their smoking patients to quit and stay smoke-free six months later.[14] Their numbers are no better for meaningful and sustained weight loss for the obese. If you as a clinician expect to fail four out of every five tries at behavior change, you will soon try less often. You will turn instead to interventions that reward your efforts and avoid those that frustrate you.

By the time these patients and their stress-related conditions get to the specialists, they are often part of a complex set of multiple chronic illnesses and behaviors that defy single interventions and fifteen-minute appointments. And yet, primary care is the setting where most people should and could get the most timely and effective help with toxic stress. If only we could see it.

Ian and I will learn in later appointments with me that he has obsessive compulsive disorder and attention deficit disorder, in addition to the scar of having watched his father die when Ian was ten, an experience that convinced him you can't be too careful in this world. His anxiety symptom severity rating, if he had completed one during that first primary care visit, would fall in the severe range on a self-report symptom scale. That finding would have surprised Ian and his primary care doctor, since Ian's a handsome, impeccably well-dressed, tightly wrapped guy who is good at sparing others the terrors of his inner world.

The weather is not the only thing Ian obsesses about. He has five other active targets for his obsessions and compulsions that interfere mostly with his relationship with his wife: dirt, money, time, food, and the law. And by the three-month follow-up visit scheduled by his primary care doctor, their baby will be two months old. Ian may be living at home, or he may not. He may be employed, or he may not. When Ian told his wife about his doctor's assessment and recommendations, she yelled at him, "If you don't see that therapist this week, you and your Weather Channel are moving out!"

The Mind Matters for Seeing Our Blind Spot

Teresa Langford was a frequent patient at the Cincinnati VA Medical Center for thirteen years before any of her doctors referred her to me for psychological help. Stress had never been a target of discussion for her or her doctors.

At the age of thirty-four when she first came for a routine checkup, she had dealt with these major stressors: parental separation at age eight, her mother's imprisonment for four months, untreated ADHD, a decade of alcohol abuse from ages thirteen to twenty-three, her closet gay orientation in the military, including a cover marriage to a man for fifteen years, a rape at twenty-one by a superior officer that went unreported, a crush injury to her left kneecap leading to her discharge from the Army, and the sudden death of her brother when he was twenty-nine.

But nobody was counting such events as stressors back then. Only the death of her brother was noted by her primary care doctor.

And at age forty-six it was only the threat of having to apply for disability after her four months in the hospital that prompted her first appointment with a psychologist. Then she and her team of clinicians began to piece together her story.

Let's take a close look at what we know and don't know about the stress–illness relationship, as scientists, doctors, and patients. I am among those who believe severe and persistent stress responses influence the course of common chronic illnesses. Not all my medical colleagues agree. You can judge for yourself.

Nearsighted Scientists, Perched on the Elephant

I was well into the third decade of my career as a psychiatrist working in an academic medical center when I was first introduced to this blind spot about stress as a major public health problem. In 2003 I watched Stevo Julius, MD, a Hungarian-born specialist

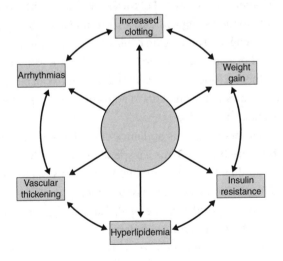

Figure 2.1 A common factor for common conditions?

in hypertension at the University of Michigan, talk to a group of health psychologists and other mental health specialists at the annual meeting of the American Psychosomatic Society, which happened to be in Barcelona that year. This man knew how to live and work and talk across cultures.

He introduced us to this blind spot through a series of slides, which I will summarize with three of my own. In the first, we see six common medical problems arranged in a circle around a central spot. Arrows pointing outward indicate that the spot has some effect on thickening of the heart and blood vessels, arrhythmias of the heart, high cholesterol and lipids, insulin resistance, weight gain, and the tendency to blood clotting.

In Figure 2.2, we add the names of the targets of some of our most common public health initiatives: heart disease, hypertension (high blood pressure), stroke, atherosclerosis (thickening of heart arteries), diabetes, obesity, and sudden death. And the arrows around the outside make the point that each of these illnesses and their mechanisms also affect the others.

Many patients have several of these conditions. The overweight patient with diabetes, high blood pressure, and high cholesterol has become a cliché in primary care clinics. These patients take a pill to lower blood pressure, a statin to lower lipids (cholesterol), insulin to lower glucose, blood thinners to reduce the risk of clotting, and anti-arrhythmics or pacemakers to adjust irregular heartbeats, like so many fingers in the dike.

Dr. Julius said to us, this audience of cutting-edge neuroscientists, "These are the problems we spend our public health dollars on. What do they have in common? What is this black spot?" He waited. We gave him an embarrassed silence.

"Sympathetic overdrive," he said, "and low parasympathetic tone. We call that autonomic imbalance."

The term *autonomic imbalance* is medspeak for an excessive or dysregulated stress response in the autonomic nervous

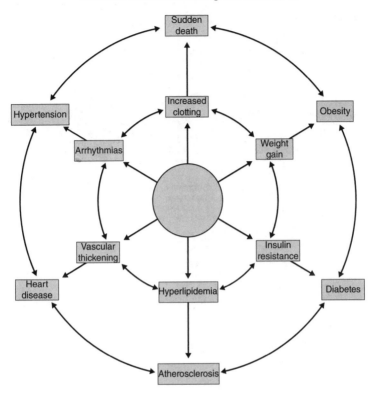

Figure 2.2 Public health targets.

system – something we all knew about in the lab but had not thought of in those public health terms. Here was a hypertension expert schooling us in our specialty of psychosomatic medicine. He told us about how commonly hypertension physicians overlook the meaning of high resting heart rates, one simple indicator of sympathetic overdrive and low parasympathetic tone.

To simply define for you, the autonomic nervous system balances the exciting effects of the sympathetic nerves with the relaxing effects of the parasympathetic nerves. Too much sympathetic activity for long periods is considered autonomic imbalance.

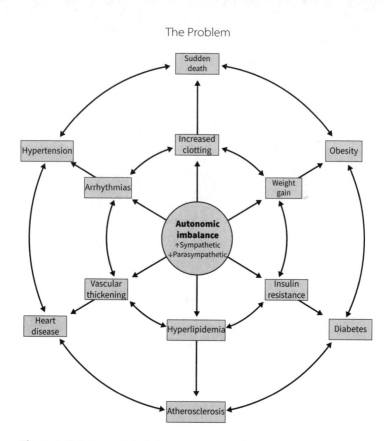

Figure 2.3 Autonomic imbalance: a common factor.

And Dr. Julius reminded us that a resting heart rate of 90 beats per minute triples the early death rate, compared to a resting heart rate of 60 beats per minute. Doctors know this, but we overlook these alarming resting heart rates for a variety of reasons – the focus of later chapters.

The lesson I've taken from Dr. Julius's talk and his work, a lesson I've tested many times since in my own talks and published papers, is that the culture of modern medicine is the creation of many nearsighted scientists, each perched on the elephant of the stress response system. Most of us clinicians are so preoccupied with our own organ systems and our stable of diseases and our specialty areas of medicine that we can't see or appreciate the big picture, the whole stress response system. We forget that our survival as individuals and as a species has been built on the whole of the stress response system.[1]

The history of medicine is marked by the discoveries of our scientific blind spots and by the invention of new ways of seeing what had previously kept disease processes invisible to doctors.

The infectious disease process, for example, was revealed in the nineteenth and twentieth centuries by technology for identifying and studying bacteria and viruses.

The early stages of most cancers were invisible to clinicians until the mid-twentieth century when X-rays and other body imaging techniques and blood tests showed us the growth of cancers.

Until sophisticated brain imaging developed in the last decades of the twentieth century, the brain and its many disorders were invisible, except to the most astute neurologists. Is it plausible that the stress response system and stress-related disorders are one of our current blind spots?

Dismissing the Mind

As a former English major and a closet science phobe during my first year of medical school in 1974, I felt like an outsider, maybe an impostor. So did plenty of my classmates, but, unlike them, after two years I took a leave from medical school, unsure whether I belonged in the culture of medicine. Then, after a year of odd jobs, writing, and an enlightening three months working in a missionary hospital in Cameroon, I came back and found a fit during a two-month summer elective on the psychosomatic medicine unit, a ten-bed specialty inpatient service at University Hospital in Cincinnati.

This unit offered me a grounding point within medicine in the way it approached the tough ones, the patients with complex sets of problems that the other services could not manage, such as the medically unstable woman with anorexia nervosa who abused diet pills and swallowed pens, as well as the abrasive chronic pain patient with brittle diabetes and borderline personality disorder.

Caring for these people on this unit required a challenging blend of behavioral analysis, aggressive medical regimens, token economies (in other words, bribing them to practice good behaviors), and psychopharmacology (drugs to change their brain chemicals) – for me an exciting mix of disciplines and languages and skills. This was my first taste of the integration of the care of the mind and the body, and it was thrilling for both what it accomplished and what it promised.

But that experience proved to be a tease, a small island in the sea of medicine and a promise shared by only a few. In the rest of our medical center, and across the country, the territory inhabited by those who cared for the mind (psychiatry and psychology) was usually set far from those who cared for the body, set apart both physically and socially from the rest of medicine in separate hospitals, community mental health centers, psychiatrists' offices, and the separate funding streams of state mental health systems.

In my first academic job in the late 1980s, I ran the psychiatric consultation service providing psychiatric services to patients on medical and surgical wards at the University Hospital in Cincinnati. That experience taught me a lot about the pecking order of the culture of medicine. It was impressive how some of the brightest among these academic physicians could be so dismissive about the workings of the mind and the brain. Many still are.

In the 1980s the brain was still a black box to many doctors, and disturbances of the mind even more of a mystery. Descartes's legacy and the division between the mind and the body lent an intellectual immunity to those who preferred to dismiss the work-ings of the mind and brain from the workings of the liver or the heart or the pancreas.

In the coronary care units and the surgical intensive care units, the mind did not matter much. Not in those days. The stigma that buried mental illness from general awareness kept the stress response system buried as well. Out of sight and out of mind.

I've spent my career reaching across this gap between psychi-atry and the rest of medicine. I often moved in one workday from an internal medicine clinic at the VA to an outpatient psychiatry practice at the university to a family medicine clinic at a commu-nity hospital.

Although among my colleagues in psychology and psychiatry, stress is a big deal – the focus of assessments and a target for drug and talk therapy – among my primary care colleagues a few find stress fascinating, but most don't. In fact, they steer clear of stress as too messy, complex, and unrewarding. Most of them don't read the journals or go to the professional meetings on stress and illness that I find so fascinating and promising. With good reason, most primary care docs stick with what they do well.

The Birth of Stress Neuroscience in Humans and Zebras

It's tempting for those of us who read a lot about it to take the neuroscience of stress as definitive evidence that chronic stress is lethal, and leave it at that. Too much of the wrong kind of stress for too long is bad for our health. On one level we know this is true, as true as the promise of the sunrise in the morning. We have plenty of folklore as well as plenty of science to support this belief.

Yet a generation ago it was neither common wisdom nor accepted dogma in medical circles that stress plays an important role in illness. And many doctors still dismiss stress as a minor contributor to illness. They do this with impunity in part because stress neuroscience is still young and remains too easily overlooked by the rest of medicine. And, as we will see in the next chapter, answering the question whether stress contributes to illness is a tricky task that in some ways defies the traditional scientific method.

A few good books over the years have summarized the state of stress research at the time, beginning with Hans Selye's *The Stress of Life* (1956). In 1994 Robert Sapolsky published what is still the most readable, entertaining, and comprehensive review of the scientific evidence for the ways stress leads to illness: *Why Zebras Don't Get Ulcers*.

Sapolsky's *Zebras*, revised for a third edition in 2004, is 515 pages, the last nearly 100 of which contain scholarly notes and references to original studies. This diligent scholar gives us both a short and a long answer: zebras don't get ulcers and other stress-related conditions because they don't worry the way we do. Most of their stress comes through acute threats to their safety. Sapolsky also spells out in detail the long answer: the disruptions in our human stress response system that can lead to disorders in the endocrine, metabolic, cardiovascular, immune, and central nervous systems.

This mountain of evidence has continued to build since then, making a strong case for chronic stress as a major contributing factor to the onset and the progression of a range of our most common chronic conditions, specifically coronary heart disease, type 2 diabetes, obesity, and major depression.

The recent growth of stress research has been substantial enough to support the emergence in the last half-century of at least fourteen professional societies and seven scientific journals devoted to exploring the relationship between stress and health or illness.

For at least two generations a large and increasing number of scientists have devoted their careers to this fascinating and elusive question. Divisions of health psychology and psychosomatic medicine have become commonplace in most sizable academic departments of psychology and psychiatry in our universities and around the developed world. During my lifetime the value of the stress–illness relationship has become harder for modern medicine to ignore.

Not Whether, But How

The evidence for a link between toxic stress and specific illnesses is now persuasive on many levels – from large-scale studies of stress in human populations down to laboratory and observational studies of people and animals, and down further to cellular mechanisms of stress and disease that are common across species. And the contribution of severe and persistent stress is not trivial.

The magnitude of the stress effect on illness outcomes in many studies is comparable to the magnitude of traditional risk factors for heart disease and diabetes.[2] If you immerse yourself in this evidence, the urgent question becomes no longer *whether* chronic stress contributes to specific illnesses, but *how*.

When you ask how, you learn what you don't know or what you prefer to ignore. When you ask how the sun rises, you learn that it doesn't literally rise. And once you learn about earth turns instead of sunrises, you can make sense of climate changes and the complexity of the ecology of our planet in our solar system, and many other wonderful truths.

Therefore, when we ask how certain patterns of stress exposures and responses make us sick, we also learn what we don't know or tend to ignore. We see the gaps more clearly, and we learn how we might change the role of chronic stress responses to prevent or relieve illness.

The Other Way to Think and See

While stress neuroscientists carve their niches in the mountain of evidence supporting the role for chronic stress in the development of coronary artery disease or diabetes, what does stress look like in the real world of primary care and specialty medicine? Where does stress fit into the management of these illnesses?

The American Diabetes Association lists these risk factors for diabetes:

- Family history of diabetes in first-degree relatives (mother, father, sister, brother)
- High blood pressure
- Age
- Race/ethnicity
- Male gender
- Physical inactivity
- Body mass index (greater than 25).

No sign of any measure of stress on this list. And the list of diabetes risk factors has looked like this for many years.

Now check the American Heart Association. If you dig around for the risk factors for heart attacks on their website, you find a list that looks like this:

Major factors that can't be changed:
Age
Male gender
Heredity (family history of heart disease, ethnicity)

Major factors that can be changed:
Smoking
Cholesterol (LDL, HDL, and triglycerides)
High blood pressure

Physical inactivity

Obesity and overweight

Diabetes

Other factors that contribute to heart disease risk:

Stress

Excessive alcohol

Poor diet and nutrition

For the first twenty years of this century, the entry for stress was just five lines long. It's worth quoting as an illustration of the AHA's level of conviction about the strength of stress's contribution to heart disease:

> Individual response to stress may be a contributing factor. Some scientists have noted a relationship between coronary heart disease risk and stress in a person's life, their health behaviors and socioeconomic status. These factors may affect established risk factors. For example, people under stress may overeat, start smoking or smoke more than they otherwise would.

Note the tentative, cautious tone of this paragraph. Stress *might* lead you to practice some unhealthy habits. No definition of stress exposures or responses.

Recently this website description has been expanded to include more elaborate tips on managing stress, the relationship between mental illness and heart disease, and how social factors like gender and race affect heart disease. These are promising recent improvements that finally recognize publicly that in 2014 the AHA officially recognized depression as a risk factor for the progression of coronary heart disease, the most common source of heart attacks.[3] And that recommendation followed the AHA's officially endorsing back in 2008 the practice of screening for depression in patients with coronary heart disease.

The content on the AHA website about stress has improved, but remember that for the ten years between 2008 and 2018 the level of attention the AHA paid on its official website to the role of chronic stress in heart disease was nearly invisible. The same has been true for the invisibility of stress in diabetes.

Stress-Free Practice Guidelines

More importantly for the clinicians who treat diabetes and heart disease, the standards of practice for the management of these two diseases have had little to say about stress in any form, and that has been true for many years.

What is not rare or harmless is the 20 percent rate of depression that complicates coronary heart disease and doubles the death risk within the first six months after a heart attack. If your doctor follows these AHA guidelines, as most primary care physicians do, your doctor will think your risk for a heart attack rests on your EKG and your troponin levels and your Beta-type natriuretic peptide levels – not on how much adrenaline you're churning out during your bouts of road rage or how low heart rate variability dips during your sleepless nights with your partner.

And none of the doctor's colleagues will think them sloppy for overlooking these psychosocial factors. Look in vain for any measure of any remotely psychological or social variable related to acute or chronic distress in the recommended risk estimation methods for calculating who is likely to have a heart attack.[4]

In the horse race for recognition as a major risk factor, depression competes with over a hundred other "novel" risk factors for heart disease, each of them vying for acceptance and influence in the AHA culture.

These brief looks at the AHA and ADA websites and treatment guidelines reflect the state of the art of treating these two disorders, and they reflect the vision problem that is a theme in this book. While stress is not even on the radar screen of most doctors as they manage heart disease and diabetes, stress also remains invisible to the healthcare system in which most of us practice or seek care.

The message from Dr. Julius is that modern medicine's blind spot for the role of stress and autonomic imbalance in chronic illness is an expensive oversight deeply embedded in the culture of medicine. It reaches far beyond diabetes and heart disease. How long can doctors afford to look the other way and dismiss the impact of severe stress?

Does Depression Kill?

In May 1994, as I was wondering about my place in the academic pecking order and what it would take to elevate depression to the status of a respectable illness on a par with cancer, heart disease, or diabetes, I met for my annual lunch with my mentor George Vaillant, who had been my program director during my psychiatry residency at Massachusetts Mental Health Center in the early 1980s.

We were both attending the annual meeting of the American Psychiatric Association in Washington, DC. Over egg rolls and chop suey in Chinatown, I asked him that day, "Why do people with depression die younger?"

As director of the Harvard Study of Adult Development, he had access to data on depression and mortality in his study subjects, and the wisdom to know that neither he nor anyone else knew the answer to my question. We decided then to try to write a systematic review of the mortality of depression. It took us four years to complete the review and get it published.[5]

We found, as others have since, that depression roughly doubles the early death rate, mostly through high rates of heart disease. This finding was true for both the rigorous studies and the sloppy ones.

That project turned my career for a while to focus on this curiosity about disease and the mechanisms that could explain how depression kills. What is the toxic element in depression? How can a mood disorder transform into a blood vessel disorder that can stop a human heart?

Now we know not only that depression does kill, but that severe mental illness of any kind reduces life expectancy by ten to twenty years. This fact is just one of the more dramatic and under-recognized contributions to our declining life expectancy rates in the US.[6]

Depression, like most major mental illnesses, poses a dilemma for those who study stress, as we shall see in more detail in the next chapter. Depression can be both a source of and a product of severe or chronic stress. In the early stages of depression before it takes on a life of its own, the timing of a depressive episode is often triggered by stressful life events. At the same time, like any acute or chronic condition, the depression itself acts as a stressor, setting up a potentially vicious cycle that takes months to resolve.[7]

In the mid-1990s, bending against the same winds that had marginalized psychiatry, I helped create a five-year residency program at the University of Cincinnati that combines family medicine and psychiatry, training one physician to practice both. A few other programs that combined internal medicine and psychiatry or pediatrics and psychiatry already existed at the time.

This kind of combined training seemed to me to offer the ultimate way to deliver on that promise of integrated care that had lured me back into medicine many years before. Maybe we could train doctors who are adept at working on both the mind and the body over the lifespan, which is the scope of family medicine. Maybe this could be one way of shaping our healthcare system toward a broader vision of health and illness, toward a system that could reduce the impact of severe and persistent distress on our declining life expectancy rates.

From Rescue to Incremental Medicine

Atul Gawande, MD, MPH, after twenty years of articulate and wise writing about medicine in our society, published a confession of sorts in a 2017 *New Yorker* article titled "The heroism of incremental care."[8] Following a detailed account of a four-year intensive treatment plan for a man who eventually recovered from chronic migraine headaches, Dr. Gawande, a general surgeon, admitted to realizing in midcareer that in his younger years he had opted for rescue medicine, assuming that greater gains could be had by doing life-saving deeds in times of crisis: "I was drawn to medicine by the aura of heroism."

But a primary care colleague of his had recently challenged him with persuasive amounts of data showing that primary care clinicians contribute more benefit to the public health of a population than the rescue medicine disciplines (such as surgery, intensive care, emergency medicine, and cardiology). Dr. Gawande was eventually convinced that managing chronic illness is the future of modern medicine, as he said:

> Our ability to use information to understand and reshape the future is accelerating in multiple ways.... The potential of this information is so enormous it is almost scary.... Instead of once-a-year checkups in which people are like bridges undergoing annual inspection, we will increasingly be able to use smartphones and wearables to continuously monitor our heart rhythm, breathing, sleep, and activity, registering signs of illness as well as the effectiveness and side effects of treatments.

In Dr. Gawande's account of his awakening to the value of incremental medicine, he never alludes to growing up in Athens, Ohio, where his mother practiced primary care as a pediatrician, and his father was a urologist. Dr. Gawande the son opted for the father's heroism of surgery. Even a wise man can take a long time to appreciate the heroism of his mother.

His personal account of his recent appreciation for the power of effective primary care to improve incrementally our public health captures both the problem and the opportunity for modern medicine in the US. Like Gawande, modern medicine has been fascinated by the rescue role. Every large medical center touts its helicopter.

Over the last century the healthcare system in the US has been built with a focus on managing acute care through costly procedures performed by subspecialists who work in subspecialty centers. This system has flourished into a lucrative business for the hospitals, healthcare systems, health insurance companies, and the health industries that support this system. These business forces have fought to protect the current system that has been so good to them, and they will continue that fight. And, like it or not, the priorities of the doctors we go to for the care of our stress-related conditions are set in part by the systems they work in.

Not My Job? Well, Then, Whose Is It?

The attentive, empathic, efficient primary care doctors that I work with often do well with the first few steps of assessing patients with chronic and toxic stress-related conditions, but their options for going further are limited by the systems in which we practice.

Their lack of easy access to stress symptom measures that are readily tracked in their electronic medical record is a mundane but common barrier.

Their limited access to mental health specialists for "curbside" consulting (two doctors passing in the hallway with a quick conversation like, "What do you think about this plan for this patient?") prior to formal referrals or collaboration prevents the kinds of creative thinking that save time and money and hassle in the rush of a primary care schedule.

Their traditional schedule of fifteen-minute appointments means that those patients who most need attention to chronic stress, the ones with multiple chronic conditions, are least likely to get it. And financial constraints on patients' access to mental health specialty services narrow the options for referral, often to the point that the doctor avoids making the referral.

The list of barriers goes on. No wonder good primary care docs think the assessment and management of stress is not their job.

And just as we clinicians tend to ignore or overlook what we can't measure, we tend to ignore or refer out those conditions we don't treat well. In general, most primary care doctors don't expect themselves to treat chronic stress well, and no one else does either. As we have seen, neither the American Heart Association nor the American Diabetes Association has traditionally given more than two nods to stress in their public education efforts about heart disease or diabetes. Nor do the latest treatment guidelines for these illnesses expect clinicians to pay attention to stress.[9]

In that sense, stress does not yet matter enough to the average primary care doctor to play a major role in treatment planning.

Toxic stress will only begin to matter as effective treatments become accessible to a wide range of healthcare providers, beginning with primary care. The promising news is that the toolkit for treating chronic stress has grown rapidly in recent years along with the science to support these treatments. Graduates from medical schools and other health professions now have a broader understanding of the psychological and social determinants of health than their elders in the profession.

Ornish against the Current

Back in the early 1980s, against the current of rescue medicine and the excitement about cardiac bypass surgery and heart transplants,

Dean Ornish, MD, made a high-risk career move. Fresh out of internal medicine residency at Massachusetts General Hospital, he moved to San Francisco to build a career on a hunch – the potential for lifestyle changes to prevent heart disease.

This was not a popular career path. He banked on the promising results of two small studies he had conducted as a medical student just a few years earlier, counting on his capacity for relentless pursuit that he had inherited from his mother. Dr. Ornish set up the Preventive Medicine Research Institute in Sausalito and focused his efforts on establishing the Lifestyle Heart Trial. This was not a cool thing to do.[10]

What kind of young man – he was thirty-one then – had the moxie to attempt such an unpopular approach fresh out of residency in a new city? Dr. Ornish was no stranger to stepping out of the mainstream. He had dropped out of the grind of being a pre-med biochemistry major at Rice University after his sophomore year, during the throes of a psychotic depressive episode with intentions to kill himself.

Instead of doing the deed, he moved home, met Swami Satchidananda, started practicing yoga, engaged in psychotherapy, and adopted a vegetarian diet. He now recalls that experience as transformative, opening his eyes to the power of the mind and his curiosity about the experience of suffering and the art of healing. Something in him resisted being reduced to a technician.

As a second-year medical student at Baylor College of Medicine, Dr. Ornish assisted on enough coronary artery bypass operations on Michael DeBakey's surgical service to see that a number of them required bypassing the previous bypasses. He recognized, "we were literally bypassing the problem without addressing the underlying causes." He had read that high-fat diets, lack of exercise, and chronic stress could cause heart disease in animals, and changing those same factors could reverse the heart disease. He wondered why this was not so in humans.

He was restless and curious and energetic enough to take a year off from medical school after his second year to run a small experiment. He persuaded the Plaza Hotel in Houston to donate eleven hotel rooms and a meeting space for thirty days. And he persuaded ten people with severe, inoperable heart disease and angina (chest pain) to spend a month in this hotel meeting and eating together with him.

Dean Ornish was twenty-four. What did he know about the ten people in his study who were in their sixties and seventies, dealing with seven to ten episodes of angina a day and facing death by inoperable heart disease? Not much.

But not-yet-doctor Ornish taught them yoga classes and meditation and gave them the scientific rationale for this intensive approach. They exercised together twice a day and ate together three times a day for thirty days. He hired a chef to prepare low-fat (10 percent) vegetarian meals. He did all this with a $5,000 grant from a local foundation, despite the skepticism of his medical school advisor.

At the end of the month he retested their cardiac function. They showed improved myocardial perfusion on thallium scans (a measure of blood supply to the heart) and were nearly free of chest pains – in just one month, with people who were so sick they were considered inoperable. His advisor told him no journal would publish the small study.

"I was surprised at the level of resistance we got to the data, because they were so exciting to me. This study didn't fit the paradigm, and people didn't quite know what to make of it," Ornish said. So he started planning his next study.

Two years later in 1980, instead of starting directly into a residency after medical school, now Dr. Ornish took another year off to conduct his second study – this time a randomized controlled trial of a more systematic intervention on a broader selection of patients with ischemic heart disease (narrowing of arteries so there is less blood and oxygen going to the heart).

This time he selected from 125 eligible patients with ischemic heart disease, twenty-three for the intervention and twenty-three for the control group. He took the intervention group to a retreat center in Horseshoe Bay, outside of Austin, Texas, for twenty-four days of stress management training and diet. They practiced stretching and relaxation and meditation while eating a vegan diet and abstaining from alcohol, caffeine, salt, and sugar.

The blind testing done in Houston before and after the intervention (in other words, the testers didn't know which people had done the stress management training and diet intervention or which were in the control group and had just gone home to sit in their La-Z-Boys and watch football) showed that after one month in the intervention group cholesterol, blood pressure, chest pain, and cardiac function improved significantly compared to the control group.

Three years later while Dr. Ornish was a resident in internal medicine at Massachusetts General Hospital, the results of this study were finally published in the *Journal of the American Medical Association* under the title "Effects of stress management training and dietary changes in treating ischemic heart disease."[11]

Nothing short of revolutionary.

Since that publication Dr. Ornish has grown over his career into an engine of culture change within our healthcare system. He has expanded the scientific basis for reversing coronary (or ischemic) heart disease through lifestyle changes, has broadened the application of his interventions to other conditions such as heart failure and prostate cancer, and has raised his influence on Medicare policies, the fast-food industry, and public health awareness.

In short, he has demonstrated convincingly that changing high-risk health behaviors such as toxic diets and toxic stress patterns is feasible, practical, and the most cost-effective way to prevent and often reverse coronary heart disease and other stress-related conditions. Dr. Ornish has shown us how we can put a hose to this firestorm. He has shown us how much toxic stress matters.

What Good Is Good Science?

But good science doesn't change medical practice. Much good science ferments in the silos of academia and research centers, never influencing medical practices in your doctor's exam room. And Dean Ornish's work, though gaining influence recently, is still dismissed by those who set practice standards for diabetes and heart disease.

Many of my primary care colleagues have only a dim idea of the evidence supporting his approach, and they rarely refer a patient to an Ornish cardiac rehab program. Fifteen years ago Dr. Ornish wondered aloud to his colleague William Roberts, "How did we get to a point in medicine where interventions such as radioactive stents, coronary angioplasty, and bypass surgery are considered conventional, whereas eating vegetables, walking, meditating, and participating in support groups are considered radical?"

This backward thinking still holds sway today.

If not science, maybe money changes behavior. After a career of investing in good science, now Dr. Ornish is focusing some of his energy on changing how doctors are reimbursed. That might change medical practice more than good science, he hopes. In 2010 Medicare finally agreed to pay for the eight weekend sessions over nine weeks in the Ornish Program for Reversing Heart Disease as a form of intensive cardiac rehabilitation. Some insurance companies have followed.

He jokes that that triumph only took about sixteen years to achieve for people who already have heart disease. Now who knows what it will take for Medicare to pay for the Ornish program that *prevents* heart disease in people at high risk.

Dr. Ornish has contributed to a wave that has not yet crested. He says, "We're getting bigger changes in lifestyle, better clinical outcomes, bigger cost savings, and better adherence than anyone has ever shown. There's a convergence of forces that make this [Lifestyle Medicine] the right idea at the right time."

But Dr. Ornish admits that making lifestyle changes sufficient to prevent or reverse chronic illness is difficult and requires sustained effort – as difficult and as powerful as many of the other meaningful things we do over the long haul, such as marriage, raising children, and working our jobs. But people stick with what's meaningful to them, so Dr. Ornish has reported impressive adherence rates for his programs.[12]

And in the 1980s, as he was designing his first studies, neither he nor anyone else understood the physiologic pathways by which meditation or yoga or walking or a vegan diet might reverse the plaque formation and blockage in coronary arteries. He made his good guess then more by intuition than by science.[13] A closer look now at the nature of our stress response system reveals why it's difficult to change how we respond to chronic stress, and why it's so powerful when we do.

3

. . . . .

Before We Climb
This Mountain

Our fuzzy "vision" for the concept of stress has been perpetuated by fuzzy language about stress. In casual conversation we can afford to speak casually about stress, but when patients talk with their doctors about stress they both need clarity. It's harder to see something clearly if you don't know how to talk about it clearly. This is true for most complex health concepts.

In the 1950s in the US when Masters and Johnson began studying the human sexual response with scientific discipline, common talk about sex was wrapped in the fuzzy language of euphemisms and embarrassment. Well-educated people knew little about the frequency in the general population of masturbation, homosexual encounters, or extramarital sex.

Since then, science has slowly sharpened our ability to see and understand the complex concept of the human sexual response, in part by teaching us how to talk about it with clarity. High school and college health classes now routinely teach the facts about the human sexual response. In the same way, clear talk about stress and the stress response system will improve our ability to study it, understand it, and manage it.

How good is the science linking stress and illness? Where is the front edge of our understanding, the line between what we know and don't know? If scientists wrestle with these dilemmas, no wonder the rest of us do too. Answering these questions is like taking the measure of the mountain we're about to climb. So, before we look closer at how the stress response system works, a few tips on the language of stress and the dilemmas of studying stress will provide a quick guide for the early part of our journey.

This fair warning about the complexities of the terrain aims to heighten our appreciation of both the difficulties and the rewards for those who make the journey. Suit up.

To Talk about *Stress* …

The first term we must manage with clarity is the tired word *stress*, which has been a source of confusion for the half-century since Hans Selye published *The Stress of Life* in 1956. In scientific papers as well as common speech the word *stress* has been used as a noun, a verb, and an adjective: "Damn, this stress headache is stressing me out! Can't take any more stress." In addition to playing multiple grammatical roles, the term has implied a challenging event or a response to an event on every point along the spectrum of severity, from the trivial to the disastrous.

To limit the confusion, I will limit my use of stress by itself to the umbrella term that refers to the process of a person responding to demands that appear to exceed the available resources. Note the emphasis on the person's perception or appraisal of demands, whether accurate or not, because appraisal, both conscious and unconscious, drives the whole stress response process. All living organisms have to adapt by maintaining a complex dynamic equilibrium, or homeostasis, in the face of demands from within the organism and from the environment. So, demands or challenges are common in everyday life.

For the good or tolerable types of stress exposures in everyday life, for which the resources appear ample, I will use *challenges* or *demands* or some synonym, reserving *stressors* for the more severe end of the severity spectrum.[1] Though technically the mild challenges of daily life qualify as demands that also require some form of adaptive stress response, as we will see in the next few chapters, these challenges rarely compromise health or safety and may in fact be fortifying.

In the context of healthcare, *stressor* denotes events or experiences that compromise or threaten a person's safety, health, or adaptiveness for more than a few hours. For example, the stressor of air travel is limited in time, while the stressor of childhood abuse lingers.

Stress Exposures

Embedded in this definition of stress is the essential fact that the stress process consists of stress exposures and our responses to them. The severity of these exposures, often called stressors, may be mild, moderate, or severe, such as a bad cup of coffee, a fender bender, an insult from a friend, or a sudden discovery of cancer. The duration or pattern of exposures may be brief, intermittent, or longer lasting, or some combination of these.

Most stressors are brief or acute; some are episodic, persistent, or relentlessly chronic. A useful duration cutoff for persistent or chronic stress exposures is six months.[2] In general we cope better with brief stressors (air travel or a flat tire) than with chronic stressors (a dread diagnosis of cancer or spousal abuse).

Good measures of stress exposures assess the severity, frequency, duration, type of demand (financial, physical, psychological, or social, for example), and the age of the person at the time of the exposure during some interval of interest (past week, month, year, or lifetime). It matters whether we have had one fender bender in the past month, or four. Patterns of stressors often mean something.

For some people the pattern of a relentless run of daily hassles over many months (bill collectors keep calling, commuter traffic thicker than ever, kids sassing back at home, spouse is late again) can have as much impact on health as a single severe event like a life-threatening car accident.

In the northern region of the Netherlands, earthquakes used to be brief, mild, and rare. In the past ten years since fracking became common, earthquakes in some areas have become nearly a weekly occurrence and an intermittent threat. In the minds of the more vulnerable Dutch in this region, the frequency and unpredictability of earthquakes now make this threat a persistent stress exposure, and the health of the population in that region is beginning to show the effects.[3]

Other kinds of persistent stress exposures, such as hearing loss, chronic pain, the threat of discrimination, and responsibility for family members who require daily care also exemplify persistent or chronic stress exposures that may threaten or compromise a person's health. The health impact of any one exposure depends on the age of the person during the exposure, the severity and duration of the exposure, and the total cumulative burden of other stress exposures over the person's lifetime. Soldiers who grew up with multiple childhood traumas, for example, are more likely to come home after combat with PTSD than soldiers who grew up in safe homes.

If we try to make sense of the effects of stress on health and illness, perhaps the most important, and often overlooked, concept in research on stress exposures is cumulative life stress. We only get one stress response system for our lifetime, and though this body can replenish itself in some ways, the cumulative demands of daily life take their toll – a toll we pay as we go and eventually recognize as aging. The record of that toll is kept in our genes and in the structures of our organs, as well as in our fickle memories.

If you and I are in the same car accident, what for you might be no more than the tolerable stress of an inconvenient crunch to the rear passenger door could for me be the toxic stress of a paralyzing near-death experience that confines me to my apartment and a life of disability. The difference for us may be that prior to that accident I had accumulated a burdensome load of stressors and a stress response system that was already worn out nearly to its limits, physiologically speaking, perhaps "decades" older than yours, even though we were born in the same year.

Stress Responses

Although it may be easier for us to identify major stressors such as earthquakes and car crashes, the more important aspect of the stress experience for its impact on health is the person's set of stress responses. Just as stressor implies stress exposures, the term *distress* implies responses to stress exposures. Because we vary widely from one person to another in how we respond to the same events, understanding how the stress experience affects health requires clear definitions of the key dimensions of distress or stress responses.

Most stress responses involve four types: cognitive, emotional, behavioral, and physiological responses.

Cognitive stress responses include the ways we consciously appraise an event or a stressor, as well as our unconscious appraisals of danger or safety. If a guy pulls up next to me at a stop sign and flips me the bird, laughing, I may think of this gesture as an invitation to a fight, or a pathetic joke. How I think about or appraise this event will determine whether I feel anger or amusement. And this combination of my cognitive and emotional responses will determine whether I pull out my AK-47 and make Swiss cheese out of his truck, or whether I give him a smile and turn up the radio.

Cognitive appraisal also involves an intuitive guess about whether the demands of the stressor exceed our resources for managing it. When my confidence is high and my sense of humor keen, I may appraise this flipping of the bird by this stranger as a minor threat for which I have plenty of resources. So I smile and turn up the radio. My heart never skips a beat.

On the other hand, if I'm half-drunk after hitting the neighborhood bar after working the night shift and have just been humiliated at work and this guy reminds me of my ex's new boyfriend, I may assess this gesture as an insult and the last straw. My AK-47 is in the trunk instead of under my driver's seat. I've got nothing to respond with. Demands exceed resources. My stress response system kicks into high gear. Fear and rage run the show. My chest thumps and beads of sweat wet my upper lip and screaming rage rips at my throat.

Behavioral stress responses do not always match cognitive and emotional responses, as all good poker players know well. And physiological responses, such as a racing heart or a sweating upper lip, sometimes reveal a perception of threat that escapes our cognitive and emotional awareness. Some phobias trigger runaway heart rates and sweating in response to the admittedly benign black cat or a spider-shaped ornament. The unconscious often overthrows our conscious reason and better judgment.

Stress is a complex process, and so is measuring it.

Good, Tolerable, and Toxic

From birth to death, our daily lives are full of demands and sometimes stressors that challenge us to adapt. Some of these demands give us pleasure – the solvable problems, the hunger satisfied by a

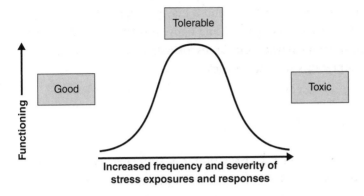

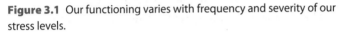

Figure 3.1 Our functioning varies with frequency and severity of our stress levels.

sandwich, a roll in bed with honey. Others are tolerable, such as the drudgery tasks at work or cleaning up our messes at home. When trying to understand what makes a stressor toxic, it's helpful to think about the inverted U along the spectrum of stress exposures and responses.

Our adaptive functioning rises as the challenges rise through the range of most mild to moderate stressors. However, as the severity of the stressors increases, our functioning levels off in the zone of tolerable stress. In this middle zone we are stretching the limits of our capacity to function well, and sensing this limitation reduces our intuitive pleasure and sense of safety. This zone is no longer easy and fun, but it's manageable, and we know it's limited to an endurable time. Schools aim to stretch students into this zone long enough to master new skills. We can recover at the end of the task, the end of the day, or the end of the week.

But the toxic zone begins at the point where our functioning starts declining as the severity of the stressors rises further. This point of toxicity, where exposure to the stressor drains the resources available, varies from person to person, from stressor to stressor, and even within a person, and it may vary depending on the person's current state of mind and body. This fact about the individual variation in what constitutes toxic stress makes measuring and interpreting stress ratings tricky.

Resilience

The capacity of the stress response system to bounce back in response to a challenge, to bend without breaking, to adapt to adversity and then regain balance is often referred to as resilience. Most humans are remarkably resilient, even in the face of life-threatening events such as a heart attack.[4] This capacity to recover and return to the resting state, known as homeostasis, is synonymous with health and an efficiently operating stress response system.

When your heart doctor asks you to walk on a treadmill, one of the numbers he or she will check is your heart rate recovery time after you stop walking. How long does it take for your heart rate to return to its resting level, say from 160 beats per minute back down to 70 beats per minute? Rapid recovery times for heart rates after an exercise treadmill test reflect cardiovascular resilience, and slow recovery times predict future trouble with heart disease.[5]

So when considering the impact of stressors and distress on health, it's not enough to measure exposures and responses. We also have to evaluate the resources you believe are available for coping with these demands. This means not just material resources, such as money and shelter, but social resources (confidants, helpers, comforters), physical resources (strength, energy, skills), and psychological as well as spiritual resources. In some resource-poor countries, faith and tribal affiliations provide believers enough resilience to weather famines and survive violent conflicts.

Stress Accumulates over a Lifetime

Even the healthiest people pay a price for resilience, and that price is now known as biological aging or allostatic load – in other words, the cumulative burden on the body gathered over a lifetime of responding to or adapting to stress exposures. A number of studies have shown that this burden can be assessed by combining selected measures of endocrine, immune, metabolic, and cardiovascular functioning into an index called the allostatic load index.[6]

Although the allostatic load index is not yet standardized for use in clinical practice, and your doctor isn't going to ask you about your allostatic load, both allostatic load and cumulative life stress exposures have been associated with accelerated biological aging and with the earlier onset and more rapid progression of common chronic illnesses such heart disease and diabetes. If that sounds troubling, it is also reassuring that we can buffer some of the effects of cumulative life stress on aging because we are psychologically and biologically resilient.[7]

So if we want to understand the relationship between stress and illness, and how resilience protects us, it's not sufficient to assess current or recent stress exposures and responses. We must also pay attention to cumulative stress over the course of our lives.

Junk Science on the Stress Research Mountain

One of the factors that has contributed to the relative invisibility of the stress–illness relationship has been the difficulty of studying it. Fuzzy terminology for stress in scientific circles only accounts for a small part of this difficulty.

Before we look more closely in the coming chapters at what we know and don't know about stress and illness, it's helpful to attend to a few of the more common criticisms of this scientific literature on stress and consider how these criticisms highlight the difficulties of measuring stress. The dilemmas faced by stress researchers offer a few guides for the dilemmas faced by patients with stress-related disorders and their doctors.

The first line of attack in any scientific debate usually aims to expose shabby scientific methods, and there's plenty of junk science on the stress research mountain. Stress neuroscience is relatively young, compared to the science of heart disease or diabetes. Any young science begins with methods that are not up to snuff, and the stress–illness question poses some unusual problems. In fact, if you had to choose a topic that defies traditional scientific methods and quick results, the study of the effects of chronic stress on chronic illness would be a good choice. Here's why.

Complexity of exposures and outcomes. The scientific method in healthcare works well when you can design an experiment that tests one exposure variable while holding the other important variables constant. Does dose Y of a topical antibiotic X decrease the rate of wound infections in women who have Cesarean sections? The exposure (the antibiotic) and the outcome (rate of wound infections) are both relatively simple, measurable events and the story is a short one, a matter of a few weeks.

The scientific method does not work as well for questions that involve complex exposures and complex outcomes over long periods. As we have seen, measuring chronic stress exposures and responses requires identifying patterns of triggering events, repeated subjective appraisals of the severity of the events, and multiple stress responses across multiple organ systems to get a picture of this intricate process of adaptation. How do you measure all of that?

And that's just the early part of the process. The illness outcomes we're interested in are just as complex. What is diabetes or heart disease? There is no simple measure of either disease.

If you have symptoms of chest pain and five risk factors for heart disease but have not yet taken an ambulance ride to the ER with a heart attack, do you have heart disease, or just sort of? And are you more or less sick than someone who is well treated for heart disease with two medications and has been free of symptoms for two years? Both people may have coronary heart disease, but at different stages and severities of illness.

Diabetes, heart disease, obesity, and depression are complex chronic conditions that vary dramatically over time and with treatment. Both the exposures and the outcomes in the stress–illness question are complex moving targets, not ideally suited for the scientific method.

But science is like bricklaying, so some of the best stress research has focused on acute stress and short-term outcomes. Lay enough of those short-term bricks side by side, and you can learn something about the long run of chronic stress and chronic illness.

One disease or many. Most research on exposures or outcomes for a disease limits the study sample to those who might develop the disease of interest. This is the traditional one-disease-at-a-time approach. Chronic illnesses are complex and messy enough disorders by themselves. Therefore, potential study participants who have more than one chronic condition, such as heart disease and cancer, have often been excluded from studies of heart disease in order to reduce the confusion in the data about a cause or an effect on heart disease because of the cancer. As a result, we know relatively little about the 60 million Americans who live with four or more chronic conditions.

Only recently has that approach begun to change. Because chronic stress exposures disrupt multiple systems at the same time, this rapidly growing and costly group of our population is now becoming the target of new studies of the impact of severe and chronic stress on multiple chronic illnesses – studies that take advantage of recent advances in systems analytics, big data analysis methods, and machine learning.[8]

Measurement. If you don't measure it, you can't study it. That's one tenet of the scientific method. As we will see in more detail in later chapters, the measurement of psychological and physiological processes has come a long way in the past fifty years, and stress neuroscience has developed a rich menu of stress measures for laboratory settings,[9] but relatively few stress measures have made it into the clinic setting.

We do not yet have one signature stress measure that, like blood pressure for hypertension or blood glucose for diabetes, can represent the tip of the iceberg for stress-related chronic illness. Without a simple standard stress measure, busy primary care doctors tend to ignore stress as a focus of treatment. They face too much pressure to treat the established array of numbers that capture key features of a risk factor or an illness, and that pressure is not likely to change soon.

Symptom severity measures (these are self-report questionnaires), like the PHQ 9 for depression symptoms and the GAD 7 for anxiety symptoms, represent a way to measure the patient's response to or appraisal of some aspects of chronic stress. These severity measures provide a number to target, and during the past ten years some primary care doctors have tried them out with patients so they can assess and improve the treatment of depression and anxiety of their patients in their practices.[10]

And often the hidden toll of chronic stress exposures and responses is only revealed by the underlying biology. A patient's high resting heart rate and high blood pressure may reveal the price paid for stoically enduring the tension in a marriage or conflict with a bullying boss. In those people who deny anything is wrong or tough it out, and who minimize their symptoms, unstable biology may provide the only signal of their distress. And if cumulative stress accelerates the aging process and some illnesses, how do we measure multiple aspects of the stress response system over time to identify the imbalances that lead to disease?

Time spans. Studying anything complex in a scientifically rigorous manner is challenging, even if the event only lasts a few seconds. Consider the difficulties of studying the effects of a ten-second sprint on Olympic-class athlete Usain Bolt's immune system. Then consider studying the effects of twenty-seven years of incarceration on Nelson Mandela's immune system. As the time span of a study increases, the number of other variables that can influence the outcomes multiplies.

The time spans for the study of chronic stress range from days to decades for most of the illnesses that are related to chronic stress. Like the archeologists and geologists who must use different methods to measure time than the laboratory biologist, the study of the effects of chronic stress on illness requires repeated measurements over days, months, years, and sometimes decades.

This kind of study also requires collecting data on the cumulative biological and psychological effects of stressors, using fancy statistical models that can manage patterns in large numbers of variables over long intervals, and using methods of estimation to fill in the unavoidable data gaps.

In general, it's harder to do research on processes that have long time spans than on short ones. For most adults facing the risk of illness, our ideal interval of interest is our lifespan, and the variable we should be most interested in is our cumulative life stress.

Unit of interest. Stress operates at every level of our physical and social lives. That poses a tough choice for those who study stress. Are we going to examine the impact of a stressor such as the 9/11 attack on the World Trade Center on the social group, such as the family? Or do we focus on one person, or one organ system, or one cell, or some specific genes, to name just a few possibilities?

It's difficult to conduct these investigations of the stress response system on more than a couple of levels. Funding agencies for laboratory science spend millions of dollars on molecular and cellular processes – they're not going to fund population studies. And the technical equipment and knowledge for studying chronic stress in a test tube rarely carries over to higher-order levels, such as collecting psychological inventories in people or mapping of disease patterns in populations across a city.

Luckily, visionaries with that rare blend of talents like Robert Sapolsky, Dean Ornish, or Viola Vaccarino (you'll meet her later) manage to tackle the problem of studying chronic stress on multiple levels using multiple lenses. And they dedicate their whole careers to this feat.

What goes around. The scientific method works neatly when it's clear what the cause and the effect might be, or what the exposure and the outcome might be. If the sound of the starter gun jolts Usain Bolt's heart rate from 68 beats per minute up to 120 beats per minute within five seconds, even though he's just sitting on the bench watching others race, that's a relatively neat cause-and-effect sequence showing his modified conditioned response to the stressor of the sound of starter guns. The exposure is clear and so is the outcome.

But when chronic stressors contribute to conditions like depression or diabetes or chest pain or insomnia, conditions that in turn function as stressors, the circle is closed. When a heart attack is the outcome of a persistent stressor, it also becomes an exposure, a source of more demands. The effect becomes a cause again, and around we go.

When studying stress over long intervals, it can be difficult to tease out the exposures from the outcomes and the causes from the effects. That's when the disease process becomes a vicious cycle, a confusion of causes and effects.

Confounders. When studying the relationship between two things, such as stress exposures and illness, it's exciting to see that a change in the exposure is associated with a change in the outcome, especially if the magnitude and direction of the change fits what you predicted. It's tempting then to assume that the first thing directly influenced the second.

But the more likely possibility in complex systems is that the effect was indirect, through other variables. These other variables are fondly called confounders because they complicate the equation and confound the investigators' wishes for a simple answer.

Statistical methods can adjust or control for a limited number of confounders, as long as the investigators bother to measure these other factors properly. But in the real world, when investigators have limited funds and limited time, which is almost always true, they are forced to choose just a few potential confounders to measure.

When we reviewed the fifty or so studies of a link between depression and death in the late 1990s, my team and I identified five common potential confounders of the relationship between depression and early death, and we rated the studies on how many of these confounders each study controlled for.[11] By controlled, we mean they accounted for other factors and determined the other factors did not confuse the data. None controlled for all five; the better studies controlled for three; and the weaker studies controlled for one or none.

More recently, when I participated in a group that reviewed the studies of depression as a risk factor for the progression of coronary heart disease, we found a similar range of attention to confounders.[12] Few studies controlled for more than four of the many possible confounders. The quality of these kinds of large studies of real people, not cells in test tubes, depends in part on the rigor with which they control for potential confounders. More is usually better, up to a limit.

The triumphs of the researchers that appear in the chapters of this book remind us of the possibilities and the promises, as well as the barriers.[13] For neuroscientists, the stress–illness mountain will always be a difficult climb. For the rest of us, it's enough to keep in mind these barriers that have made understanding the stress response system and its role in chronic illness a slow but revealing journey.

Part II

The System

4

• • • • •

Our Resilient Stress Response System

On Ted Daley's drive to work, the SHINE PDA alerted him with a vibration and its signature ding-dong tone. He had fifteen minutes to respond. He pulled into the next Shell station and tapped in his mood ratings (fair), his sleep data (six hours, four awakenings), and his stress level (mild). In the comments box he wrote, "Another day at the races. This BP cuff is too tight. Can you drop the PSI?"

He doubted that blood pressure cuffs use the same measure as car tires, but maybe the tech would get the point. It took him about four minutes to enter his data. When he noticed the card reader on the gas pump was out of order, he blurted, "Crap!" and slammed his car roof, surprised at his short fuse and how much his hand stung. Inside the station he paid cash for his gas, tossing in three bags of Dorito barbecue chips and a family pack of M&M's, just in case the day was a downer.

Ted had found out about this SHINE study (Shyness and Inhibition in New Experiences) through emails from the U Pitt Research Office. They were always looking for guinea pigs and this one caught Ted's eye. Most studies cover the participant's expenses, but this one offered $400 more, for the inconveniences and the duration. And he figured maybe he'd learn something about what happens to his blood pressure under stress.

Five years ago, out of the blue, Ted's older brother had died at thirty-eight. Just dropped dead, home alone, on a Thursday evening. Nothing suspicious, probably a heart attack, they said. Ted didn't know much more than that. He asked his sister, but she didn't know. Their brother lived alone and kept his worries to himself.

"In our family we bury our stress," said Ted. "If you don't talk about it, it'll go away." He knew his brother had had trouble with his anger, blew his stack a lot. Life got rough for him in his twenties and stayed that way. Maybe that's why he kept his distance. He knew his brother saw a psychiatrist once, but he never would tell Ted much about it. Then all of a sudden he was dead. Can stress do that?

Ted blows his stack sometimes, but only when he's alone – throws things, smashed a plate once and another time a bobblehead, but that's about it. His coworkers think of him as mellow, but he knows his boss ticks him off more than is good for him. These things seem to sneak up on him, catch him by surprise, and suddenly he explodes, but only when he's alone. In a few minutes it's over. Could his anger be like his brother's? His next birthday will be his thirty-eighth. Could he end up on his floor some Thursday evening?

Your Stress Silhouette

This chapter introduces our stress response system and how it works in the sprints of life. Under the best of circumstances and when we are in the pink of health, our stress response system functions like a finely conducted orchestra, and we hardly notice what a marvel of orchestration we live by.

Aside from minor but important differences from person to person, we all live and die by the same system for coping with daily stressors. And as with our faces and our fingerprints and our voiceprints, though we all share some common features in our stress response systems, it's our distinguishing differences that make our stress response systems unique for each of us.

How is your system different from mine? Most of us don't know, or we would have a hard time articulating how our stress response systems set us apart. Our first access to tips about stress and stress management all too often comes on the job or in a crisis when we're facing a health scare, burnout, or collapse. That's too little too late.

The outline of the physical features of your face is so distinctive that you and those who know you well could pick your silhouette out of a lineup with little trouble. Consider how your stress response profile – a sketch of how you react to and recover from the stressors that are relevant to your physical and emotional health – might define the way you approach an illness.

Are you a gut reactor (nausea or heartburn), a vascular reactor (tension headaches or high blood pressure), an immune reactor (allergies or asthma), or some combination? Does it take you hours, days, or weeks to recover from troubling challenges? What gives you the resilience to recover rapidly? If you knew your stress response profile, you could see more clearly how close you might be to developing diabetes or heart disease, and what you might do to change that course. We'll take a closer look at stress profiles in another chapter, but let's consider Ted's.

Ted's silhouette looks something like this. He's a combination of a gut and vascular reactor. His capacity for keeping his composure around others means that at times of high demands, he appears mellow to others. He may misread the signals from his stomach, mistaking for hunger the pattern of stomach churning triggered by anxiety. He has learned to expect these distress signals from his stomach, and he knows they can be calmed by snacks. Thus the Doritos and M&M's – an inexpensive effort that comes with the price of extra calories and a touch of nagging guilt.

Later he will learn from the study data report that his blood pressure rises on workdays and comes back down on the weekend – news to him, but hardly surprising that his vascular system stays on high alert much of the week, day and night.

Ted doesn't think much about these patterns. They're just part of who he is. He doesn't think about his stress response system and certainly doesn't talk with his wife or friends about it. Or his doctor. He doesn't have to. Yet.

Transcending Trouble

In the fall of 1972 at the start of my junior year of college, I slept badly, night after night. The previous summer I'd been dumped by my girlfriend of sophomore year, and she now lived in the same large dorm. Occasionally I'd see her from a distance in the dining hall or walking with her roommate to and from the dorm. I just couldn't forget about her. My jaws ached from clenching in the night. My mental jaws ached too. I couldn't stop chewing on life, day and night. Could true love ever happen to me? Is medical school worth the work? Will I ever start on the soccer team? Why can't I read faster? Who am I?

My friend Derrick told me I should open my pores and come with him to find out about transcendental meditation. Explore the East. Tune into what George Harrison channeled from Ravi Shankar. There was a TM Center on Garden Street, blessed by the guru Maharishi Mahesh Yogi.

I attended the first session with Derrick. I went back for the second and the third. I got initiated with a mantra I swore to tell no one, and my initiator told me to practice twice a day for thirty minutes before meals. If I could rise above my troubles while diving deep into relaxation, that kind of magic was worth a try.

It took me a month to get the hang of it, but once I found the habit, it changed my life. I started worrying less, sleeping more efficiently, studying with less self-doubt, concentrating better under deadline pressures, and playing soccer with more focus. It didn't do much for my love life, but this habit of meditating twice a day slowed down the pace of my life, and the pace of my mind, so at least I felt less troubled by what I was missing.

"Be here now," Baba Ram Dass told our generation. Was this really some private spiritual journey, or had I been brainwashed by the Maharishi and Ram Dass? It felt so good I didn't dare push the question. My roommates were getting high on weed while I was getting high on TM, but I couldn't brag about it. Back then it was square to do anything that healthy.

Part of what intrigued me about this transformation of my jaws, my daydreams, and my night dreams was the awareness that somewhere across the Charles River at the Beth Israel Hospital there was an internist in a white coat, Herbert Benson, MD, who was studying what TM did to heart rate, blood pressure, oxygen consumption, and skin resistance.

The potential medical student in me liked this science angle on this ancient Eastern spiritual practice. The TM Center wanted us to know that Western medicine was finding that TM is not all in your head, not just a spiritual flight. TM changed your physiology while you were meditating, changed it for the better, and after months of practice for me, TM brought on the cumulative benefit of "restful alertness" even when you were not meditating. Seasoned meditators generally had lower resting heart rates than novices, and much lower than the average uptight college kid.

Dr. Benson published *The Relaxation Response* in 1975. When I read it. I realized that while I had been transcending my troubles in college with the help of my mantra (*iihhm* – shh, don't tell!) under the influence of the Maharishi, Dr. Benson across the river had been training his subjects to achieve the same effects by repeating the word *one* in a calming rhythm.

Dr. Benson established the secular dimensions of the relaxation response[1] and popularized its application to stress management through a series of books, including *Beyond the Relaxation Response* (1984), and most recently *Relaxation Revolution* (2010). He and Joan Borysenko, PhD, started the Mind Body Institute at Beth Israel Hospital, and from that work she wrote her popular *Minding the Body, Mending the Mind* (1987). Their example of West meets East paved the way for the work of Deepak Chopra and Jon Kabat-Zinn, two leaders who helped make a place in mainstream medicine for their modifications of the Eastern healing practices of acupuncture and meditation.

Soon after Dr. Benson published his early validations by Western science of the health benefits of TM, the Maharishi invited him to join the TM world and travel with the Maharishi.

"The Maharishi and I were very close," Dr. Benson told me recently. "He wanted me to spend my life with him. My wife said no way."

Instead, Dr. Benson, a cardiologist, chose to stay with the physiology department at Harvard Medical School, earning himself an early dismissal from the favors of the Maharishi. At the same time, his studies of TM were often dismissed by his colleagues as no more than "Herb's crazy thing."

He recalls, "I started to get death threats. When a committee was set up to decide whether I could accept a grant to study the physiology of meditation, the dean, Bob Ebert, said to me, 'If Harvard can't make an occasional mistake, who can? Take the money.'"

So with the dean's backhanded blessing, Dr. Benson persisted with his "crazy thing" and clinical applications.

When he set up his Mind Body Institute in the late 1970s, he had the foresight and good fortune to put on the institute's board

84

a man who would later save him, John Henry. After the Beth Israel Hospital "threw us out" in the crunch of a hospital merger in the early 2000s, Dr. Benson's institute was homeless for a few long years. His bid to move the institute to the Massachusetts General Hospital was rejected by MGH until 2006.

Then John Henry, owner of the Boston Red Sox and the *Boston Globe*, offered to fund the institute with $20 million, and Bill Coors (of beer fame) offered to establish a professorship for Dr. Benson. That broke the ice of the conservative MGH culture. The Mind Body Institute introduced integrated care into the MGH culture as a principle that has found a respectable place there.

Eventually Herbert Benson's persistence triumphed. His legacy now (he died in 2022), takes the form of the Benson-Henry Institute for Mind Body Medicine at the Massachusetts General Hospital, directed by Gregory Fricchione, who recently coedited a most readable and beautifully illustrated book on the stress response system, *The Science of Stress: Living under Pressure.*[2] This book aims to educate the general reader about the latest concepts from stress neuroscience as they affect our public health approaches to heart disease, depression, diabetes, and other common noncommunicable stress-related diseases.

With his relaxation response, Dr. Benson brought Hans Selye's science of stress closer to the everyday practice of medicine. To appreciate what an invisible marvel the stress response system is, let's focus now on the features that distinguish it from other systems we may be more familiar with.

It's essential. The first feature to appreciate about our stress response system is that we can't live without it. When we're healthy, it works well, and when it breaks down, we feel it first as distress, later as illness, finally as death.

Evolution has spent millions of years refining this system, not only in our species but in all primate species before us, and it works pretty well most of the time for coping with acute stress – well enough to allow us to survive long enough to procreate, and to help others in our tribe to procreate, which is one of the reasons we're still here.

It's complex. The second feature to appreciate is that the stress response system is complex, the way an orchestra is a complex system with many sections of instruments for playing a piece of music, whether the music is simple or sophisticated. Think of our stress response system as an everyday miracle of orchestration of our many organs to keep our body's internal environment relatively stable in the face of the demands of daily life.

Six main organ systems play major roles in our stress responses: the nervous system for information management, the heart and lungs for oxygen delivery to the tissues, the gut for turning food into energy, hormones for signaling and regulating, the immune system for defense and healing, and the musculoskeletal system for motion.

It's a good thing we don't have to think about all the moving parts of this symphony that have to work to keep our temperature within a few degrees of 98.6 F, our blood volume within a few tablespoons of five liters, our heart rates between 50 and 150 beats per minute, and our blood pressure close to 120 over 80 most of the time.

When these sections of our body's orchestra play in harmony with each other, it's called coherence, a state of maximum efficiency that feels good. Intuitively we strive for coherence in our stress response systems. When we lose that coherence, when we drift into incoherence, we feel anxious. We sense trouble, and if we can't adjust, eventually we sense illness.[3]

It's self-regulating. For the most part, the system operates automatically without a user manual. We don't think much about reacting to stressors – we just react by instinct. For the most part, our stress response system regulates itself. The command center resides mostly in the unconscious parts of our nervous system: the subcortical parts of our brain, the bulk of the central nervous system, the peripheral nervous system that includes all the branches outside the skull and spine, and the autonomic nervous system, which is a network of self-regulating reflex arcs, all with intricate attachments to every other major organ system.

Through a complex series of feedback loops, each organ system keeps itself operating within certain limits that are compatible with life. If our blood pressure drops, our heart rate jumps enough to compensate so blood continues to flow everywhere we need it. Each subsystem, and the stress response system as a whole, keeps a certain order, or more properly a certain balance between order and disorder.

Good health requires a certain amount of order, but not too much. Some variability in heart rates is healthy, within certain limits. Too much order in the form of a narrow range of heartbeats makes cardiologists worry that their patients' hearts can't adjust to the various demands of activity and rest. In a similar way, a trained neurologist looking at electrical tracings of brain activity can distinguish the healthy kinds of order in brain functioning from the chaos of delirium or the flat lines of coma.

When one part of the stress response system veers too much toward disorder, alarm bells go off not only in that subsystem but in others, and we sense distress. For example, if you lose blood from your left hand after you slice it with a dirty knife, that wound disrupts both your cardiovascular system and your immune system, both of which automatically react to correct that bit of disorder.

Your gut also reacts, possibly with nausea to avoid eating while coping with the cut, and your nervous system reacts with pain signals and dizziness and the urge to retreat to rest.

Each of these responses represents the evolutionary selection for subsystems that not only regulate themselves but also respond to the other subsystems in ways that foster their self-regulation. Persistent malfunction in any one organ system may mean prolonged distress, disease, or death. And when the stress response system falters or breaks down in this way, understanding the basics about our stress response system is likely to be handy.

Good stress, or a challenge well managed, actually improves the fine-tuning of our stress response system. Tolerable stressors impose demands and cause more distress with greater short-term costs, but usually result in adaptive growth or a sense of resilience, a weathering of the storm: getting the chores done, resolving a dispute about money in a marriage, recovering from a cut to the left hand, coping with unemployment by finding a better job than the last one. Most good jobs and good marriages challenge us with a blend of good and tolerable stressors most of the time, resulting in a fit stress response system.

On the other side of that fine line around what's tolerable, toxic stress challenges us in ways that overwhelm some part of our stress response system's ability to self-regulate, to adjust, and to return to rest. Toxic stress costs us dearly now and in the near or distant future – psychologically, socially, physiologically, or in all three ways. So, in its broadest definition, stress is a constant feature of everyday life and can either promote or damage our health.[4]

It cycles through work and rest. Another feature that is crucial to understanding the stress response system is that the optimal state of the stress response system, similar to the optimal state of the heart, is a cycle of work and rest – not full rest and not endless work, but cycles of work and rest. Think of the work phase as the stimulus or acute stressor that both challenges and resets the system.

Just as the heart functions best when rhythmically alternating contractions with relaxations, at around 60 beats per minute, the larger stress response system functions best when rhythmically alternating work and rest, activation and relaxation, stress reaction and recovery. Some rhythms of the stress response system span cycles of seconds; others span minutes, hours, or the full day.

All these work–rest cycles are needed for regulating the system. We tune up by alternating action and relaxation. Evolution has selected for normal organ functions that regulate themselves in this way.

The longest of these work–rest cycles is the sleep–wake cycle or the circadian rhythm. The timekeeper for this cycle is mostly in the hypothalamus, but is also in other organs outside the brain, such as the adrenal glands. Within our eight hours of sleep there are sub-rhythms of activity, as in the three or four REM sleep phases and the deep rest of stage IV sleep.

Within our sleep–wake cycles we also live by hunger–feeding cycles, eating about three times a day in subrhythms of hunger and satiety every four to six hours, also a form of work and rest.

Less tied to the clock are the various tasks or mild acute demands that tax our stress response systems during our waking hours, often followed by some form of relaxation: climbing stairs followed by sitting, difficult meetings followed by bathroom breaks, digging the ditch followed by a cigarette, conversations followed by quiet.

We pace ourselves each day, negotiating work and rest, in response to the pull between the demands for work and the demands for rest, which we experience as various signals of fatigue. These fatigue signals come to us as sensations in a body part: cramping in a hand, weakness in the legs, a foggy sensation in the mind, a dwindling of interest, or eventually the urge to sit, lie down, or sleep.

Within a wide range of variations we tune up our systems every day through regular sleep, work, exercise, meals, sex, games, and relaxation. Too much stimulation or too much rest or too little of these work–rest rhythms for too long disrupts this self-regulation process, paving the way for illness. In the next chapter we'll look more closely at the kinds of stress exposures and responses that are powerful and persistent enough to lead to illness.

It's both indiscriminate and specific. Our stress response system responds to challenges of any type, good or bad, appealing or threatening, with a set of general reactions that are primitive, like a dog's reaction: heightened attention and focus, rising heart rate, shift in blood flow from the gut to the muscles, and sympathetic nerve activity while inhibiting the vagus or parasympathetic nerves. That's the indiscriminate aspect of the stress response system. And in humans, depending on how we judge a challenge, our system may respond quite specifically to one stressor and quite differently to some others.

In the early 1950s Hans Selye defined stress as "the non-specific response of the body to any demand."[5] That may sound too vague for good science, but the definition has survived. The point is that your stress response system responds automatically to any demand or stressor in some ways that are not specific to the stressor, whether the stressor is toxic or delightful.

In the short run, insults and victories both make our heart rates jump and rob us of our appetites for a while and shunt blood to our large muscles, making us want to jump and shout. In other ways our responses to insults are quite specific and different from our responses to victories. And what insults me might delight you, but more on that later.

It's always on alert. If you had to design a warning system for a house or a neighborhood, would you err on the side of sounding the alarm too early or too late, too often or too little? Better safe than sorry? Even if false alarms make you bonkers with anxiety from false threats?

Imagine if you had to check your fire alarms and door locks and security system every day to make sure you were safe in your house. As inefficient as it seems, evolution has selected for such a threat warning system in humans, one that is always on, always ready to kick into action, and requires effort to prevent our stress response system from firing.

Nature's default assumption is that the world is not safe, not until we verify safety, which we do again and again and again. Deep in our psyches, deep in our primitive nervous systems, the fire chief in us keeps the engine idling and the firefighters sleeping in their overalls with their boots waiting at the bottom of the pole.[6]

One of the tasks of the healthy brain is to inhibit or restrain the stress response system. That job goes partly to one of the most evolutionarily advanced parts of our brains, the prefrontal cortex, which sits up front over our eyes.

The prefrontal cortex orchestrates the activities of the limbic system or the emotional brain. This is the modern brain restraining the primitive brain. Along busy nerve tracts from the prefrontal cortex back to the amygdala in the emotional brain, the inhibition of the stress response system keeps the lid on most of the time. This set of circuits linking those two areas allows us to regulate our feelings of alarm using our hard-earned judgment. Judgment counts when evaluating threats and safety.

But for best survival, the system must react fast and be always ready. So when the brain perceives threat or senses unsafety, that inhibition drops fast and the amygdala is released to take action, sometimes gradually, other times as fast as fire.

In the body the release of the stress response passes to all organs first through the vagus nerve.[7] The process is called vagal withdrawal, for the withdrawing of the usual vagal inhibition of sympathetic activity. This is like releasing the brake of a truck on a steep slope. Let it rip.

Understanding this anatomical and evolutionary fact about the stress response system being always on and often inhibited only by a prefrontal cortex that perceives safety and a vagus nerve that keeps the brake on the sympathetic nervous system helps us make sense of the fact that signs of stress reactions often persist long after we consciously know the stressor has passed.

After a trauma or a threat (real or imagined), deep in our limbic systems and in our prefrontal cortexes, we sense the world is not yet a safe place. We're still on high alert. Our firemen still have their boots on. It can take a while to regain that sense of safety both up front in our brains and down deep.

It's redundant and elastic. Redundancy is one of the ways nature achieves resilience or the capacity to continue to function when a part is broken. Ten violas can cover for one fainting violist.

For example, pairs of genes are redundant, and they provide some resilience for survival when one gene mutates or breaks down.

On a system level, if both nerves and hormones send out alarm signals about approaching danger, the signal is more likely to reach its target organs than if only one organ system performed the messenger task. Likewise, if more than one artery feeds a section of an organ, the injury from a clot in that artery can be offset by the blood flowing in the other artery. Our cardiovascular system is thick with extra vessels. Up to a point, a redundant system is a resilient system, and for the stress response system, longevity relies on resilience.

Each of the organ systems serving the stress response system is elastic, within limits. So orchestrating the stress response system is a more sophisticated task than operating your car, in which most of the parts are rigid or relatively inflexible. For example, whereas the volume of space inside your car engine for circulating oil and gas does not change significantly as you speed up, the total volume of your cardiovascular system can expand to 5.5 liters and shrink to 4.5 liters, depending on your size, gender, blood pressure, your current activity level, how much you've been sweating, how much water you drank today, what burdens you face tomorrow, and lots of other factors.

And where your blood flows (such as away from your stomach and into your large muscles if you're running for your life from a tiger) also varies with your state of mind and the competing demands within your body. The types and numbers of cells and molecules (killer T cells and cytokines, for example) that pour into your circulation, especially to injured areas, vary widely with the demands of an injury or an infection, but usually within healthy limits. We recognize those healthy limits in part through the ranges of normal for blood pressure, temperature, white blood cell counts, and blood sugar levels, for example.

Elastic systems are defined by that wonderful tendency to return to some sort of resting state, after flexing to an extreme. In response to an injury, your count of white blood cells may shoot up within minutes from 9,000 to 15,000, but drop down within hours if there's no infection to fight. The fit sprinter's heart rate hits 160 beats per minute or more within seconds of the starting gun and, if the runner is fit, returns to the low 60s within fifteen minutes of crossing the finish line.

On the other hand, if the runner is flabby and unfit, it might take an hour or more for your pizza delivery guy's heartbeat to return to its resting rate after he sprints to your doorway in the rain, only to find you gave him no tip for being forty-five minutes late.

The time required to return to the resting rate is called the heart rate recovery, and it's one of the best measures of the resilience of a person's cardiovascular system. The stress response system balances activation and relaxation, accelerator and brake, the tone in our sympathetic and our parasympathetic nervous systems.

When both work well, we cope and we stay nimble and our doctors give us good news at our annual checkups. Herbert Benson coined the term *relaxation response* to emphasize the recovery phase of this process, which is our capacity to counter or recover from the fight-or-flight response. But when overactivation, acceleration, and sympathetic tone persistently overrule the relaxation, the brake, and the parasympathetic tone, we're in trouble. We're stuck in a state of hyperactivation. The relaxation response is not relaxing our system. Illness eventually emerges. That system needs help re-regulating itself.

When all our organ systems are working in harmony with each other, we meet our challenges well. When they slip out of sync, we feel it as distress, and if that disharmony goes on long enough, illness is more likely to creep in.[8]

In Sync

Homeostasis is the term Walter Cannon gave in 1932 to this relatively stable internal environment we so effortlessly achieve every day we are healthy. We raise our heart rates in anticipation of warm breast milk or a cold beer, and we lower them when satisfied. For a ten-second sprint we draw glucose from liver stores and fat cells; we distribute it out to the muscles of our thighs, backs, and arms; and we shunt blood away from our stomachs.

That's our brain, heart, adrenal glands, sweat glands, lungs, every artery and vein, even our immune systems, all in sync, dancing through a sprint – no big deal. And then we and each of our activated organ systems calm down, all in sync – also requiring no apparent effort by us. (It seems improbably brilliant, but, in fact, anything less effective has just not been good enough to survive and reproduce itself.)

For coping with short threats, this harmonious elasticity of all our organ systems is all we need. But what happens if a car accident leaves you with one leg shorter than the other, or your job exposes you every day to sulfur fumes and grinding noises, or your mind plays tricks on you constantly with whispering voices hassling you all day long?

These demands don't kill you, but they raise the burden you have to cope with day in and day out. Your stress response system can't bring you back to your previous resting state. Without thinking about it, you find a new normal, a new set of set points for the system.

About thirty years ago a new term came into the stress lingo: *allostasis*. Thanks in part to Bruce McEwen, PhD, at Rockefeller University. Allostasis describes the relatively steady state achieved after accommodating to some chronic stressor. Extreme stress can bump the stress response system from its most efficient state to a less efficient state associated with a chronic condition like diabetes or depression.

In later chapters we'll return to this concept of allostatic load, a measure of the burden of our accommodations to stress that we accumulate over many years. Eventually, we all have to figure out how to accommodate to the persistent nags and demands in our lives, the ones that don't go away, and if you stick around long enough, we call that aging.

This all points to the conclusion that evolution has favored a stress response system designed to cope with quick trouble, the sprints of daily life. As long as we can recover to face the next quick trouble, we do okay.

But what if the trouble does not go away? Are we less well equipped to cope with troubles that hound us day and night, week after week, and month after month? The short answer is yes. Stressors that allow for recovery disturb our stress response systems briefly, and they tune it up. We feel fit and hearty. But stressors that persist and don't allow full recovery eventually wear us down under the weight of our allostatic load.

Modern civilized life has thankfully reduced the acute threats our ancestors once faced, while serving us a new menu of troubles that don't go away.

Since so much of the stress response takes place automatically and involuntarily, in ways we find hard to understand, though we know the physical sensations well, you may ask why we should bother understanding something so beyond our ability to know, measure, or control.

Because in the next few chapters we will see that you can both measure and control your stress responses, within certain limitations, and the length and quality of your life depends on how well you do that.

But first, what can we learn from the world's fastest runner?

5

Symphony in 10-Flat by Usain Bolt

Imagine one of the maestros of the stress response orchestra, Usain Bolt, that thirty-one-year-old sprint marvel from Jamaica, about to run his 143rd and final 100-meter sprint on August 5, 2017, in London. It's the final race of his professional career.

He's run this race countless times in competition and training. Running it again requires another challenge to his homeostasis (that stable internal environment discussed in the last chapter) – a challenge he has studied the same way Leonard Bernstein studied the musical scores of the pieces he conducted, even those he had written himself.

Since setting the 100-meter world record of 9.58 seconds in 2009, Bolt has been trying to find that magic balance, that edge that could match or beat his own performance. How do you fine-tune the nearly perfect instrument, the nearly perfect orchestra? What's the chance he could find the perfect tuning on his final race? He's been having trouble with his starts, not as quick out of the blocks as before. What's the fix for that?

One scenario could go like this. Two hours before the race, Bolt fuels up with his usual high-carb meal, knowing that the circulation that now flows freely to his gut to take in all this fast energy will soon shift away from his digestive system to the vast vessel beds that lace his large skeletal muscles, the ones that move this body forward so efficiently. This last phase of preparation begins in his brain.

The decisions about strategy were all finalized yesterday (lane position, shoe selection, start plan), and he knows these decisions so well by now that they need no conscious rehearsing. He begins carefully crafting his mellow state of mind, that trance that detaches him from distractions, narrows his focus, and heightens his awareness as he scans his inner physical landscape: "Where am I soft or hard, warm or cool, tense or loose? Is this vigor, fatigue, or butterflies I sense in my belly?"

The conductor is wandering around the orchestra floor as the instrumentalists tune up, the conductor sensing who is on today and who might have had a hard night and need some extra attention: "Does my lung section need more graded deep breathing than usual? Does that tight right hamstring require heat pads, massage, or more focused mental relaxation in the next twenty minutes? Do I have time for all three treatments?"

Bolt knows too much thinking will derail him. Thoughts about strategy drift into thoughts about how the press will cover this race. Could Gatlin or Coleman steal it? And then thoughts about his life after retiring from racing.

But the maestro banishes these thoughts, like kicking intruders out of the rehearsal hall. Instead, he plays his mantra, shunts his mind away from these distractions to the task at hand. Wisdom in this moment requires pattern recognition, matching his current sensations of his body's landscape with his memories of his best performances. Wisdom requires honest readings of his shifting emotional states to gauge his confidence against his fears.

These feelings are gold currency for experienced runners like Bolt, who knows better than anyone in his field how to use them to make adjustments that will sharpen his performance. He will have a hard time after the race telling his coach and the reporters just what he did in the hours before or during the ten seconds of the race that made the difference, because at this point he has no meters to read and not much language for how he adjusts his hormone surges and heart rates and breathing patterns and the circulation volume to his hamstrings. But at the deepest level he knows.

For the hour after the meal and the calming rituals, his parasympathetic nervous system rules, signaling his gut through the long reaches of his vagus nerve to digest and move food along, signaling insulin to store the energy absorbed from that meal, store it in the liver, fat, and muscles for quick access later, signaling the heart to lope along gently for now. He limits his mind to easy thoughts, circling around the race, shrinking his attention down to this one task. He's in slow mode, restful alertness, relaxation with eyes wide open to his inner world.

An hour before the race a few familiar words with his coach trigger his cortex to tell his hypothalamus to jack things up, to raise the secretion of CRH (corticotropin-releasing hormone) to the pituitary, but just a bit for now. And his cortex tells his sympathetic nervous system to signal his adrenal glands to squeeze into his bloodstream new epinephrine, but just a bit for now.

The signal is rippling through every section of the orchestra. Casual warm-up is over. The silence of preparation descends. The parasympathetic now yields to the sympathetic nervous system. Cortisol starts dripping from the adrenals into the bloodstream. Heart rate starts climbing from the low 50s into the 60s then 70s.

Respirations occasionally go deep, sounding the call to every collapsed alveolus asleep in the dark regions of his lungs – stretch and get ready for full oxygen infusions. All alveoli at full inflation will be needed. As heart rate and blood pressure rise, the amount of blood flowing out of his left ventricle rises too, moving oxygen more efficiently now from lung through heart pump and arteries to skeletal muscle, but just a bit for now.

The timing of this controlled excitation is exquisite, like prolonged foreplay designed for the perfectly timed climax. His insulin levels are dropping, his glucagon levels are rising, and the stored blood glucose starts pouring into his bloodstream.

As Bolt stretches his limbs in ritual warm-up, the tiny blood vessel beds in these trunk muscles open up gradually, letting blood in like flood water seeking out marsh beds, soaking the fibers with oxygen, stimulating activity in cells that were dormant just a few hours ago. This is another form of recruitment, all hands ready to play.

His muscles can taste this fuel and, in their way, ask for more. The cortisol amplifies their capacity to gobble up glucose and to contract with force, ramping up their kinetic power in carefully calibrated steps. Bolt orchestrates this phase through a series of minor exercise revvings followed by relaxings, attending each time to where there's harmony and to where something's out of touch. He is tuning and retuning in a sawtooth climb toward a state of heightened excitation that is both exquisite and sophisticated, compared to what you and I do in our weekend warrior excitements.

When the gun cracks and Bolt jumps from the blocks, his heart rate is already in the low 100s. Within the first strides, the burst of epinephrine and sympathetic nerve activity jolts that rate into the high 100s. Was his start fast enough, fast enough to be his best? He thinks not. Needs something more.

Epinephrine jolts the glycolysis process into high gear to dump more glucose into the blood in higher amounts. His stride rate climbs, breathing rate climbs, cardiac output climbs, and every other system climbs in tight step as he reaches peak velocity at 30 meters, three seconds down. Cortisol and endorphins pour their full juice on straining cells, making this explosion of force possible, tolerable. Now to hold this peak velocity, hold all the outputs that have made it possible, hold it longer than the others can. Stretch that peak. Consume all energy stores.

At 70 meters Bolt sees Gatlin and Coleman on either side: they're too close. His frontal cortex calls for something more, but what? More power, more forward leaning, more short strides? Then it's over. The line crossed, the push is over.

Now the stride shift, the turning, the realization that Gatlin had bested him, and so had Coleman. On the big board he's just under 10-flat. Bolt feels a release, an enormous release, but can't sense any more than that as he slows his stride.

This downshifting is as rapid, as automatic, as familiar as his start. Sympathetic activity now yields to the rise of parasympathetic activity, slowly yields. Epinephrine levels decline while acetylcholine and vagus nerve activity take over the relaxation process. This, too, is a carefully orchestrated wind-down of each system in concert with the others.

While his heart rate drops gradually, his respiratory system has to keep oxygenating at high levels to clear the lactic acid that has built up in the last ten seconds. He inhales long and deep breaths. His musculoskeletal system has to clean up the minor damage in its fibers with help from the scavengers of the immune system, and his glucagon declines so insulin can later restore the food stocks in the cells. And his brain conducts every phase of this movement of the symphony with almost as much care as the earlier escalation.

As Bolt becomes aware of the crowd booing and the positions of Gatlin and Coleman nearby, he tunes in to that physical sense of release again and finds the sensation a welcome one. In a flicker like a dream fragment, his full career flashes before him and then vanishes.

"This is okay," he says to himself. "I've been a lucky man. I've been the best for a long stretch. And today is not my day, not for winning."

Instead of feeling frustration or humiliation or a tightening, he feels something large, a loosening, something warm for his rivals and gratitude for his disappointed fans. He embraces Gatlin first, then Coleman, and then waves to the crowd. These thoughts from his brain ease the recovery role for his parasympathetic nervous system. The conductor now has his full orchestra confidently in yield mode.

If Bolt had resented this loss or harbored bitterness for his rivals, his mind and his body would have remained in fight mode, heart and mind still racing though his legs were walking. Not this day for this wise man.

Instead, he senses the greater glory of his many triumphs, not the burn of this one defeat. That choice from his cerebral cortex eases the toll on his heart and his adrenal glands and every other organ in the orchestra. And that choice allows him to lay a gentle hand on the parasympathetic nervous systems of the other runners and of all fans who watch him as he reaches out to his rivals and up to the fans in this enormous stadium.

The boos are gone. The cheers now take over. The crowd joins him in a chorus of release and relaxation, thousands of vagus nerves to the rescue. The fight is over. This is recovery. The longer race is done, a new form of rest now won.

Orchestra of Organs

As marvelous as such feats are, I do not want to leave you with the impression that they are nature's magic. We can understand much of what the component organs are doing. More mysterious still, even to the experts, is the orchestration of these organs under stress, which we understand less well. But let's look closer at three of the major component organs of the stress response system during an acute stressor like this sprint or a sudden fright in a dark alley.

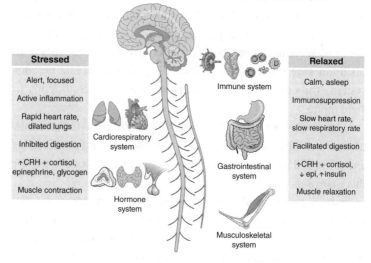

Figure 5.1 The major organs of the stress response system.

Understanding the mechanisms at work in each organ helps us appreciate the marvel of orchestrating the whole stress response system over a lifetime. The major players in this stress response orchestra are our brain and its nerves, our heart and lungs and their vessels, our glands and their hormones, our gut for energy metabolism, our immune system, and our musculoskeletal system for fighting, fleeing, or freezing.

Every other organ also joins in to varying degrees – the immune system can't do it without the skin, the muscles can't do it without the genito-urinary system knowing when to shut down – the proportions of each activity varying in part with the demands of the stressor.

Brain and nerves. The anatomical parts of the nervous system play lead roles in each stress response. The cortex of the brain, where conscious thought takes place, and the limbic system, which conducts much of our emotional lives, often beneath our awareness, run the command center.

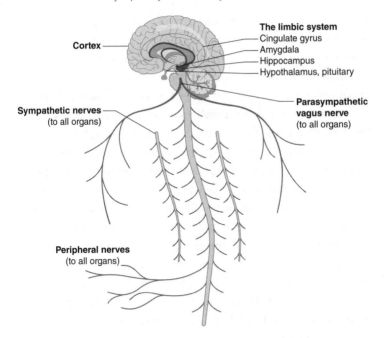

Figure 5.2 The nervous system: our conductor.

The limbic system includes the hippocampus and amygdala in the temporal lobes, the hypothalamus more centrally, and the pituitary gland that hangs just below the hypothalamus.

Branching out from these centers, the cranial and peripheral nerves that play major roles in the stress response system include the vagus nerve that runs from the brain stem down to nearly all the organs in our chest, abdomen, and pelvis, providing most of the parasympathetic or relaxing effects, and serving as the brain's window into the body.

Operating in counterpoint to the parasympathetic vagus nerve is the sympathetic nerve chain, the other half of the autonomic nervous system, that runs up and down both sides of the spine and reaches into nearly all those same organs to provide the activating

103

stimulus or accelerator. And throughout our bodies run the sensory and pain fibers that usually alert us to threats from inside or out.

Our stress response systems can be tripped into action from above or below. That is, we can switch the system on by thoughts in our cortex above ("This dark alley is not a safe place and I better split, now!") or by reflexes from below. At the first scuffle of shoes in the dark alley, I'm in the air, jumping back, lightning fast, my heart already leaping. All this is directed by reflexes from below, well before my cortex registers that some heavy-set man making such a noise in this darkness is likely to pounce on me, so close that I better jump back fast before he kills me with a crowbar or a pistol.

The shorter, quicker reflex path from below that has me jumping before thinking runs from my sensory nerves up to my thalamus and hypothalamus, out to my hippocampus and amygdala, where it is checked against my library of past dark alley threats, and down to my motor cortex. That rapid reflex arc triggers the stereotypical jump reaction that is hardwired in my motor system to excite my fight-or-flight response.

The longer path triggered by the scuffling noise runs from my thalamus forward to my frontal cortex where, with a little more time and thought, the CEO in my brain can think twice about that noise and decide whether this is a threat to be fought or to run from. Or perhaps I realize that this is just another practical joke by my jerk of a friend because of course this is Halloween! That's my judgment restraining my reflex response.

In the dark alley I'm now so focused on those scuffling shoe sounds that the song I was singing in my head and the list of errands that was nagging me and that half-trance that floated me into this alley have vanished – my brain can't think about anything other than my enemy in this darkness.

I'm on full alert, my pupils are wide open, my sympathetic synapses are firing, I feel no pain, and I'm ready suddenly for I don't know what. I'm crouching and ready to fight, well before I realize

I'm scared to death, well before I know what made that scuffling noise. That's my nervous system in sympathetic activation mode, phase one of my stress response.

Meanwhile, my heart rate speeds up and my blood pressure rises, forcing open vessel beds in my muscles that were shut just before I turned into the alley in my absent-minded trance.

All this sympathetic activity paradoxically widens some arteries to increase flow to muscles and brain while contracting others to decrease flow to my gut and kidneys, shunting blood where it most needs to go to survive the impending threat.

The central nervous system is a use-it-or-lose-it organ. Athletes and musicians know that daily use of some brain circuits is necessary to perform at their peaks. Stroke victims know that losing some circuits to a blood clot forces them to learn to walk or speak again by retraining other brain circuits to adopt those functions.

Neuroplasticity is the capacity to modify the functioning of circuits in the brain by stimulating dormant circuits or training new circuits to perform new functions. A workaround, if you will. Neuroplasticity is one of the features that facilitates homeostasis, allostasis, and resilience – it's the tendency of the brain to regulate itself by remodeling circuits under the pressure of practice.

Some changes come within days and others take months or years to establish themselves. In later chapters we will see in detail how treatments for stress-related disorders capitalize on neuroplasticity, such as the example of researchers at the University of Wisconsin who have developed a lollipop-like device that stimulates neuroplasticity in the brain stem for the treatment of neurologic disorders.[1]

Hormones. Among our hundreds of hormones, the ones that matter most to the stress response system are those that play prominent roles in the hypothalamic-pituitary-adrenal (HPA) axis, the hormonal pillar of the many ways we respond to stress. Variations on this HPA axis operate at every level of the evolutionary ladder of

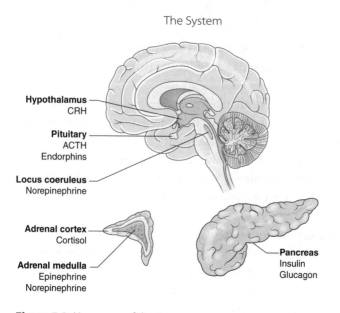

Figure 5.3 Hormones of the stress response system.

primates, so it's worth understanding. (Endocrinologists can't talk about their favorite hormones without their acronyms and abbreviations, so I'll use some of their lingo. And I recognize that this discussion can get bogged down in medical terms.)

The job of these stress hormones is to regulate autonomic nervous system activity, energy metabolism, immune function, and even certain behaviors such as fighting or fleeing, sleeping or working.

The first hormone secreted in response to the perception of a threat is usually corticotropin-releasing hormone or CRH, secreted by the hypothalamus, one of the most primitive but important centers deep in our brains.

The hypothalamus controls much of our daily rhythms. We don't think of it as a gland, but technically the hypothalamus serves the function of a gland by secreting CRH into a set of blood vessels that run just centimeters below to the pituitary gland. This is the everyday alchemy miracle: we transform a thought into a molecule that triggers a cascade of other molecules into the bloodstream that then trigger complex behaviors that save our lives.

When CRH circulates in the bloodstream down to the anterior pituitary gland, it triggers the secretion into the bloodstream of adrenocorticotropic hormone (ACTH, or corticotropin), a name that reminds us that its function is to stimulate the cortex of the adrenal glands. The adrenal glands sit like pyramid-shaped hats on the tops of the kidneys. There in the cortex of the adrenal glands the ACTH stimulates the secretion of cortisol. (Cortisol, or hydrocortisone, is classified as a glucocorticoid molecule, or one that affects *glucose*, comes from the adrenal *cortex*, and is a *steroid*, as are estrogen and testosterone.)

In an example of nature's brilliant redundancy, a second line of response to stress follows the sympathetic nervous system to the adrenal gland, also called the sympathetic-adrenal-medullary (SAM) axis. While the cortex or outer layer of the adrenal gland is secreting cortisol, the medulla or inner core of the adrenal gland is secreting epinephrine (also known as adrenaline) and norepinephrine to do similar and complementary work in the service of stress management.

Epinephrine is your body's rapid responder (seconds); whereas, cortisol supports the fight-or-flight response over minutes and hours. Epinephrine and norepinephrine also regulate autonomic nervous system activity, energy metabolism, immune function, and fighting or fleeing, sleeping or working. Harmony between these two parallel axes of the stress response system, the HPA and SAM axes, allows for efficiency and rapid return to a resting state; disharmony is alarming and uncomfortable – the kind of discomfort that eventually drives people to doctors with fatigue, anxiety, chronic pain, or insomnia.

After the alarm triggered by the scuffling in the alley, I'm ready to fight. My engine is primed for action. Where's the fuel? One of the functions of this surge of these specific hormones is to pull lots of glucose from the glycogen, protein, and triglycerides of the storage cells in my liver, muscles, and fat into my blood where the glucose can feed the energy needs of my brain, muscles, heart, and lungs, as they kick into high gear.

Playing counter to insulin is glucagon, also secreted by the pancreas. Insulin and glucagon sit on opposite ends of the energy seesaw. Insulin moves glucose from the blood into the cells; glucagon moves it out. Acute stress lowers insulin levels and activity while raising glucagon levels and activity.

The acute stress response robs us of our appetite because during a crisis all our energy must go to flooding our circulation with the glucose we already have in us. We can't afford the time it takes to eat and metabolize new forms of energy, a process that requires hours and consumes precious resources. This shift to consuming stored energy during a crisis is accomplished in part by CRH and glucagon inhibiting appetite. We can eat later, if we survive.

And we can feel pain later, if we survive. The acute stress response includes surges of endorphins, our body's narcotic to temporarily spare us the full pain of injury during the fight or the flight. To our endorphins we owe the mixed blessing of hurting more after the extreme challenges of a fight or a rugby match than during the event. Both the temporary anesthetic of endorphins and the later return of pain at the site of the injury improve our chances of survival.

Immune system. The organ system we may be least aware of during any phase of the stress response is the immune system. Since the function of our immune system is to guard against invasions, it must respond to early signs of trouble.

The first wave of response is triggered by the effects of epinephrine, norepinephrine, and sympathetic nerve activation on the stores of immune cells in our vessels, bone marrow, thymus, lymph nodes, and spleen, where the immune cells hang out like troops in barracks, waiting for the call to arms.

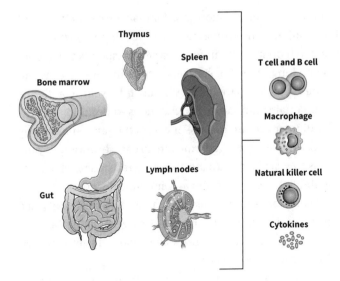

Figure 5.4 Your immune system.

The number of white cells, such as lymphocytes, macrophages, and natural killer cells, circulating in the bloodstream rises within seconds and minutes of the stressor. This call to arms helps us get ready for fighting injuries, if they come. Mild elevations in white cell counts are common in emergency department patients with acute physical trauma, well before infection could account for such a rise.

After activation comes suppression of this acute immune response, often bringing the number of circulating white cells back to normal levels within an hour or two. However, if I've been assaulted, beaten, and robbed in that dark alley, and if I replay my terror through flashbacks many times a day, the suppression of my immune function may go too far and drift into a state of chronic low-grade inflammation, commonly associated with chronic stress.

As we will see in the next few chapters, excessive CRH and cortisol can do this too. Chronic high levels of cortisol can suppress our immunity. Too much endorphins for too long can do this. And chronic activation of the sympathetic nerve chain can do this.

The research on how the immune system responds to stress in the short and long run is not simple, because the immune system is not simple. It's full of paradoxes. Stimuli under some conditions will activate certain immune cells or functions while inhibiting others; under different conditions the effects of the same stimuli may be reversed. And the prolonged exposure to cortisol during chronic stress exposures can lead to a state of cortisol resistance, which sets up vulnerabilities to infection and autoimmune disorders.

The key point for us to appreciate from this quick review of just a few of the organ systems involved in the stress response is the intricate coordination across all organ systems required to mount even the most mundane stress response.

You and I are not world-class sprinters, but our stress response system kicks in when a project is due at work, or the Wi-Fi goes out during a critical Zoom meeting, or our aging mother falls yet again.

Our bodies, like Usain's, often sound the call to action, meet the demand, and then relax to a state of relatively low output. At its best, our body's stress response is a miracle of elastic harmony by a large and invisible orchestra. But what happens when we are not so resilient? And how does the trouble accumulate over our lifetimes?

6

Resilience for Life – Yours

As recently as the 1990s, it was common to talk about trying to find the cause of cancer. Or the cause of heart disease. Or the cause of diabetes. The simplicity of the goal seemed irresistible. And has always proved to be elusive.

One of the hard lessons we have learned from decades of research on these common chronic conditions is that we will never find "the cause" of any of them. The processes by which we develop these conditions are far too complex to be reduced to any single cause. Even with infections like tuberculosis, other factors in addition to the presence of the TB bug must contribute to the disease process. The *tubercle bacillus* alone does not "cause" tuberculosis, but it's a key contributing factor.

The language we now use for talking about the contributing factors of coronary heart disease, for example, begins with the eight major risk factors: age, gender, family history, diabetes, smoking, high blood pressure, obesity, and physical inactivity. This concept of risk factors recognizes that many factors in various combinations may contribute to the emergence of a single chronic condition. Predicting who will get that condition has become a numbers game. Are you willing to roll the dice with your health?

Teresa Langford has a higher probability of dying by heart attack before fifty than Usain Bolt. She has at least five risk factors, and, so far, he has none. How does a severe chronic stressor raise our risks for chronic illness? Can building resilience protect us from the risk factors and stressors we can't change? Understanding the basics of how the stress response system works in both the short and long run helps us make sense of the elaborate, varied, surprising, and sometimes contradictory research on stress and illness.

Stress-Related Illnesses

The degree to which toxic stress contributes to an illness varies with the illness and the person. And one person's sensitivity to stress may vary over their lifetime. Psychiatric illnesses are in general sensitive to stressful events, especially during the early years of depression, bipolar disorder, and schizophrenia. Common physical illnesses like diabetes and heart disease may also be sensitive to stress in some people at some stages of the illness.

The determination of how stress-related an illness might be depends on careful tracking of the course of the illness relative to your levels of distress over an extended period. Making the determination that a specific aspect of an illness is related to specific stressors can be useful for making treatment decisions, such as knowing when to adjust medications or do more careful monitoring or engage in intensive psychotherapy.

The Stress–Illness Log

- Before deciding that stress plays a role in an illness, try keeping a stress–illness log for a month or two.
- Choose one or two types of stress (arguments, paying bills) that happen frequently and can be measured simply (mild–moderate–severe, or 0 to 10 scale).
- Choose one or two illness measures that vary with time and reflect the severity of the illness such as levels of pain (0–10), resting heart rate, or severity of depressive symptoms.
- Use a calendar, journal, or app to log daily ratings.
- Share these data with the people who help you manage the illness; look for patterns.
- Consider what other factors you did not measure that might affect the patterns. Can you improve your log for next month?

Resilience over the Long Run

Resilience, like stress, operates at every level: genes, the cell, every organ system, the organism, the individual, the family, the group, the tribe, the society. Resilience is the capacity of the stress response system to find its "home base" (I've introduced the term *homeostasis*) after a disturbance. Resilience is our buffer against disease, and disease is evidence of failures in resilience.

We develop an intuitive sense of our resilience through life's daily tests. Our confidence in our health is rooted in this acquired intuition about our capacity to meet life's stressors. This means that acquiring wisdom about health depends on knowing about stressors and what makes one stressor more manageable or threatening than another.

Children who shine at school in spite of abuse at home, soldiers who thrive in boot camp and on the battlefield, prisoners who stay fit through rounds of punishing deprivation – these survivors remind us that the exposure to severe stressors is not the only variable in the equation, or even the most important one, relating stress to illness.

The capacity of the stress response system to regulate itself through work–rest cycles tells us that our risk for illness depends not only on the stressors we're exposed to but on our responses to those stressors, our resilience, our capacity to recover and repair.

In general, as the number, severity, and frequency of acute stressors increase, our risk for illness should increase. But the studies of stress and illness are full of exceptions to this expectation, and one explanation for these exceptions comes from the often forgotten variable of resilience.

Some people stay healthy in spite of long exposures to high levels of stress because they have plenty of resources for bouncing back. These resources may be as varied as religious faith, optimistic personality traits (glass is half full), financial wealth, physical vigor, a robust immune system, or a rich social network.

Teresa Langford remained apparently healthy during her twenties and thirties in spite of plenty of tough stuff in her life. But during her forties her resilience dropped as her stressors mounted and her reserves became depleted. The result eventually was a gang-up of chronic physical and mental illnesses.

This reciprocal relationship between stress and resilience shows up in a number of good studies. For example, after many studies had shown that depression in the period following a heart attack roughly doubles a person's risk of dying within six months, resilience researcher George Bonanno, PhD, looked carefully at who dies and who does not die.

He examined the data for over 2,000 older adults with depression from at least three time points during the ten years surrounding their first reported heart attack. He identified four trajectories: The largest group (68.3 percent) was the resilient group with low levels of depression symptoms throughout the ten years. The chronic depression group (14 percent), who reported stable levels of depressive symptoms before and after the heart attack, and the group with depression before the heart attack whose depression symptoms later improved (6.8 percent) were not at greater risk for dying. The only trajectory with increased mortality was the group that developed depression *after* the heart attack (10.9 percent).

New onset of depression after the heart attack reflected a stress response system that was having trouble recovering. Trouble in the cardiovascular system had created trouble in the central nervous system. The personality trait of optimism was the key variable that differentiated the large resilient group from the three other groups with different trajectories of depression.[1]

The lesson from this study is that 90 percent of us are remarkably resilient. Resilience is the rule, not the exception. We bounce back from heart attacks, and optimism helps us to be resilient. Even most of us who have had trouble with depression before will bounce back after a heart attack. But the 10 percent of us who develop depression after the heart attack are in an unstable state, both in our brains and in our hearts. We're less resilient and more likely to die soon.

These people deserve urgent and careful attention during the six months after a first heart attack. Their heart disease has triggered a disruption in their central nervous system – that's stress-sensitive or stress-related heart disease. Identifying these people as high risk in a timely way has been a difficult lesson for cardiologists and primary care doctors to adopt in practice.

Optimism provides a buffer against heart disease. So does the capacity to regulate our emotions. So does life satisfaction and emotional vitality and positivity. These are traits that have come to be known under the term *positive psychology* – a relatively new term in the psychology lexicon.

Positive psychology translates into resilience, which prolongs life by reducing the burden of heart disease.[2] As we learn to see the anatomic, hormonal, neural, and immunologic consequences of these forms of positive psychology, it becomes clearer how patterns of "feeling good" can make for longer, healthier lives, even when life throws you high levels of stressors.

For the lucky few, optimism may come naturally, a matter of temperament or personality. For the rest of us, optimism can be learned. Martin Seligman, PhD, a psychologist whose first book (with Christopher Peterson and Steven Maier) was *Learned Helplessness*, is also the author of *Learned Optimism: How to Change Your Mind and Your Life* (2006). As one of the leading voices in positive psychology, Dr. Seligman has shown how common principles of cognitive behavior therapy can be applied to the learning of optimistic approaches to life that lead to measurable health benefits.

Love Hunger

Today most of us can see and talk with anyone we choose anywhere in the world at the tap of a phone screen, even in war zones, for less than the price of a postage stamp. We now make social connections with an ease that was unimaginable just a generation ago. We smartphone owners should be well connected and socially well fed.

Not true, said a recent Cigna survey of loneliness in over 20,000 US adults.[3] This study is just the most recent to underscore the paradox that in this age of hyperconnection, loneliness and social isolation remain a major public health problem.

Using the UCLA Loneliness Scale to measure loneliness, this survey found that 27 percent of people in the study reported feeling rarely or never understood by others. Over 40 percent felt their relationships were sometimes or always not meaningful. One in five felt rarely or never close to people. The age group that reported the highest rates of loneliness were those aged eighteen to twenty-two. Surprised?

The larger context for this recent survey was a 2015 review of seventy of the best studies of the effects of loneliness or social isolation on mortality.[4] Whether you're lonely or merely choose to live alone raises your risk of early death by 25 to 30 percent – as large an effect as the more traditional risk factors of obesity, smoking, or physical inactivity. The effect of loneliness on death hits hardest not on the elderly but on those in middle age. Although loneliness is now more common among the young, it is more lethal among the middle aged.

One of the believers in this loneliness epidemic is Vivek Murthy, MD, whom you may recognize as the former Surgeon General of the US (2014–2017).

"We live in the most technologically connected age in the history of civilization," he said, following his article "Work and the loneliness epidemic," in the *Harvard Business Review*, "yet rates of loneliness are increasing."[5]

According to one expert, since the 1980s the percentage of American adults who say they're lonely has doubled from 20 percent to 40 percent.[6] Dr. Murthy attributes this epidemic to our increasing geographic mobility, our growing preferences for texting and email over direct conversation, and the recent shift in work efficiencies and habits that isolate workers from their colleagues. The isolations imposed by efforts to manage the COVID epidemic have magnified this effect.

How can we understand how such apparent progress in social networking could fuel a rise in loneliness with measurably poor consequences for our health? Evolution has not prepared us for these unprecedented levels of self-sufficiency that have come with first-world rates of progress. We evolved to function best in small, tight families and tribes, but over the last half-century, in developed countries, we may have grown efficient and self-reliant to a fault, dispersing ourselves far from the social structures of our origins.

We have isolated ourselves through our houses, our cars, our access to information without talking to anyone, our work spaces, and our recent dependence on screens and devices. This efficiency and comfort come at the unintended expense of direct conversations, eye contact, handshakes, hugs, and the smells of each other. We forget that we need to belong to groups that need us. The isolations imposed by COVID have forced this lesson on us in a way that should be hard to forget.

Is loneliness a reasonable price to pay for our progress? And how does loneliness pertain to toxic stress?

Consider the physical costs of social isolation. If we could examine the inner workings of loneliness, what would we find? For all but the most introverted and isolated hermit, here's what the lonely feel:

- Resting heart rates generally go up when we're alone, and, over the long run, high heart rates strain the cardiovascular system.
- Acute stress hormones, such as adrenaline and cortisol, rise and stay elevated when we're alone, reducing resilience.
- Sleep becomes less restful and less efficient when we feel lonely – meaning we don't recover from fatigue well.
- Inflammation levels creep up, and infections too, both reflecting a struggling immune system.
- Self-care goes down. Why not skip that shower? Who needs to brush teeth if no one's around to be offended? Cooking for one is no fun.
- Cognitive processing slows with loneliness: more errors on the crossword puzzle, more forgetfulness, fewer problems solved, fewer contacts made.

When mental agility and judgment slide, sometimes that opens the way for people with depression to consider suicide. Solitude is one of the universal preconditions for suicide attempts. Almost no one tries to kill themself in the presence of another; the social prohibitions are too great. Deadly combinations of these physical and psychological undercurrents of loneliness pave the pathways to heart disease, diabetes, depression, and early death.

So, loneliness, like hunger and thirst, is an adaptive signal, if we learn to pay attention to it and respond by establishing meaningful social connections. But the seductions of modern self-sufficiency are hard to resist, and poor health poses only a distant threat compared to current comforts, so a substantial number of us choose to pay this steep price of loneliness. And yet our resources for combating the seductions of self-sufficiency also have never been greater.

If we don't get smart – smarter than our phones – about feeding our love hunger, our loneliness may starve us to early deaths.

Depression: Searching for the Toxic Stress in Heart Disease

In 2009 when the American Heart Association (AHA) convened a writing group to consider depression as a risk factor for coronary heart disease, the AHA Science Advisory and Coordinating Committee asked the American Psychiatric Association (APA) to participate.

When the AHA invitation came in, the president of the APA that year, Carolyn Rabinowitz, and I had just presented a symposium on depression and heart disease at our annual meeting, so she asked me to join the AHA writing group. How could I say no to this promising opportunity to contribute to the AHA's potential stamp of approval on a large body of evidence that could clarify and promote the role of depression care in the management of heart disease? I was flattered.

This writing group included nearly twenty of the leading researchers in the field: health psychologists, cardiologists, internists, sociologists, nurses, statisticians, and me as the lone and perhaps token psychiatrist. Of course I said yes. I hoped this project would clarify for all of us not just the magnitude of the effect of depression on heart disease but the mechanisms that explain how depression contributes to the development of heart disease and early death.

For this academic exercise we chose to think of clinical depression as the stressor – the toxic burden that challenges the cardiovascular system, sometimes to the extremes of illness. This role of depression as the exposure or trigger for a physical illness can be confused with the other role clinical depression also plays, which is the outcome, or the mental illness that may result from overwhelming stressors, such as losing your cat, your job, and your driver's license (that humiliating DUI!), all in one miserable month.

Clinical depression, especially in the early years of the course of recurrent depression, is often triggered by stressful events. The resulting depression in turn adds to the stressful demands, creating a cycle during which it's hard to distinguish the eggs from the chickens, the exposures from the outcomes. For this paper the AHA was clearly interested in the contribution of the stressor clinical depression to the development and progression of coronary heart disease.[7]

We started out expecting a neat six- to twelve-month series of conference calls to review the available published data and perform a systematic analysis that would support a set of recommendations. That's what we scientists do.

Instead, we ended up spending about four years on this project. By the time we finished, just twelve of us were left, and we had tackled only half the original task. Writing by committee is rarely fun. We eventually agreed that there were not enough well-designed studies to address our original question about depression as a risk for the *onset* of heart disease. So we settled on the second question, whether depression is a risk factor for the progression of *existing* coronary heart disease. For that question we found more than fifty good studies, and that data set formed the basis for our eventual review and recommendations published in 2014.[8]

Prior to publication of our report in *Circulation*, the AHA's Scientific Review Committee gave our manuscript the AHA stamp of approval to serve as a scientific statement, the highest level of endorsement conferred by the AHA and their closest thing to defining a standard of practice. I figured we had paved the way to transforming care for depression in patients with heart disease.

And what was the toxic element of depression? Our paper includes a list of possible disturbances within the physical body in which depression may contribute to the progression of heart disease. The list is long and science-speak for "we don't know." Or "it's complicated and messy." I was disappointed that we had not found a bullet to blame for depression's toxic effects on heart disease. But not surprised.

The other truth that was emerging around this time was that the same list of potential mechanisms for how depression kills us could apply to other major mental illnesses. Depression, my "favorite" pathway to heart disease, was by no means the only mental illness with this toxic association.

Several reviews had shown that risks for early death were equally high across most other severe major mental illnesses: schizophrenia, bipolar disorder, and anxiety disorders.[9] And what these illnesses shared in common was an early age of onset, a chronic or recurrent course, and severe symptoms. Two-thirds of these early deaths were from common, long-lasting physical conditions like heart disease, lung disease, and diabetes.

Other studies confirmed what we found: The mind ravages the body. High levels of relentless "mental" stress exposures eventually wear and tear apart our organ systems in very specific patterns of physical diseases that don't seem on the surface to resemble each other. There's nothing like these afflictions of the mind to turn our body and soul old before our time.

Aging and Shoelaces

I met a ninety-four-year-old man in my exam room recently. He shuffled in with his cane in his right hand, gave me a glance with a wink of mock triumph, leaned on his cane, and, tapping one heel against the other, said, "Didn't miss a step!"

Trailing him came an elderly woman who shuffled as he did, but without a cane, bracing her steps with one hand on the door jam, then the other on the chair back. I took her for his wife, too proud perhaps to be seen in public with a cane. But then she said, "Prop your cane in the corner, Dad!"

It turned out his daughter was my age, though she looked and sounded older than her father. What gave her that look of being near the end of life? Her unsteady gait, the wrinkles and sag in her cheeks, the nicotine stains on her fingers, the fine tremor in her hands, the ponderous pace of her speech – she made me feel I was in the presence of an old and weary woman. She looked closer to death than he did.

I later learned she had always lived alone, hadn't worked since her early retirement nine years ago, had been her father's sole caretaker since then, had steered clear of doctors for herself, and didn't do much other than tend to him. He gave me a delightful lift, but she weighed heavily on me.

So what's the difference between the stressors that make us stronger (like the father) and the stressors that kill us (like the daughter)? Does taking care of your elderly father for nine years give meaning to your day or age you so rapidly that it sends you early to your grave? Or both? Stressors that age us and make us die young usually get a grip on us and won't let go for many months or years. Marriages, universally known to be stressful, usually extend life. Loneliness, including lonely marriage, usually shortens life.

Chronic stress responses and aging overlap not only in my exam room but also in the nuclei of our cells. Take a closer look at your chromosomes. You may think you know how old you are, but it's also possible now to measure the age of your cells by measuring the length of the telomeres in the chromosomes of your white blood cells.

Telomeres are the sections at the end of a chromosome that are like tightly wrapped tips of a shoelace. As cells divide, their telomeres fray and shorten. But most cells repair these tips with the help of an enzyme called telomerase. Chronic stress exposures and responses interfere with this repair process, making the correlation between stress and telomere length a tighter one in those with high exposures.

Trauma in childhood has been shown to shorten telomeres and accelerate the aging process.[10] In general, long telomeres protect us and short telomeres predict earlier onset of our common diseases of aging, such as diabetes, heart disease, and dementia.

Can boosting our telomerase slow the aging process? Theoretically and experimentally yes, but to do this in the clinic is a more difficult task.

Through this lens we can see that the aging process involves a decline in the capacity to recover from strain and a decline in the capacity to repair ourselves at every level: brain, organs, tissues, cells, and genes. The decline in one organ system may accelerate faster than in the others; heart disease may come before dementia, or depression may precede diabetes. In people with metabolic

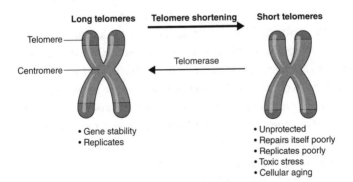

Figure 6.1 The long and short of it: telomeres.

syndrome, who have three or more risk factors but not yet heart disease or diabetes, for example, the decline seems to happen simultaneously across multiple organ systems.[11]

When our response to chronic stressors fails to recover and repair, we take another step in the aging process, another shuffling step, with or without a cane, closer to death.

What Can We Learn from the Oldest of the Old?

If resilience is what protects us from illness under stress, wouldn't it be useful to know what makes a stress response system function at its best? What are the conditions that favor the best functioning of our stress response system?

This is another way of asking what makes us healthy, if we define health as both the absence of disease and the presence of well-being. Stress research labs have given us answers to this question for short time frames. For example, optimism, rapid heart rate recovery, and intact negative feedback at a key circuit in the brain for regulating cortisol levels all favor good stress reactivity in laboratory studies of humans. But what we most want to know about resilience must come from the laboratory of life.

Medical anthropologists have helped us by asking a simple question: where do people live the longest and why? If you have never heard of Hunza, Vilcabamba, or Abkhasia, that is your first clue. You have not heard of them because they are rural villages in remote places: northern Pakistan, the mountains of Ecuador, and the foothills of the Caucasus between Russia and Georgia. These villages harbor some of the highest numbers of healthy people living to one hundred or more in the world.

The secrets to their longevity have been the subject of some compelling books and documentaries, which have led to promising community development projects in the US and elsewhere.[12] Many remote rural villages don't do so well on longevity, so studies of these select outlier villages teach us some valuable lessons about the conditions that allow their (and potentially our) stress response systems to function at their best for the longest time, relatively free of illness and blessed with well-being after a hundred years, across a variety of religions, races, geographies, and political systems.

Listen to the lessons as digested by Dan Buettner, author of *The Blue Zones: 9 Lessons for Living Longer from the People Who've Lived the Longest.* Move your body daily, and gently. Work with a purpose. Face stress and let go of stress. Belong to small groups and to communities. Care for your family. Eat a plant-based diet and drink a little wine. Live loyal to these habits.

What sets these Blue Zones villages apart from most other rural villages and all cities? In these outlier communities, the range of stressors to which these citizens are exposed is relatively narrower than the range in more complex urban environments. The demand for physical activity occurs daily, and the opportunities for rest also occur daily.

Social networks are tight at the family and tribal level, so the risk of isolation or loneliness or deviance is relatively slim. The opportunities for meaningful roles in these communities are ample, even for the ultra-elderly, so most people live their late years with a sufficient sense of purpose.

Their approach to work is unhurried, steady, and often playful. Their agrarian economies require a modest and balanced diet, mostly vegetarian. Their food supply is ample without being extravagant. Their climates are relatively free of pollution and violence. In their one-hundredth years most of these centenarians remain free of the afflictions we assume are a normal part of late aging. High blood pressure, heart disease, dementia, and arthritis are not common among these centenarians.

If this sounds like a formula for bliss, think again. Most of us raised in the US or in developed urban settings might find it fascinating to visit one of these villages, but after a month or two of living this life, we would find these villages dull, the conversation limited, the jobs simple, the food bland, and the entertainment repetitive. For a short time we could move and eat and drink and befriend and work and relax with these people who will outlive us.

But we would be outsiders who can never belong to these families, groups, and tribes in the deep sense required for the stress response system to function at its best. Our sense of purpose and meaning would not run as deep as theirs. We would always feel far from home. Almost all of us would soon find our way back home to the faster and shorter life. And Starbucks.

7

• • • • •

Fast Tracks to Dying Young

In the late 1980s Sheldon Cohen, PhD, at Carnegie Mellon University tried to infect healthy people with the cold virus. What he learned about resistance to getting the sniffles is tied to our stress response systems.

Could this study have predicted who among us came down with COVID-19? Maybe.

In his 1991 study published in the *New England Journal of Medicine*, Dr. Cohen and his colleagues reported on his efforts to see whether stress affects our vulnerability to infection with the common cold. After assessing perceived stress response levels in his study participants, he dripped one of five respiratory viruses (the common cold) into the nostrils of 394 healthy people and watched them carefully for a week.

He found that reported levels of stress response predicted the vulnerability to infection in these participants. The greater their stress levels, the greater the chance they would develop the infection, all other things considered. In other words, people with lower resilience to stress had to blow their noses.

Twenty-one years later, in 2012 Dr. Cohen was still trying to infect healthy people with the common cold and figure out who gets sick and who doesn't. But now he was also studying and reporting on why and how stress influences not only infection rates for the common cold but the course of common chronic illnesses.[1]

The short answer from the work of Dr. Cohen and others is that chronic stress damages the negative feedback loop for cortisol by making the receptors for cortisol resistant or less responsive in certain target tissues such as immune cells. So people with chronic stress end up with elevated cortisol levels. Or in the target tissues where the receptors don't work well, the cortisol is less effective. With less negative feedback, the fine-tuning of the immune response slips out of sync. The end result: low-grade inflammation. This cortisol resistance sets the stage for making other conditions such as asthma, heart disease, depression, diabetes, or possibly COVID worse.

It's no accident that the main hormones of the stress response system are tied intimately to the main hormones of the energy metabolism system – namely, insulin and glucagon. Glucose storage is a smart investment, but it takes time and energy. Withdrawing energy from our stores for crises is also expensive. Do it too often and you feel the cost as fatigue.

Fatigue is the experience of going to the pantry of our energy stores and finding the shelves mostly empty. One feature of the late stages of chronic fatigue syndrome can be persistently low levels of cortisol, which makes it hard to access whatever energy stores are there.[2]

Six fast tracks to dying young run through our lives (some we can change or control; some we can't):

1. Genes and epigenetics
2. Traumatic childhood events
3. High-risk health behaviors and relationships
4. Imbalance in parts of the nervous system
5. Cortisol resistance
6. Chronic inflammation.

There are other ways to think about how persistent stressors contribute to illness, but these features of the stress response system give us a framework for thinking about the most common pathways from chronic stress exposures to serious illness. They tap into the mind, body, and social dimensions of how we experience toxic stress.

Genes and Epigenetic Changes

Stress exposures sculpt our genome, as we have been taught by Elizabeth Blackburn and others who studied telomeres. And telomeres are not the only part of our genes that are affected by stress. If we lose a lover or learn a shocking secret or take a disfiguring wound to the face, it can haunt us day and night. Some kinds of stress have a way of getting under our skin and into our genes. We squirm, we try to shake it off, but it seems to burrow so deep there's no getting rid of it.

Here's how deep stress goes and how it goes deep. When we perceive a threat, signals from our hypothalamus start the cascade of stress hormones. Once cortisol circulates in the bloodstream, it works its magic by tickling certain receptors on certain tissues such as white blood cells that do much of the work for our immune systems.

High levels of cortisol circulating in the blood lead to cortisol seeping across cell membranes and finding certain receptors to enter cells where it flips a switch, or many switches. And some of these complex ways of flipping the switches on genes turn them on or off.[3]

These gene switches then change the type, frequency, and amount of proteins a cell churns out. Genes communicate their information through protein synthesis. These shifts in protein concentrations can alter the stress response system. And when this happens during highly sensitive periods of development, such as fetal life and infancy, they can remodel the system in lasting ways, sometimes for the better, sometimes for the worse.[4]

Remodeling could take the form of excessive production of pro-inflammatory cytokines, making the person prone to severe or prolonged reactions to injury or allergy or autoimmune diseases. Or the remodeling could take the form of the atrophy of a part of the hippocampus in the brain, or the opposite, the building of extra circuits for a sensory or memory circuit.

These are just a few examples of how stress gets under our skin, under our membranes, and onto the switches on our genes. This is how stressors remodel the circuits of some parts of our central nervous systems. No wonder we can't just do what Taylor Swift tells us to do, and "shake it off."

Changes in gene expression that change the expression without changing the structural sequence of genes are called epigenetic changes – think of this process like making revisions in software that don't change the hardware. These changes affect the way the person functions, but usually are not transmitted across generations.

From animal as well as human studies we now know that chronic stress exposure drives epigenetic changes in stress-sensitive brain tissues and in immune cells and fat cells.

Consider the genes in immune cells. A recent report examined five stress-related genes from immune cells in a study of 119 adult identical twins.[5] The question was whether exposure to childhood trauma was associated with later developing depression as an adult.

The punchline from this complex study is that genes switching on or off, in two of the five stress-related genes, accounted for about 20 percent of the risk for developing depression in people exposed to substantial childhood trauma.

The details about which gene on which chromosome are not what counts to us now. All these findings need to be confirmed. What's exciting is that this and other studies have shown it's now possible to trace a path from traumatic stress in childhood through epigenetic alterations of stress-related genes to the development of serious illness in adulthood. And part of the story is recorded in the genes of these immune cells that make them more prone to fostering chronic inflammation – one of the physical effects of chronic depression in some people.

A similar epigenetic process happens in fat cells. If chronic stressors and persistently high cortisol levels drive me to comfort eating and snacking binges to calm my emotional turmoil, I may end up with a beer-belly type of obesity and high levels of something called nuclear factor kappa B in my fat cells and circulating in my blood. My larger volume of fat cells and my high levels of this circulating factor in turn provide a fertile bed for low-grade inflammation throughout my body – and especially in the cells lining my heart arteries, where blockages called plaques narrow the arteries and can lead to heart attacks.

Here's an example of how psychological stressors can drive gene expression to fuel disease progression in the vessels of the heart. The beer belly is one outward sign of this inflammatory process that reaches into the coronary arteries.

We don't yet know the mechanisms of these epigenetic changes during the course of chronic stress. The field of the epigenetics of stress is so new that it promises more questions than answers.

- What are the critical periods for specific stress-regulating genes?
- How much stress exposure is necessary to change genes?

- Can epigenetic changes in one part of the stress response system compensate for changes in another and thereby provide a path to resilience?
- If poverty dramatically raises the risks for trauma and separation during critical periods, what hope is there for achieving resilience?
- Could some early interventions improve the chances for a child born into poverty to escape the worst of the health burdens of chronic stress in later life?[6]

Trauma and Adverse Childhood Experiences

If you work in an obesity clinic long enough, as Vincent Felitti, MD, did at Kaiser Permanente in San Diego during the 1980s and 1990s, you can't avoid asking a question that surprisingly many primary care providers never get around to: How did this obesity start?

You might think taking an obesity history and understanding the patterns of weight gain over a lifetime would be a sensible place to start, but most doctors who work with adults who struggle with obesity jump right into the diet and exercise talk.

Dr. Felitti noticed that many of his overweight patients alluded to troubled childhoods, and he wondered if the two might be linked in some way. In 1993 when he approached Robert Anda, a physician epidemiologist at the CDC, the question they wanted to answer was whether trauma and difficulties in childhood predicted the later development of obesity and other illnesses in adulthood – a sensible question that had never been rigorously tested.

At the time there was no easy way to ask these questions about trauma in childhood, so they wrote a ten-item questionnaire with yes/no answers. It had to be easy, short, and simple enough to administer to large samples over the phone as well as in person. It also had to capture enough of the range of tough childhood experiences that it could distinguish between low, medium, and high levels of exposure to trauma and adversity.

Because the questionnaire was designed for adults trying to remember events that happened as far back as forty or fifty years, it had to focus on exposures that could be reliably remembered.

At first glance, the measure seems too simple. Just ten questions about things that happened in your childhood. Just answer yes or no. Were your parents ever separated or divorced? Did a family member have a mental illness? Did you live with someone who was a problem drinker or used drugs?

Along with questions about ever having been verbally or physically or sexually abused or assaulted, any one of these questions by itself is not extraordinary in a primary care visit – embarrassing perhaps, possibly shameful, and often avoided by both patient and doctor – but legitimate questions for a doctor visit.

What is extraordinary about the Adverse Childhood Experiences Scale (ACE) is that the asking of all ten questions together and then scoring the number of yeses is amazingly simple.

In 1998, after the first retrospective study of over 17,000 middle-class participants in the San Diego Kaiser Permanente system showed promising associations between high scores on the ACE and poor adult health outcomes, critics and doubters of the study pointed to various flaws, so Drs. Felitti and Anda answered their critics with more rigorous prospective studies and expanded the reach of these studies to include an improved version of the ACE. The ACE study has since generated over seventy publications and a popular following in some circles (see www.acestoohigh.com and www.acesconnection.com).

Why is the ACE scale gaining traction? It is now clear that for this middle-class San Diego sample as well as for the samples in all the states that collected the relevant data across a wide range of socioeconomic levels, ACE scores predict over forty poor health outcomes in adulthood: diabetes, heart disease, COPD, headaches, autoimmune diseases, depression, suicide attempts, obesity, smoking, alcohol use, school performance, high school graduation, teenage pregnancy, and work absenteeism, to name a few.

In general, the higher the ACE scores, the higher the risks for each of these poor health outcomes. That puts exposure to adverse experiences, as captured by the ACE scale in the elite group of age, gender, and socioeconomic status, among the most powerful predictors of health and illness – more powerful than smoking.

How can any single risk factor have such a powerful effect on such a wide range of health outcomes?

The answer is that the risk factor must exert its impact early enough in development that it can substantially dysregulate multiple organ systems in ways that last a lifetime. The only known target for such an effect is the stress response system.

Dysregulate the stress response system during critical developmental periods (before age eighteen), and the effect can disrupt the functioning of the central nervous system (as in recurrent major depression), the endocrine system (diabetes), the immune system (autoimmune disorders like Crohn's disease or multiple sclerosis), and the cardiovascular system (coronary heart disease).

These dysregulations often take many years to contribute to the development of these disorders, along with other factors like genes and high-risk behaviors. For the majority who adapt well to these early insults, the risk vanishes. It's the minority who don't adapt that we need to identify and help, the earlier the better.

Although some parts of our popular culture have been quick to embrace the concept that childhood trauma leads to adult illness,[7] the medical culture has been slow to adopt the concept into clinical practice. Screening for adverse childhood experiences is not yet a common practice in primary care in the US or elsewhere.

At one of our finest medical centers in the early 2000s the effects of toxic stress on child health were nowhere to be found.

Nadine Burke Harris, MD, graduated in 2005 from her three-year pediatrics residency at Stanford University, confident she knew what she needed to know to set up a pediatrics clinic in one of San Francisco's poorest neighborhoods, Bayview Hunters Point.

Thirteen years later in 2018 she published a book (*The Deepest Well: Healing the Long-Term Effects of Childhood Adversity*) in which she tells how the challenges of providing care for this high-risk population eventually forced her to see what had been invisible to her during her pediatrics training: the powerful role that childhood trauma plays in her patients' risks for not only mental but also physical illnesses in childhood and early adulthood.

She argues for the value of screening for adverse childhood experiences to reduce the risks of chronic illness in childhood and adulthood. Better than a generation ago, more of these young clinicians like Dr. Harris now generally know what belongs in a good stress management toolkit. But the struggle to bring the *science* of stress to bear on the *practice* of medicine has been long and slow.

A Smoke, a Toke: The Dangers of High-Risk Health Behaviors

When public service announcements tell us to quit smoking, lose weight, and get plenty of sleep, they are targeting our high-risk health behaviors. When the advocates of Lifestyle Medicine demonstrate they can reverse diabetes or heart disease without medicine or surgery, they are targeting our health behaviors.

The example of villages in the Blue Zones where centenarians live free of the heart disease that we Americans think of as part of normal aging – they, too, reveal the power of behaviors to prolong life.

What are these high-risk behaviors that are so familiar to us and so foreign to those who live free of disease at one hundred?

Do these risky behaviors really exert such a toxic influence on our risk for illness? Addictive behaviors, compulsive worrying, physical inactivity, cheating on sleep, engaging in toxic relationships, and social isolation are some of the more common risky behaviors.

Addictions of any kind put the autonomic nervous system through a roller coaster of ups and downs. Both the stimulation and the withdrawal override the natural rhythms of the autonomic nervous system, stretching it to extremes and confusing its capacity to self-regulate. Compulsive working, eating, exercising, or worrying disrupt the natural rhythms of our sleep/wake cycles, hunger and satiety, activity and rest.

The workaholic accountant who works ten-hour days (more during tax season) and sleeps only three or four hours a night can't turn off his worries about harmless threats. He can't find the off switch. His sympathetic nerves are firing deep into the night and most of the day. He's exhausted at thirty-eight, and feels trapped.

On the other hand, idleness or physical inactivity is also a high-risk behavior and a common result of wealth. Automobiles and the Internet and elevators have elevated our standards of living to the point of idleness and isolation. In developed countries it's easy to avoid physical exertion. Our innovative efficiencies and conveniences of the last century now tether most of us to our chairs as never before in human history.

And these conveniences may shorten our lives considerably, compared to our Blue Zones brethren who walk for their water, harvest their food with their hands, climb hills to bathe or eat with family, and communicate face-to-face every day with their family, friends, and tribe members. No devices link them to strangers or separate them from those close by.

Why do we engage in these high-risk health behaviors? Because they work, in the short run. They ease our distress. A smoke, a toke, a swig, a snack – then we feel better. Often these high-risk health behaviors bring us a reinforcing relief, followed by a craving for more relief. Use leads to tolerance, which leads to more use – the vicious cycle of compulsive behaviors and addiction.

Addiction becomes a state of captivity that fears its own release. No wonder these habits are hard to break. Relief now. Pay later. Threats of distant disease can't hold a candle to the power of the immediate relief of distress.

Some people inherit genes for addictive behaviors that raise their risks for metabolic disorders. Others inherit genes for depression or ADHD, both of which raise their chances for high-risk behaviors that eventually lead to metabolic disorders. Depression at its worst sinks its victims into beds and couches, raising their health risks. ADHD may rob them of their sleep, their jobs, or effective conversations, each of which raises their health risks.

The perceived demands of chronic stressors drive us to persist with our risky behaviors. These are learned coping strategies that in some way feel good enough to continue in spite of their costs. Smoking solves my nervousness problem. Binge-watching movies deep into the night solves my insomnia problem. Saying no to a date solves my fear-of-harassment problem. We learn these strategies from our families, our friends, and the hawkers of our culture who profit from our distress.

Engaging in toxic intimate or important relationships also contributes to risk for illness. Just as too much Jack Daniels or marijuana for too long is hard on the stress response system, too much of the abusive boss or the jealous office mate or the deceiving spouse or the demented parent can pave the way to illness. These forms of chronic social stress at home and in the workplace have all been linked to poor health outcomes and early death.[8]

Equally bad for us is the absence of relationships, as former Surgeon General Murthy reminds us. Humans have evolved to be the most social of species. We thrive on certain kinds of connections. When we either lose contact or repeatedly face toxic contacts, we don't do well. The ancient ritual of shunning, the punishment of solitary confinement, and the mundane fact of loneliness in every-day life are variations on the same fast track to dying young.

Imbalance: Brain and Nerves on Edge

Your genes likely establish the initial set points for your resting heart rate, breathing rate, the tone and pace of how food moves through your small and large intestine. Those set points might rise with stressors at critical developmental stages, and experiences of effective recovery might lower them. So, as we develop, we make many adjustments to these set points. However, we don't yet know the epigenetic mechanisms by which the set points of the autonomic nervous system are switched by stressors.

Autonomic set points shape our personalities. The excitable, flamboyant, and mercurial lead actor in the school play likely has a higher resting heart rate (say 85 beats per minute), and a more reactive one, too (a greater jump in her heart rate from resting to excited, say 85 to 120), than the droll nerd slouching in the back of the class cracking dry jokes with a heart rate that never climbs above 70. Nothing's worth getting excited about, not for him.

Of course, a car accident could jack up that set point for the nerd's heart rate, especially if it maimed him for life. So could his father's loss of his job, if it introduced him to the grip of poverty. Disability and the discomforts of poverty day and night change how our hearts beat and how we breathe and how we fight infections and how we eat and how we store what we eat. Every section of the orchestra may change how it plays.

On the other hand, the lively lead actor could become infatuated with Buddhism and start meditating several hours a day and dra-matically lower both her resting heart rate and her overreactivity to stress. She could learn to be more mellow. She could train her vagus nerve and her whole parasympathetic system to play a stronger role in its dance with her sympathetic system during stressful challenges. Or she could train her amygdala to lower its set point and reactivity, toning down her whole sympathetic nervous system.

If only she could know what's going on in her amygdala. Have you ever wondered what's going on in your amygdala? And does it matter in the long run? Remember, the amygdala functions like the fire alarm security system on high alert in your brain.

Back in the mid-2000s a group of investigators at Massachusetts General Hospital followed 293 adults over age thirty with no heart disease or cancer or other chronic illness for three to five years after they had PET scans of their brains.[9] The researchers wanted to see if the activity of their amygdalas as measured by the brain images predicted the development of illness later on. And if it did, could they tell how amygdala activity made these people sick?

The investigators knew that chronic stress exerts a risk for heart disease with a prevalence and potency that is on par with the effects of smoking, high cholesterol, high blood pressure, and diabetes, but they wanted to nail down the mechanism for this effect. Could they trace the pathway from stressors to the onset of heart disease? No such studies had been done in humans.

They first established in a small cross-sectional study that high ratings of chronic stress exposures were associated with high amygdala activation, confirming the widely published observation that the amygdala is one of the first parts of the brain to be activated by perceptions of threats, whether the threat is the sound of a gunshot or a troublesome worry.

Then they found that high levels of amygdala activity – the brain's equivalent of a high resting heart rate – were associated with a significantly higher risk of developing heart disease within three to five years. This effect was not influenced by more traditional risk factors, such as high cholesterol or smoking. The higher the activity in the amygdala, the greater the risk for heart disease, and the sooner the cardiovascular event happened. Think heart attack here.

The high brain activity was also associated with high activity in the immune cells of the bone marrow and with arterial inflammation, reflecting excessive stimulation of the immune system's inflammatory response.

The full meaning of this study will require more studies like it. And someday those of us with high stress and high amygdala activity will want to know how we can turn down our sympathetic nervous systems a notch or two, in ways that reduce our risks for heart disease.[10]

The brake on the stress response system – the parasympathetic branch of the autonomic nervous system – works mostly through the many branches of the vagus nerve. Neurosurgeon Kevin Tracey sees much promise in exploring ways to stimulate or regulate specific local circuits within the vagus nerve system to correct parasympathetic imbalances that could be specific to the affected organ, such as the colon or the pancreas or the liver, in a person with, respectively, ulcerative colitis or diabetes or hepatitis.[11]

Tightly integrated to the sympathetic and the parasympathetic systems is the system that regulates pleasure and reward. You've heard about dopamine, a neurotransmitter in the brain. The brain chemicals that trigger a runner's high or a drug addict's cravings. These circuits in the brain are highly excited by certain secretions. No wonder "stress" drives me to drink. No wonder "stress" makes me take a cigarette break or gamble or binge or wash my hands for the twenty-third time today. It's a tight loop between stress and pleasure, and sometimes a vicious cycle.

One of the more startling findings from recent studies of brain imaging in people with chronic depression is the shrinking in size of two specific brain areas during episodes of severe depression: the amygdala and the hippocampus. These are the primitive parts of our emotional brain where reflex emotional reactions are programmed (amygdala) and memories of select key experiences are attached to those emotions (hippocampus).

The good news is that even after loss of cell mass in these two structures, with recovery from depression, the architecture in these two brain regions is restored – neuroplasticity to the rescue. No wonder it often takes many months to fully recover the cognitive agility that is lost during a severe depressive episode.[12] This is one example of how a persistent stressor (depression) can wear down a structure that is essential to the stress response system's capacity to self-regulate.

We will see in a later chapter how specific therapies, such as meditation, group therapy, and some forms of exercise, can restore the architecture of the stress response system after years of strain. Our bodies are resilient, and neuroplasticity is the central nervous system's capacity to rebuild its self-regulation circuits.

Hormones in Turmoil

The endocrine organs that charge into action during acute stress, as discussed earlier, are the hypothalamus, pituitary, and adrenal glands.

When all is well, cortisol sends a wake-up call to the central nervous system, promoting alertness and making sleep difficult. Cortisol turns fat into glucose to make energy available to the brain and muscles for the business of fighting or fleeing or heavy lifting. Cortisol inhibits the immune response by slowing the production and functioning of T cell lymphocytes. And if you are in good health, high cortisol levels eventually contribute to the negative feedback loop in the hypothalamus to return cortisol levels to normal ranges. That way, once the threat has resolved, this expensive output for crisis management does not exhaust the resources.

In a certain type of major depression, the receptors in the hypothalamus that register cortisol levels become resistant and the negative feedback loop fails. So the cortisol levels stay high, disrupting sleep, immunity, appetite, energy metabolism, mood, and eventually the sharpness of thinking.

Much of the misery of clinical depression can be traced to these harmful effects of excessive cortisol over long periods. Once we restore the capacity of the hypothalamus to shut down the problem, the fog of depression lifts. In that sense this subtype of depression is a disorder of the stress hormone system. This blunted cortisol response to a challenge can be a feature not only of depression but of other chronic illnesses.[13]

Is this hormonal turmoil a cause or a consequence of the illness? It can become both.

At the beginning of this chapter, I introduced you to researcher Sheldon Cohen who recruited participants for studies and gave them the virus of the common cold. He wanted to see whether stress affects our vulnerability to infection with the common cold. And the answer was yes.

It's no accident that the main hormones of the stress response system are tied intimately to the main hormones of the energy metabolism system, namely, insulin and glucagon.

Resistance to insulin. Adult-onset or type 2 diabetes is an energy storage problem that begins with insulin resistance. The high glucose levels of the metabolic syndrome and prediabetes signal this state of insulin resistance. That is, the receptors on the membranes of fat cells that need insulin to absorb and store fats stop recognizing insulin. This usually happens in fat cells that have stored too much fat, a popular problem in the US with over half of the population overweight or obese.

Each fat cell reaches a bloating point. Often we can't change our diet without also changing how we manage our stress responses, at least the ones that rule how we eat. In the early stages of prediabetes and diabetes, for many people effective stress management is essential to glucose control.

Low libido. Conditions of relentless or repeated stressors also affect other hormones. During the acute stress response, two sets of hormones that retreat or shut down temporarily are the reproductive system and the growth system. Times of threat are no time to make babies or to grow. Fight, flee, or freeze, but don't fondle.

Evolution has made sure that stress blunts libido fast, but only temporarily. In the best of health, the rising or lowering of sex hormones happens over minutes or a few hours, then reverts to the resting state. During the minutes surrounding a race, Usain Bolt's libido is low. The night after he sprints, when he's lucky, his libido works just fine. But confine Bolt in a war zone for many months or a high-crime neighborhood or rural poverty, and the persistent stress of living daily under these conditions will eventually throw off his delicate balance of hormones too.

Persistent stress reduces testosterone in men and in general reduces fertility. In women, high levels of persistent stress interrupt menstrual cycles and reduce fertility.

I grew up in the 1960s hearing that smoking stunts children's growth. Those were the early days of understanding the effects of smoking on health. That finger wagging was the older generation's way of trying to dissuade us from smoking. What is closer to the truth is that what may stunt growth is chronic severe stressors during critical growth periods.

At the extremes of psychosocial deprivation, such as in some poorly tended orphanages or abusive home environments, children with "failure to thrive" syndromes, also called "psychosocial dwarfism," fall off the growth charts and puberty comes late. The explanation is that, in growing children, prolonged activation of the HPA axis suppresses growth hormone. Equally stunning is the rapid correction in growth spurts that comes with restoring the child to a safe, nourishing environment.

This blunting of growth hormone reminds us that acute stress and chronic stress trigger catabolic states, which means we expend more energy than we store. Part of the body's response to acute stressors is to send out the signals (glucagon, the counter to insulin, and glucocorticoids are the messengers) to draw into the blood the glucose from cells that store glucose (the liver is the richest sugar warehouse), to break down fats into sugars, and to break down proteins too.

All this catabolism makes lots of energy available on short notice for the work of managing the demands of the stressor. But that's not sustainable for long, so once the storm has passed, the healthy stress response system goes back to the anabolic resting state that allows storing of energy and rebuilding of fat stores and protein.

Storms that don't pass, especially those that linger in our minds, keep us in the catabolic state too long, which means we store fat in the wrong places (our bellies), suppress bone build-up, lose muscle mass, and eventually develop a resistance to insulin, which paves the way for diabetes.

We become like Teresa Langford when many bad things happened all at once. We feel vulnerable because we are. We sense that our capacity to respond to challenges is weak, and we are right. That can be depressing. It can make us fat. And it can accelerate the onset of diabetes.

Oxytocin. The other hormone that plays a role in chronic stress is oxytocin. This hormone, which is produced by the hypothalamus and secreted by the pituitary gland, is best known for its role in facilitating the mother's breastfeeding of her baby. But children, men, and women, whether they are breastfeeding or not, have circulating levels of oxytocin that have other interesting effects.

Oxytocin stimulates the release of dopamine in our pleasure centers. It lowers cortisol levels. It stimulates endorphins to reduce pain perceptions. It decreases the fight-or-flight response and boosts the secretion of gamma-aminobutyric acid (GABA), which has a calming effect on the brain. It sharpens our attention to social cues, helping us read others better. No wonder it's so good for breastfeeding.

But these effects are also good for stress management. Add all this up and you get the opposite of fight-or-flight. You get a buffering effect that is called the tend-mend-defend response – a set of behaviors that protects infants and mothers by securing attachment behaviors.

People vary in their inborn levels of oxytocin. People with autism and antisocial personality disorder tend to have lower levels of oxytocin. Men have lower levels than women, but around the time of the birth of a baby, fathers' levels of oxytocin rise and their testosterone levels drop, both of which make them less likely to go prowling for trouble and more likely to hang around the nursery. As we'll see later, all of this raises the possibility that oxytocin might prove useful as a buffering treatment for people enduring chronic stress.

The Slow Burn: Chronic Inflammation

Like ground fires that smolder beneath the surface, low-grade chronic inflammation is a feature of many long-lasting illnesses. We have just seen how stress-related dysregulations in the brain can lead to cortisol resistance. These changes open the doors to infections (for example, the common cold and AIDS), to fibromyalgia, to chronic obstructive lung disease, to depression, and to heart disease.[14]

We have seen how chronic stress dysregulates the storage and release of glucose – a pathway to obesity and diabetes. How much does low-grade inflammation add to this process?

Usually we fight infections and toxins with a large army of immune cells that produce cytokines. Some cytokines promote and others inhibit inflammation. We make these cells and molecules in our bone marrow, spleen, thymus, and lymph glands. When healthy, our immune system self-regulates each inflammatory response, shutting it down when it has done its job. That's healing the common cold and the bruise from your loving brother.

But when the demands of daily life in poverty keep on coming in the form of hunger or violence or threats from within the home or homelessness, for a range of reasons our immune system can fail to mount a sufficient response, leaving the infection or injury to persist unchecked. Or at the other extreme, our immune system can mount an excessive immune response that attacks not only the injury site but other tissues, also leading to inflammation unchecked, as in the cytokine storms of COVID, allergies, asthma, or autoimmune diseases.

Training mothers reduces offspring inflammation measures. Edith Chen and her husband, Greg Miller, both research professors of psychology at Northwestern University, have been studying the mysteries of how poverty fosters physical illnesses. These disparities in health begin early in life, with higher rates among the poor for preterm births and infant mortality and delayed growth. Poor youth in the US have higher rates of obesity, insulin resistance leading to diabetes, and asthma.

And in later life, regardless of their socioeconomic status as adults, those who grew up poor have higher rates of stroke, heart disease, chronic lung disease, and some cancers. Something toxic about poverty in youth seems to have lifelong effects on health.

In some but not all youth.

Professors Chen and Miller noted that in a subset of "resilient" youth who avoided these illness markers, it was Mom who protected them. In retrospective studies among children raised in poverty, having a nurturing, responsive mother was associated with better regulation of inflammation.

Can good mothering protect children from some of the ravages of poverty?

By teaming up with researchers at the University of Georgia, Chen and Miller managed to identify a group of rural Black teenagers and their parents, 90 percent at a low-income level, who agreed to participate in their study when the teenagers were eleven to thirteen and be interviewed again at age nineteen.

In this randomized controlled trial, could the study train half of the mothers to be more responsive and, if so, would that mothering intervention pay off five or six years later when they examined the inflammatory markers of these teenagers at age nineteen?[15]

The short answer to both questions is yes. The Strong African American Families Program was able to train these mothers to be measurably more responsive with basic communication skills to their younger teenagers, and six to eight years later all six of the inflammatory markers in the teenagers improved significantly and remained improved, compared to the control group (the teens whose mothers had not been trained).

This study and others make the argument that by changing the environments of high-risk children, we can change the toll on their immune systems, and possibly on their risks for illness later in life.

Cortisone. One common example of stress hormones disrupting the immune system can be seen in the use of immunosuppressants to treat asthma, brain injury, or cancer. Our most common immunosuppressant is cortisone, a steroid medication form of cortisol.

For short periods this drug can be helpful in reducing the immune response, and cortisone does that. A person with a knee injury may get a cortisone shot in the knee to reduce the swelling and pain.

If cortisol levels remain elevated by chronic stress or medication use, they will inhibit the formation of T cell lymphocytes in the bone marrow and other tissues. Cortisol also facilitates the storage of existing lymphocytes, taking them out of circulation. Cortisol also inhibits the release of cytokines, the molecules that attack toxins. So on many levels the immune system is hobbled by prolonged exposure to high levels of cortisol, one of the hallmarks of chronic stress.[16]

One of the mechanisms by which persistent or repeated stressors contribute to the onset and progression of coronary heart disease is by contributing to inflammation in the arteries leading to the heart. As these coronary arteries harden and form plaques or blockages in their walls, these plaques become sites for local inflammation. Over many years these plaques eventually lead to more widespread signs of inflammation, as measured by rises in the biomarker c-reactive protein or CRP. High levels of CRP may signal a higher risk for heart disease.

Pain–fear–tension–inflammation. In a different pathway from stress to inflammation to illness, chronic pain, when it leads to anxiety or fear, increases tension in muscles and tendons, interfering with their capacity to relax and rest. Excessive, persistent muscle and tendon tension leads to minor injury in these muscle and tendon tissues. Like the plaques in coronary arteries, these injury sites become inflamed and the cytokines released by the immune cells at these sites increase the perception of pain. Pain generates anxiety and fear.

This cycle of pain, fear, tension, inflammation, and more pain can feel like a straitjacket. No wonder chronic pain is a fast track for common chronic illnesses like diabetes and depression and heart disease. Release from this straitjacket is not quick or easy.

What We Know and Don't Know

Before pulling these pieces into a coherent picture of the stress effects across the lifespan in the next chapter, let's review what the current state of the science of stress and illness boils down to:

- Chronic stress exposures and responses are important contributing factors in the development and progression of specific chronic physical illnesses (diabetes, coronary heart disease, obesity, hypertension) and most major mental illnesses (depression, anxiety, schizophrenia, bipolar disorder). The question is no longer whether there's a link between patterns of stressors and illness, but how chronic stress accelerates each specific illness process. The front edge of stress neuroscience is now focused on the mechanisms that transform stress responses into disease. (The evidence for the contribution of stressors to the many forms of cancer is less strong, and varies by cancer type.)

- The magnitude of the stress effect on these chronic illnesses is for many people as great as the effect of traditional risk factors such as smoking, not exercising, and poor diet for heart disease or diabetes. This stress effect is too big to be ignored.

- For any individual person, the magnitude of the stress effect on risks for illness depends on their age at exposure, the severity of the stressors, the duration of the exposures to stressors, and their appraisals of threat or safety during each exposure and its aftermath. In general, the higher the "dose" of stress exposures and responses, the greater the effect on the illness. And the higher the person's perception of distress, the greater the effect on the illness. The relationship between chronic stress and illness is strongest in those exposed to high levels of stressors over many years.

- Most acute stressors do not make most people sick most of the time. We are tough! We are resilient. We recover. The recovery reflex is built into the healthy stress response system.

- The mechanisms that translate chronic stress into illness are related to failures of the adaptive capacities of multiple aspects of the stress response system, beginning with dysregulation of the recovery phase of responses to acute stress. These dysregulations have been described at the level of specific genes, membrane receptors, organelles, cells, neural circuits, organs, the stress response system, the individual, the family, and society. Though a number of treatments have proven effective, we don't yet know enough about most of these mechanisms to design the most efficient treatments by targeting specific mechanisms of healing or re-regulation for a wide range of people.

149

- We don't know the answers to other compelling stress questions:
    - What determines the critical periods of child development during which severe stress can dysregulate the stress response system in a way that lasts into adulthood?
    - What makes some people sensitive and others resilient to the same stressor?
    - What determines which illness is triggered by a given pattern of chronic stress?
    - Concerning treatment, does intensive stress management make us less sick or more healthy? In general, yes to both possibilities. More robust clinical trial research is needed to understand which stress reduction treatments at what stages of illness are most effective at improving which disease outcomes. We need to devise stress reduction treatments that are affordable, easy to use, flexible for individual needs, and effective. Only then will doctors and patients adopt stress management widely and effectively. And we need *prevention* research that focuses on the impact of stress management on the prevention of specific stress-related disorders. For example, can intensive stress management approaches for people with metabolic syndrome (more on that syndrome in the next chapter) reduce the rate of developing diabetes, high blood pressure, heart disease, or obesity?

With these points in mind, consider whether we can reduce all this science to one picture that helps us tell our stories. Can we build a model for the pathways from chronic stress to chronic illness during the course of a lifetime? Such a model should guide us to think and talk more clearly about what to measure and when, what to treat and prevent, and when to try these treatments and preventions.

8

• • • • •

Scan the Lifespan

Dr. Goodachari paused outside the exam room where he would see Mrs. B for the first time since his partner retired. He had the sinking feeling from a quick scan of her short problem list, her medication list, and his partner's last note from six months ago that Mrs. B's visit could end with the addition of a third medication to get control of her high blood pressure.

More drugs is rarely a gratifying step for either the patient or the doctor. Dr. Goodachari had about twelve minutes to get to know her and negotiate a plan with her, before checking back with the teenage mother in labor down the hall. Adding a beta-blocker to Mrs. B's diuretic and ACE inhibitor could be an acceptable next step for now, if they couldn't come up with something better.

The first surprise he found was the second woman in the room. Mrs. B sat perched on the edge of the examining table, her rotund pear-shaped build dressed in a black pants suit with gold hoop earrings, long scarlet nails, and a quick nervous smile. She seemed to him a flashy sixty-two, trying to look fifty.

He reached out his hand, "I'm Dr. Sidhartha Goodachari. If that's too much of a mouthful to remember, most of my patients just call me Dr. Good."

She shook his hand, pointed to the corner chair, and said, "That's my chauffeur, Dr. Good, and my big sister."

Mrs. B's big sister was half her size, dressed in a beige skirt and matching jacket, with a book in her lap. She gave him a nod and a familiar smile. He recognized her immediately as his patient of many years and gave her a warm handshake.

"Fancy seeing you here, Madam Principal," he said. She was one of the few Black women of her generation who had been able to climb the administrative ladder of the public school system. He liked her quiet but firm confidence. She reminded him of his own mother, a public health nurse and one of the first Asian American women to enlist in the Foreign Service. In the years that he'd taken care of Mrs. B's sister, he didn't recall her mentioning this particular younger sister among her many siblings.

"How are you doing, Mrs. B? Is that your preferred name?" he said.

"That's just what everybody calls me, even my kids," she said, with a darting glance at her sister. "I woke up with an octopus in my eye." Her hand lifted and waved across her right eye and back down to her lap. "That's why I had to hire me a high-priced chauffeur," she said, nodding toward the corner.

Dr. Good felt an anxious tug in his belly and a sense that this bleeding in her eye could turn into more than a twelve-minute appointment. With his foot he hooked the stool from under the desk and sat down, now looking awkwardly up at the rotund woman above him and across at the enigmatic smile of the poised sister. He recognized also that he was facing another example of his retired partner's minimalist approach. Why was obesity not on

Mrs. B's problem list in the medical record with a BMI (body mass index) of 36? What else was not on her problem list?

Unfolding Backward

The medical stories about chronic conditions often unfold backward. The current urgent need begins the conversation – "I have a floater" or "We've got to bring your blood pressure down." When the urgency resolves, we fill in the blanks – if we're lucky, and if we're motivated to make the time for the longer story.

If Mrs. B only shows up at the clinic when the need is urgent, and the doctor only makes time to address that urgent need, the blanks remain unfilled, the story obscure. This time the good doctor sensed a long and complex story had led to the floater in her right eye and they would need several monthly visits to fill in the story. He knew that getting that story would be crucial to managing her blood pressure with fewer medications, crucial to sparing her a life on insulin shots.

The task of this chapter is to condense the essence of the last two chapters into one image of the effects of persistent toxic stress across the lifespan. The last few chapters focused on what happens mentally and physically during acute and chronic stress exposures.

We now look at these events as stress-related illnesses build across the lifespan.

Dr. Good reached his hand up to hers, saying, "Come down to this chair here where we can see each other better and you can tell me what it's been like to wake up with this octopus floating in your eye."

He flicked off the overhead lights, and, now, with her back to the shaded window, she told him in detail about the events of her morning while he listened and prompted and examined both eyes with his instruments. The fresh floater in her right eye hovered in

153

her lower medial quadrant near her optic disc. As they talked, he took her blood pressure once in each arm and listened to her neck and chest.

"Diabetes and high blood pressure run in your family?" he asked, knowing the answer. Mrs. B looked blankly at him while her sister nodded, suggesting they had talked about this before.

Dr. Good said, "Mrs. B, your pressure is still up, your weight is up, and your sugar was up the last time we checked it. And now you've got a floater. What would you like me to help you with?"

She didn't hesitate. "I gotta be able to drive, Doctor. My daughter delivers in two months. She's counting on me to sit her baby. That's my first grandbaby. I've waited too long for this dark octopus to get in my way. Can I drive with one eye closed?"

They talked about a plan for her floater, for her blood pressure, and for getting her ready for her grandbaby, if she was ready to work at it, a little bit every day. He ordered the beta-blocker, referred her to the ophthalmologist (eye specialist), and wrapped up the appointment after 12.5 minutes.

"When you come back to see me next month, we'll talk about a more comprehensive plan. In fact, why don't you make three appointments, one for each month."

By the second visit, through a fluke of luck in scheduling she had seen the ophthalmologist, her floater was shrinking, and her diastolic blood pressure was consistently under 90. He learned that she spends most of her day in a chair, much of it alone, and all the dieting she does during the day has been negated by the snacking she does at night. No wonder she's prediabetic. And the night snacking is an old habit to beat insomnia. The insomnia is a residue of partially treated depression on a timid dose of an antidepressant.

At the third visit, Mrs. B showed him pictures of the new granddaughter. And the good doctor said, "She's darling. Bring her with you next time you come. Now tell me when your weight became a problem."

Mrs. B's lip trembled and her nervous smile vanished as the tears welled up in her eyes. "Sixth grade," she said. "When my period came on."

She confided in him her terror of puberty after the chaotic years with her father's brother Binkie living in the house, with all her sisters off to marriage or college or the military. Binkie never touched her, but he talked so creepy about sex and animals that she never felt safe. He only talked that way when they were alone in the house, which was too often. Nobody believed her. They trusted him but she didn't. She wanted nothing to do with sex in any way, and eating seemed to calm her fears.

Heavy seemed to keep the boys away. Binkie eventually left her alone. It wasn't all his fault. Just forget about it. The teasing from her classmates about her weight was a small price to pay for safety from the dating game.

"It's still like that," she told him. "Nothing calms my nerves like a mug of warm milk and a plate of my brownies."

The Lifespan Lens

Though it is possible to look at stress and illness on many levels, from the cell to the society, this model focuses on the individual person across the lifespan because individual people, as opposed to organ systems or societies, are the best initiators of change.

When a group of motivated people join together to make a change, as we do for weight watching, abstinence from alcohol, political action, and barn building, the possibilities for change increase. And when groups of groups, such as communities and societies, are motivated by a common cause, we can sustain lasting change. But most change begins with motivated individuals (some of whom read books) who share an effective way of thinking about a problem.

Can a model of how severe and persistent stress exposures drive us along the pathways to illness provide the framework for conversations between doctors and patients? Can it help us choose effective treatments? Does it accurately represent the essence of the best research on how patterns of stress responses translate into illness? And can this model provide the framework for researchers to ask the revealing questions that will improve how we prevent and treat these illnesses?

The ACE Pyramid

A good example of a model for how stress leads to illness across the lifespan comes to us from the Adverse Childhood Experiences Study.[1] This model, mentioned earlier, emerged from the many studies that showed a dose–response relationship between exposure to adverse events in childhood and illnesses in adulthood – chronic physical illnesses, mental illnesses, and high-risk health behaviors.

In medical lingo a dose–response relationship means that, as the "dose" of the medicine rises, the response, such as pain relief or reduced itching, also rises. It implies a strong relationship between the medicine and its effects. In this case, the dose (the more adverse experiences reported) predicts the response (the greater the chances of illness later).

The ACE model proposes that early exposure to a range of adverse experiences during critical periods of childhood leads to disruptions in the development of the brain and the central nervous system. These disruptions later show up during school years as social, emotional, or cognitive impairments or all three, sometimes subtle, sometimes severe. These impairments lay the platform for high-risk health behaviors in adolescence and early adulthood, such as unsafe sex, smoking, violence, and drug and alcohol misuse.

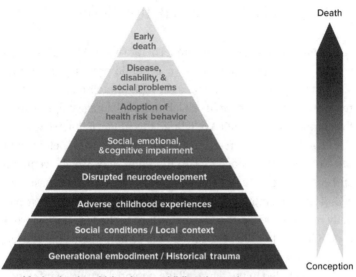

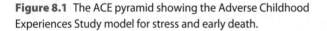

Mechanism by which adverse childhood experiences influence health and well-being throughout the lifespan

Figure 8.1 The ACE pyramid showing the Adverse Childhood Experiences Study model for stress and early death.

Decades later these stress-related behaviors may foster the development of stress-related illnesses such as asthma, diabetes, depression, heart disease, addictions, chronic obstructive pulmonary disease, autoimmune conditions, and some cancers. These are the illnesses that kill us early, especially those of us who were exposed to four or more adverse experiences early in life.

The ACE pyramid provides a visual summary of the stress and illness story across the lifespan. In later chapters we will return to how the ACE study has shined a light on the healers' blind spot, but to think creatively about ways to reduce or prevent these poor outcomes we need more specifics and a finer level of detail than this ACE pyramid provides.

Caution While Building a Better Model

A few cautions about our new model before we build it.[2] First, these will be static representations of a dynamic process, the equivalent of trying to capture a dance through photographs. The stress response system never holds still, but the still image helps us study the components in detail. We'll build this model in four stages.

Second, the model reads from birth to death, from left to right. Most of the arrows move toward the right, since we all eventually end on the right side of the page. However, some of these processes also operate in a circular fashion, or can be at least partially reversed, suggesting the arrow flips to the left, such as when Mrs. B lowers her blood sugar enough to move herself to the left, out of the metabolic syndrome and prediabetes zone.

If we included in the figure all the potential arrows of influence, it would create a more accurate but chaotic picture, which would defeat the purpose of the figure. So the arrows we show represent selected vectors of influence that dominate the progression toward metabolic illnesses.

Third, the relative importance or effect size of any single component of the model, such as genes or trauma or stress hormones, may shift over time for any person or groups of people. This effect size of a single component could be represented by the size of the box for that component, the size of the font, or color highlighting. However, because it's currently difficult to measure consistently over time the relative contributions of each component and these contributions are always changing, the model appears to attribute equal importance to all components across time.

Imagine, however, that each component may change over time, and, for any one person, a single component may exert a stronger influence on the stress and illness process than would be observed in a twin, a sibling, or an age mate from a different family or culture.

For example, inflammation may play a larger role for you in your thirties, while autonomic imbalance may play a larger role for your high-strung brother in his thirties or for you later in life.

Each of the components of this model have been introduced in earlier chapters. To serve as a useful guide for research, each component must be defined and measurable. My goal is to create a model that can help conversations about stress between patients like Mrs. B and her good doctor and you and your doctor so we can improve treatment plans.

Genes, Stress, and Death

We begin with a few simple truths. At the point of conception we are a packet of genes in a fertilized egg struggling to survive in an environment, initially our mother's endometrial bed, with one certain outcome, death, in the near or far future – either in a few days or, with luck and love, many decades.

We begin with these few facts about the extremes of life, and much room in between for the many unanswered questions that will determine our pathways from birth to death.

The box in the upper left labeled Genes in the figure represents all the genetic material that is relevant to our survival and particularly to our stress response system. As we saw in the last chapter, this includes the development of the structures of the key organ systems and the regulation of their functioning in response to a range of challenges. Although much is still unknown, the current challenge is to build the genetic library to understand what the stress-relevant genes are, what they do, and how stress turns them on and off.

The box in the lower left that stretches across the length of the lifespan represents the role of stressors in general and, in particular, chronic or episodic severe stressors. The shape of the stress

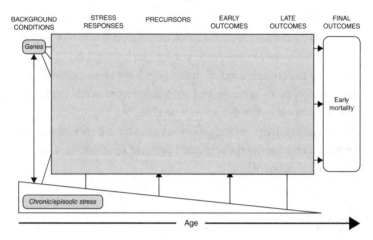

Figure 8.2 Genes, stress, and death.

exposure triangle suggests that stressors, though present through-out life, vary during the course of each life, posing their great-est challenges early in life. The tougher the early adversities, the steeper the slope and the faster the acceleration to metabolic risk and aging. The two-way arrow between genes and stress reminds us that from the start genes influence stress and stress influences genes in their eventual impact on the development of illness.

The mother's womb is just the first of many environments that will shape the expression of our genes. Mothers who struggle with famine or severe depression during pregnancy are more likely to deliver babies with low birth weight – the earliest example of how stress inhibits growth hormone.[3] That kind of effect requires turn-ing off a lot of genes, for example, genes for bone growth, that would rather be turned on.

Low birth weights also predict health risks in adulthood, such as a large increase in risk for heart disease.[4] Findings such as these represent examples of a stressful maternal environment shaping the infant's genetic expression in ways that endure for life.

In a similar way, the mother's stress hormones, such as cortisol, cross the placenta and alert the fetus about the level of stress "out there," in effect training the fetus to raise its production of cortisol. Prenatally stressed rats grow into adults with high levels of cortisol. That kind of lasting effect requires turning on some genes for excessive cortisol production that, in a kinder and gentler world, would have been turned off.

Genes shape our environment at every stage of life, beginning with the genes of the fetus shaping its embryonic environment. For example, the genes for obesity, such as Mrs. B may have inherited, can invite grade school bullying, a stressor that further fuels the expression of those obesity genes. Remember how chronic stress promotes the deposition of fat in the abdomen.

We don't know enough yet about our genetic profiles and our epigenetic expressions of our genes to verify such a guess. But it's not hard to imagine that someday soon genetic profiling will alert us to our vulnerabilities to common disorders like diabetes and heart disease in a way that improves on the current lack of precision from family histories alone.

Mrs. B and her sister shared the same family history but developed different health risks, possibly due in part to different genetic profiles. It's also likely that more precise genetic profiling could identify stress vulnerability and resilience profiles that will alert us to whether our diabetes or heart disease is likely to be particularly sensitive to stress.

Surprises and Black Boxes

What are Mrs. B or her sister or you most likely to die from?

Working backward from death, the next figure narrows our focus to a few common pathways to death: heart disease, diabetes, and obesity. This narrowing of our focus acknowledges the limitations of the page, the imagination, and science. We choose to focus here on these three sets of conditions because they are common, costly, and lethal, and research about their relationships to stress is the most robust.

And they serve as examples of the principles that guide variations of this model that could be applied to the pathways to other chronic conditions, such as COPD, cancer of various types, liver disease, kidney disease, and autoimmune disorders. We place these three sets of conditions just to the left of death because they often cluster together and are among the commonly listed "causes" of death.

For many of us who considered ourselves healthy until our first heart attack or our first diagnosis of diabetes, the story seems to start with the onset of the illness. High blood pressure. Boom. Sudden heart attack. The big surprise. It hits us in our fifties, in our sixties, or if we're lucky or female, in our seventies. The black box between birth and the onset of heart disease or diabetes is often a mystery in retrospect. Here again is the blind spot we would rather not see or think about.

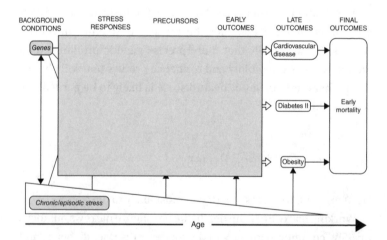

Figure 8.3 Heart disease, diabetes, and obesity: common causes of death.

And because of the urgency of managing the newly diagnosed illness, the long process in our life that preceded the diagnosis too often remains a mystery. Those three twenty-minute visits scheduled by the good doctor with Mrs. B don't happen often enough in practice, because she ends up in the hospital for a new urgent unrelated problem (possible skin cancer with complications), or she becomes preoccupied with the congenital abnormality of her grandchild and puts her own care on the back burner, or some other distraction interferes. But when we look carefully, we often find the pathways – the early part of the story.

Metabolic Syndrome

One component of the black box that often precedes the diagnosis of various types of heart disease, diabetes, and obesity-related conditions is called the metabolic syndrome.

In the late 1980s and early 1990s, this concept of metabolic syndrome emerged in the medical literature in recognition that these risk factors for heart disease rarely occurred alone for long. If you had mild elevations in your lipids (measures of cholesterol such as triglycerides or LDL), you were more likely also to have mildly high blood sugars or mildly high blood pressure. If you had high waist circumference because of fat in your belly, you were more likely also to have high cholesterol or high blood pressure or high blood sugar, or all three!

And once you had three of the five risk factors – high blood pressure, high glucose, high triglycerides, low HDL (the good cholesterol), and high waist circumference – your likelihood of developing diabetes or heart disease rose dramatically, compared to having just one or two risk factors. Clusters of mild risk factors in your thirties and forties meant trouble sooner or later for most, roughly doubling the risk for heart disease.

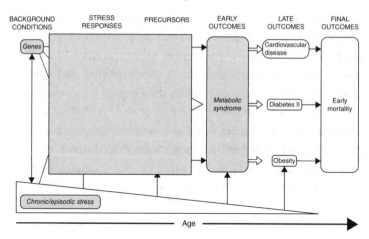

Figure 8.4 Metabolic syndrome may show up before a diagnosis of heart disease, diabetes, or obesity.

Notice that the thresholds for each component of the metabolic syndrome are lower than most clinicians and patients would find alarming.[5] And any one of these laboratory findings alone rarely causes symptoms or distress, so they are "silent" and often unrecognized or ignored. By themselves they don't usually require treatment. But when they appear in clusters, they raise a red flag, if you bother to look for it. The concept of metabolic syndrome invites us to ask, "When do metabolic disorders begin?"

The concept of metabolic syndrome has survived scrutiny over thirty years because it is one of the few early indicators of trouble in multiple organ systems: cardiovascular (heart), endocrine (diabetes), and energy metabolism (obesity). That makes metabolic syndrome a useful concept if you want to look under the hood of your stress response system. It's a check engine light.

Before he walked into the exam room, Dr. Good knew from her chart that Mrs. B had three of the five criteria for metabolic syndrome: high blood pressure, high blood sugar, and high waist circumference. He knew before he met her that correcting her blood pressure was not the whole story. They would likely need a series of appointments to negotiate a plan to try to tune up her blood sugars, lipids, and likely her central nervous system too.

Metabolic syndrome is a valuable concept for another reason. It's easier to reverse metabolic syndrome than to reverse the illnesses it leads to. Once you develop heart disease or diabetes or morbid obesity, the chances of reversing the course of that illness are small, unless you're willing to invest in intensive treatment for extended periods.

In contrast, it's relatively easier to reduce mildly high blood sugars and mildly high blood pressures and being overweight using a regimen that combines medications, exercise, and diets that are good for all three problems.

Trouble in the Box

Working backward, it's useful to now ask what sets up the conditions for metabolic syndrome. Take a closer look at how the key contributing factors to the development of metabolic syndrome have been conspiring for many years before the emergence of a metabolic disorder.

In the model, we see the six fast tracks in relationship to each other over the lifespan. We see that genes and stress have been affecting hormones and energy metabolism, fueling high-risk behaviors, stoking low-grade inflammation, and tipping the autonomic nervous system out of balance to lay down these pathways to metabolic dysregulation and eventually metabolic disorders.

The arrangement within the black box contains some important messages. First, we can understand better the mysteries of how illnesses like diabetes and heart disease develop if we ask what was going on in each of the key sections on the left side of the figure in

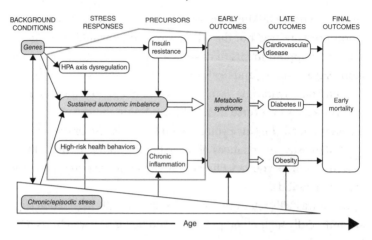

Figure 8.5 Pathways from stress to death.

childhood and early adulthood. Since these pathways each influence the others to some degree, we can't grasp the whole process if we ignore some or most of the organ systems.

Second, each of these pathways is measurable, as we will see in greater detail in the next chapter. So it is theoretically possible to capture the state of the whole system through a series of snapshots of each of the subsystems across time. The research project that Ted participated in (the guy who wore the monitors and cuffs and spit into a tube every so often for the SHINE study) attempts to measure a selected piece of this process through ecological momentary assessment of most of these factors.

Third, since the system is always in flux, the relative importance of any one section on the functioning of the whole person will vary with time. And it will vary from one person to another.

On the day of her appointment, Mrs. B's floater and the threat of not being able to drive when her grandbaby was born may raise her cortisol in a way that also raises her blood sugar and her heart rate and her blood pressure. That's behavior and hormones affecting energy metabolism and autonomic tone in ways that, if they persist, will accelerate her chances of crossing the line into diabetes or a stroke or heart disease.

Meanwhile, her lean sister leads a more disciplined life and contends with fewer intense emotions, and likely less of a cortisol load. Her sister's prefrontal cortex holds a tighter rein on her limbic system and her stress hormones. And maybe her sister's limbic system is easier to rein in than hers is.

On the other hand, Dr. Good's engaging Mrs. B to change her diet and sleep habits and blood pressure could slow or reverse that process that has contributed to her high blood pressure. If he can persuade her to engage in programs that help her change her high-risk health behaviors, such as the Diabetes Prevention Program (I'll talk about this in more detail soon) or the Ornish Lifestyle Medicine Program, she can improve her chances of grandmothering for many years. Sometimes it takes a full-court press on all aspects of the stress response system to secure a new normal, to change the allostatic set points.

The model also illustrates why it's difficult and expensive to conduct comprehensive research on this process. The ideal research study of the contributions of chronic stress exposures and responses to the development of any chronic illness would assess several measures of each of these six factors (genes, trauma and chronic stress, hormones and energy metabolism, high-risk health behaviors, autonomic imbalance, and immunity) across fifty or sixty years in a large number of people (several thousand) while monitoring for a large number of illness outcomes and causes of death.

Can you imagine the costs and logistics of such a study? But it's not impossible. Since beginning in the 1940s, the Harvard Study of Adult Development is studying its second generation, and the Framingham Heart Study is studying its third generation. It can be done, once the political will is strong enough to drive the science through the halls of the federal government agencies that fund these grants.

The model also illustrates how the task of the doctor often begins late in the game, in a sterile exam room, at the time of an acute event for a major illness. By the time most people come to their doctors with a serious problem, the groundwork for diagnosing these chronic conditions has been laid.

It's difficult to prevent a process that has been quietly incubating for ten or twenty years. It's hard to change the outcome, but it can be done. Remember that Dean Ornish's first study drew on people who were so far to the right of heart disease depicted in the model that they were deemed inoperable – a euphemism in those days for terminal heart disease. In one very intensive month, young Ornish moved these twelve people back from the edge of the cliff.

If my model suggests a process too complex for our meager efforts as patients or doctors, it also promises many points of intervention, as we will see in later chapters. The long triangle across the base of the figure suggests that the rate of acceleration of this process depends on the severity and long-lasting effects of the stressors that feed the process along the way.

If timely, effective stress management reduces this factor, it can change the other factors too. The Diabetes Prevention Program has proven that timely intervention in high-risk young adults can prevent or delay the onset of diabetes. Dean Ornish has shown repeatedly that a full-court press of intensive stress management and vegetarian diet and social support, when provided in concert, can tilt that triangle in the other direction and "reverse" or redirect the process of coronary heart disease within six to nine months, even for people in their sixties and seventies with advanced heart disease.[6]

Effective management of blood sugars in Mrs. B, if bolstered by changes in her autonomic nervous system, her stress hormones, and her late-night snacking, is more likely to re-regulate her stress response system than a single drug for her blood pressure or her blood sugar.

But changing behaviors can be tough. Too much too soon is often a waste of effort with little to show for it. Too little too late is certainly frustrating if not futile. It's not yet clear in any one person's life when the optimal time is to intervene, because such a decision depends on so many variables. Teresa's story is one example.

No Longer a Symphony

During Usain Bolt's gifted life as a professional sprinter his genes and his circumstances have been relatively kind to his stress response system. In his early thirties, every section of his orchestra still played well, whether he was sprinting for a medal or navigating the daily hazards of his celebrity status as our fastest man. So far as we know, he does not yet face any signs of metabolic risks or illness. Usain Bolt is a symphony, a model of harmonious adaptation.

But what does this model teach us about how to understand my patient Teresa Langford, who suddenly at the age of forty-six found herself lying in an intensive care unit bed in April 2011, recovering from surgery after a bout of necrotizing pancreatitis? By what pathways had she found herself straitjacketed into six chronic conditions with a raging inflammation in her belly?

Unlike Mr. Bolt, who volunteered for his stress as a sprinter, Teresa had faced demands on her stress response system that were uninvited, unpredictable, hard to control, persistent, and too numerous and invisible to count. These demands had mounted gradually over many years, layer by layer, then escalated suddenly with the inflammation in her pancreas.

For the first weeks in her hospital bed, she was aware only of feeling overwhelmed, and she could not have come up then with a laundry list of the troubles that had landed her there. How had she gone from her peak as an ammunitions ordnance corporal in the Army and later a production manager on a manufacturing line for

Procter & Gamble to being fat, financially dependent on her partner, and physically disabled, in pain much of the time – now lying
at death's door? Consider her pathways.

Genes. The Langford family history was riddled with early
deaths. At thirteen Teresa moved in with her maternal grandparents to escape the vagabond life of her mother in Florida. She
moved in partly to help her grandfather take care of her grandmother, who had recently been diagnosed with breast cancer.
Within months her grandmother died in her sixties, and later two
aunts developed breast cancer. At twenty-eight Teresa lost her
brother to a heart attack, after he refused to seek help for chest
pains and high cholesterol. He was twenty-nine. She knew that
high cholesterol ran in the family. Her mother had three heart
attacks before she reached fifty, and when Teresa first came to
the Cincinnati VA in 1999 at the age of thirty-four, she was taking
Zocor for her high cholesterol and nifedipine for her blood pressure. She knew that her older sister had developed diabetes in her
early thirties.

It's hard to measure the toll of growing up knowing you may
carry some dangerous genes, but by her early thirties Teresa knew
she could expect hand-me-down trouble in some form.

Adverse Childhood Experiences. Teresa does not think of herself
has having lived a traumatic childhood, nor did her doctors. She's
proud of the fact that through hard times she was never beaten, or
assaulted, or sexually mistreated by those in charge of her. On the
contrary, she feels close to many members of her family and credits
them with coming to her rescue when she needed it, especially her
grandfather.

Yet here's the list of eight adverse experiences that qualify as
severe or persistent stressors in the lives of most children under
eighteen: parental separation, mother's imprisonment, poverty,
unstable home life, discrimination against her gay mother, discrimination against her own gay identity, which she at first denied

then concealed during her teens and in the Army, probable undiagnosed and untreated ADHD, and frequent alcohol abuse.

Chronic Pain. The aunt and uncle who helped her grandfather raise her during her high school years had no children. Teresa would spend weekends with them and quickly developed a strong bond with her uncle, who had spent three years in the Army in World War II. In high school Teresa played every sport she could to build up her fitness. She vowed to follow her uncle's example and enlist in the Army, which she did in 1984 at age nineteen, fully intending on a career as an officer. After her first three-year enlistment term, she reenlisted and was selected for drill sergeant training. She was climbing the ranks and was promoted to corporal.

Then one day in August while on duty setting up the camo netting on a tent pole, the guy supporting her loosened his grip and she fell, crushing her left kneecap on the metal crossbar of the cot, fracturing the kneecap and tearing some tendons. The healing did not go well and left her with traumatic arthritis in that knee and chronic pain that bothers her to this day. Her injury eventually led to a medical discharge after six years in the Army. Her disappointment cut deep. Now she had to start over at twenty-five.

Fitness had been one of the things that set her apart from her fellow soldiers and won her respect. Now she struggled day and night with walking and standing. Pain ruled. That persistent sense of physical insecurity surely took a toll on her stress hormones and her autonomic nervous system, though no one knew how much. Deep rest was hard to come by.

High-Risk Health Behaviors. Early in her Army years, while stationed in South Korea, after a long night at the bar Teresa left a group of drinking buddies to walk back to the barracks. One of her fellow soldiers caught up with her, steered her into an alley, and, in her words, "forced me to have sex with him." Soon after, she met her first girlfriend.

So alcohol, which Teresa viewed as her shield, one of her ways of coping with being both gay and a woman in the Army, contributed to her experience of what the VA now recognizes as "military sexual trauma (MST)." It was not until she was forty-eight that Teresa opened up enough to let this incident and its consequences become a part of her medical record.

After ten years of hitting alcohol harder than most of her peers and several years after her "military sexual trauma," Teresa gave up alcohol suddenly when, after a night of heavy drinking, a friend of hers drove home alone and ran into an oncoming car, killing both herself and the other driver.

Teresa felt stunned, angry, sad, and scared: "That could have been me," she said to herself, and she made a promise to her lost friend that she would never drink like that again, a promise she has kept.

The two other high-risk health behaviors that emerged after her cracked kneecap were physical inactivity and overeating. Teresa could no longer work out her anxieties through drills and heavy lifting on the job. And without alcohol, food offered the safest way to calm her storms: Pepsi and growing portion sizes. Over the next ten years, this new combination of overeating and hours on the couch jacked her body mass index (BMI) up from that of a fit soldier to one that put her in the range of severe obesity (36).

And chronic stress has its own lopsided way of putting weight on us. The fat cells inside our abdomen, the abdominal omentum, are particularly sensitive to elevations in the stress hormone cortisol. So Teresa's high cortisol from worries, hustle on the job, and knee pain may have turned her Pepsis and hefty portions into a "beer belly." This belly shifted her center of gravity forward, straining her lower back, requiring her stress response system to find a new set of normals for her gait, her heart rate each time she rose from the chair, and her breathing volume now that there was less room in her belly for her diaphragm to pull downward.

One of the later consequences of her obesity was insomnia. For many years after losing her job to layoffs, she felt tired most of the time, which was out of character for her high-energy approach to life. At age forty-four a sleep study discovered that she had developed obstructive sleep apnea, often a complication of obesity when the accumulation of fat in the soft palate causes constriction of the airway during some phases of sleep. If her stress led to her obesity, and her obesity led to her sleep apnea, the insomnia from her sleep apnea only made her experience of stress more vicious. No wonder she felt trapped.

Sleep serves many functions, only a few of which we understand well. One of the features we understand is the crucial function of deep sleep in achieving states of deep rest. During deep sleep the sympathetic nervous system takes a break and the parasympathetic system takes over, relatively unopposed. The EEG slows down into a characteristic slow wave pattern. Heart rate and respirations go down. Muscle movement and activity in the motor cortex also relax. Energy stores in the brain and the body increase. The cells' tanks fill up, the circuits reset, the whole central nervous system can reboot.

During a good night, deep sleep lasts forty to sixty minutes each cycle and occurs two or three times during those precious eight hours. Teresa may have been lucky to get one or two rounds of deep sleep a night, and some nights none. Day and night her sympathetic system was working overtime while her parasympathetic system was rarely able to do the restoring.

Insulin Resistance. By the time Teresa was forty, she was working in her best job ever as a production manager at a manufacturing site for Procter & Gamble's baby wipes. She was on her feet and on the go most of the day. It was tough and she was good at it, as long as her adrenaline kept pumping on the job. But what price was she paying?

Her BMI had climbed to 38 and her hemoglobin A1C had climbed to 6.8, high enough to secure the diagnosis of diabetes. Over the years her pathway to diabetes had been paved by genes, overeating leading to central abdominal obesity, and nearly two decades of persistent and moderately high stress living. That translates into higher than normal levels of cortisol and glucose, both of which also contribute to the receptors on fat cells becoming resistant to insulin, the hallmark of type 2 diabetes. She needed insulin from a syringe.

Inflammation. Teresa's last pathway to metabolic trouble, inflammation, was the one that nearly killed her, but inflammation was not an overt part of her health record until 2011. In 1999, after she had her gallbladder taken out, she had developed pancreatitis, requiring a two-week hospitalization, but she recovered and did okay for seven years before diabetes was diagnosed. In addition to her diabetes, the major factor contributing to her vulnerability to inflammation was her obesity, which in many people fosters a low-grade chronic inflammatory state related to fat cells harboring large amounts of inflammatory cytokines. This kind of low-grade inflammation feels like having a cold or the mild flu: low energy, easy fatigability, apathy, excessive sleep. It's often confused with or overlaps with clinical depression.

Low-grade inflammation saps our energy and our self-esteem as we do less and less. As our self-esteem plummets, the negative thinking of depression accelerates this downward spiral.

As with most people who develop pancreatitis, the original problem or cause of Teresa's condition was never found. The signature feature of pancreatitis is that instead of secreting its enzymes into the small intestine where they can digest food, the pancreatic enzymes get clogged up in the pancreas and start digesting the pancreas itself. Perhaps it starts as a simple plumbing problem, an inflamed duct that closes, or with an infection that interferes with secretion. In any case, once the inflammation sets in, it spreads. If inflammation spreads fast and deep enough, as with Teresa's, the inflammation destroys the tissues of the pancreas, hence "necrotizing" that part of the organ.

Several failures in the immune system regulation have to happen for Teresa's pancreas to start digesting itself. The negative feedback to the hypothalamus (as cortisol levels rise during acute inflammation) fails to suppress the cortisol. And the inflammatory cells' capacity to recognize its own pancreas tissue as self (not foreign) becomes impaired, allowing extensive attack and tissue destruction. So, it's likely that before the forest fire of her pancreatitis lit up, Teresa had harbored a smoldering ground fire of low-grade inflammation for many years.

Underemployment. Though she initially thrived in the Army and had a good job for three years as a production manager, overall Teresa feels frustrated that she has not been able to do more. After she got laid off from Procter & Gamble in 2005, she enrolled at Xavier University and graduated in 2009 with a degree in special education. She chose this field partly because she knew that her older sister had a learning disability and she suspected that she herself had some kind of problem with learning.

In addition to having a high-energy temperament, she remembers grade school and high school as being frustrating experiences academically. She had a hard time sitting still and staying focused for long periods. She had to work extra hours to get average grades. In 2009 she failed her first two special education licensing exams because they were all essays. With her professor she narrowed the problem down. They figured out that with extra effort she could learn things and could discuss them in class, but consistently she could not write her answers in essay form. In contrast, she had thrived as an ammunitions ordnance officer and as a production manager because those jobs required her to be on her feet and on the move most of the time. Not much paperwork, no staring at a screen. When her adrenaline was pumping, she could think more clearly.

It took a couple of years of getting to know her before Teresa and I could trace this pattern of difficulty with schoolwork and testing to a coherent history of attention deficit disorder, soon confirmed by her robust response to a trial of ADHD medication. What had those years of academic frustrations contributed to the toll on her stress response system? Her self-doubt, her repeated experiences of failures in school and some types of work, her dogged extra efforts at the expense of sleep – all could have contributed to what is likely to have been excessive cortisol levels adding abdominal fat to her belly, and excessive epinephrine levels driving her hypertension, and excessive carbohydrate intake overwhelming her insulin stores.

Her reward for her struggles: obesity, hypertension, and diabetes in her forties – the fertile field for her near-death experience. Yet now, recovering from her near-death experience, she was a certified special education teacher, looking for another chance to serve.

By the time I met Teresa she already had diagnosed diabetes, obesity, hypertension, asthma, arthritis, sleep apnea, and a nearly lethal bout of pancreatitis. Our challenge was to see if we could slow down this process and turn it around. Every section of her orchestra was out of tune. And the conductor was out for a long lunch break. Or maybe the conductor had quit and was never coming back.

Where do we find hope? What do we try next? We will return to her journey through treatment later.

We can't fix what we can't measure, and that's the topic as we enter the next section.

Part III

Measuring Toxic Stress

Part III

Measuring Psychosis

9

. . . . .

Managing Begins with Measuring

Before he met Mrs. B for the first time, Dr. Good glanced at the pattern of her blood pressure readings over the previous several years. He could see from her chart the fitful climb of her pressures in spite of his partner's additions of first one medication and then a second, each with several dose increases. The picture of uncontrolled high blood pressure despite medication jumped out at him.

Dr. Good also glanced at the patterns of her glucose levels, her cholesterol, and her body mass index, all of which were climbing in the wrong direction. It took him just a few glances through her labs to adjust his hunches, and with one hand on the door knob, the focus of his attention went to her central nervous system. What did he know about the state of her central nervous system? He had some guesses, but he knew better than to search for lab values. He knew he wouldn't find any.

We don't measure nerves or nervousness or the central nervous system in the clinic. We don't measure stress or the stress response system. We talk about it, but we don't capture the essence of that talk in numbers, not usually. And our talk about stress is general, impressionistic, passionate, and often hard to translate into action.

The aim of this chapter is to describe the range of approaches to measuring stress that is available to researchers, to doctors, and to their patients in order to appreciate the kinds of choices we must make when trying to measure stress in the clinic. An appreciation of the dilemmas of stress measurement sets the stage for understanding in this chapter what the essential components of a clinically useful stress profile are.

Making a Model Work

The concept of stress has been around a long time, and building a model for how stress leads to illness is, relatively speaking, the easy part. The harder part is putting the model to work in places where it counts for patients and their docs, such as the primary care clinic, where the mission is treatment planning.

The first hurdle we face in making this model useful is measurement. Scientists generally ignore what can't be measured. And busy primary care doctors have to treat the numbers. What numbers for stress do they treat? Very few. And if we're hoping to motivate distressed people to change their high-risk health behaviors, we know that measurement can be a powerful motivator.

Why Not Measure?

It's not only stress that we clinicians avoid measuring. The history of medical science includes numerous examples of our reluctance to admit measurement into the art of medicine. An article by Tony Rousmaniere[1] reminds us that in the mid-1800s, 250 years after its invention, many physicians were reluctant to use the thermometer to manage fever. In 1868 Carl Wunderlich "proposed the radical idea of tracking a febrile [fever] illness by reading the patient's temperature at regular intervals."

Good doctors at the time used touch and observation and intuition to track fevers. Thermometers were cumbersome and often not reliable. As technology improved along with the science of fevers, reluctance yielded eventually to including thermometer data for fever management. The switch to temperature monitoring required several decades. Now every parent knows how to watch a child's fever of 99 degrees F, and knows to rush a fever of 104 degrees F to the emergency room. And during the worst days of COVID, we were all taking temperatures at home and at entrances to a business or health clinic.

Until the late 1990s in the US, physical pain, though common, remained unmeasured, mostly underappreciated, and often inefficiently treated. Only with the adoption in the late 1990s of the rating of pain on a 0 to 10 scale, initially in VA medical centers and later around the country, did pain become "visible" and consistently measured with a simple question.[2]

We doctors are often reluctant to measure a patient's mood, which has clouded the practice of psychotherapy and psychiatry, perpetuating our confusion about what works to relieve mental suffering.

And as the technology and science of measuring stress and other physical and psychological processes improve, our reluctance to measure is gradually yielding to the practice of measuring the workings of the brain and the mind. In fact, the healthcare reform movement in the US is embracing measurement-based care as a key principle for improving the quality of healthcare. Has the time arrived for effectively measuring some aspects of the stress response system when you see your doctor?

The Sophisticated Lab Approach

To appreciate what it takes to look deeper into the workings of the stress response system, beneath our conscious awareness, I followed Nancy Murrah, RN, BSN, a nurse, deep into the basement of the Emory Hospital Clinic Building in Atlanta one Tuesday morning. Murrah has been coordinating clinical research studies at Emory for thirty years, and she still does it with enthusiasm and affection for her patients and colleagues.

At the time she was coordinating five studies run by Viola Vaccarino, MD, PhD, the chair of the department of epidemiology at Emory's Rollins School of Public Health. Dr. Vaccarino is a cardiovascular epidemiologist married to a research psychiatrist, Doug Bremner, MD, and this marriage is part of what has spurred her to focus her career on psychosocial risk factors for heart disease.

The study I was about to observe is called the PTSD and Ischemic Heart Disease Progression: A Longitudinal Twin Study. All the twin pairs in this study are Vietnam veterans, and the question the study aimed to answer was whether and how PTSD might contribute to heart disease over twelve years. The twin design would allow the investigators to tease out genetic and environmental influences on heart disease.

Murrah led me to a suite of rooms off a main corridor in the basement where a team of three research assistants in white coats was already setting up Mr. F for the morning protocol. She handed me a white coat, we glanced in at the waiting room where Mr. F's heavy-set twin brother was dozing, and then entered the recording room.

Mr. F sat still in a full-backed recliner chair with six EKG wires stuck on his chest trailing out from under his green checked shirt tails, four wires clipped to carotid sensors on each side of his neck, a clear IV tube for blood drawing inserted in his right arm, a blood pressure cuff on his upper left arm, a respiratory belt around his chest, and sensors clipped on three fingers of each hand.

He was an average-sized man who looked pretty fit for sixty-four, and he smiled calmly at me when I was introduced, offering me his wired hand for a shake, amused and accommodating and apparently expecting me. He had spent the previous day doing similar procedures for this study, and twelve years before, he and his twin brother had completed the baseline version of this study. So Mr. F was a study veteran as well as a military veteran. This was familiar duty for him.

Steve, the head tech, sat to his right by the BIOPAC console and screen, chatting with Mr. F, arranging the wires, and tinkering with the leads, while Belal, the assistant on Mr. F's left, circulated to help with the setup. From where I sat on a stool behind Steve and facing Mr. F, I could watch the readouts on the screen and him. Light banter among the three of them kept the mood friendly.

I learned from the banter that Mr. F and his brother, who live in Wisconsin about a five-hour drive from each other, had flown to Atlanta Sunday on separate planes, one from Madison and the other from Milwaukee. Mr. F told me his brother got lost in the Atlanta airport for four hours and couldn't figure out how to call him.

"Something's not right with him," Mr. F said in his matter-of-fact understated way. "I hadn't seen him for the better part of a year until we got here Sunday. I don't know what's going on, but he's changed."

After Steve ran the baseline tracings for heart rate and heart rate variability, Belal took the blood draw for cortisol, epinephrine, and norepinephrine, and the oral swab for sampling the microbiome of Mr. F's GI tract.

Then a third research assistant, Stacey, came in to run "the scripts." She explained to him that she would play the scripts through the headphones while they would record various measures with all the wires and bands adorning his body. All he had to do was attend to the scripts.

She asked first for Mr. F to rate his emotions and his level of distress. Then she put headphones on him and played the series of four scripts, two neutral ones followed by two "traumatic events," which he had chosen from his life and described the day before.

Stacey's team had edited his description of these events into two scripts of a few minutes each. After she played each script, she asked him about his specific feelings (nervous, anxious, fearful, high, angry) and asked him to rate his level of distress from 0 to 100.

The video camera and I watched him during these scripts. He looked calm and untroubled by all these wires and recording devices and strangers attending to him. For the first two neutral scripts, he reported no emotions and no distress. For the first trauma script he reported mild anger and mild anxiety, but rated his distress level 0. Here is what he was listening to [KIAs are service members killed in action]:

> In August of 1969, I was involved in a combat assault. The duties we were performing were to pick up KIAs. We landed the helicopter, and the people on the ground loaded three or four KIAs into the helicopter. On the way back to the base camp, the KIA's shifted and fell over. One of the KIA's body cavity released some blood. I got very angry. I still think of why I had that reaction, what had I become.

For the second trauma script, Mr. F reported mild anxiety and rated his distress at 20 out of 100. I wondered what it would take to rattle this man and raise his distress rating over 50! See for yourself:

> I was driving to the store one summer day and saw some guys tossing a football around. I also noted that two cars about a half a mile ahead were staging to race. They came up to where the guys were playing football, traveling around 90 miles per hour. The football rolled into the road and one guy ran after it. He saw the cars and stopped, but then he tried to make it to the football. The car hit him

so hard that he bounced like a rag doll. I tried to help, but he was gone. He died at the edge of the road.

I could see on the monitor that Mr. F's blood pressure readings were up in the range of hypertension: at baseline 167/85, up around 153/90 during the first trauma script and the second, and back down to 136/78 after Steve asked him to relax at the end of the procedure. His heart rate rose from a baseline of 59 to the high 70s and back down to the low 60s.

"My blood pressure is usually pretty low," he volunteered, unaware of what his readings had been. He then talked again about concern for his brother's confusion, and Steve noted his blood pressure rise when he talked about his brother and then return to normal during the relaxation phase at the end. Here we could see the cardiovascular reaction in his stress response system as he experienced what he called mild anger, anxiety, and distress.

Mr. F had spent the previous night in the Emory sleep lab, and after he finished this morning's recording session, he would spend the afternoon in a PET scan of his heart to study blood flow during rest and during a drug-induced stress test. That evening he and his brother would fly back to Wisconsin, having twice donated their time, confidences, and body fluids to one of the state-of-the-art studies of stress across a crucial section of their lifespans.

Like Ted Daley who was wearing all the monitors and filling out logs for the SHINE study, Mr. F is among our unsung heroes. As are our friends and neighbors who agree to be in phase 1, 2, or 3 studies of treatments for cancer or who rolled up their sleeves to try out the COVID-19 vaccines.

People who sign up for and qualify to be in research studies that benefit the advancement of science and eventually lead to advances in treatment for each one of us are never thanked enough. We researchers learn so much from their unselfish gifts.

Dr. Vaccarino's team plans to mine gold from these 283 twin pairs of veterans with data on their genetic, endocrine, cardiovascular, immune, metabolic, gastrointestinal, and autonomic and central nervous systems. That gold mine will produce one of the most comprehensive pictures of the stress response system in action, the whole system and its parts. Yet this study is just one of several like it that Dr. Vaccarino's team has completed, exploring the effects of stress on heart disease.

The silent strains that I could see on the blood pressure and heart rate monitors during Mr. F's recording session are just the tip of the iceberg of his stress response system that Dr. Vaccarino's study measures in detail. And what will his brother's system look like, the one who has been struggling with PTSD for decades and now can't find his way out of an airport? Dr. Vaccarino hopes to show us in detail how those two facts of Mr. F's twin brother's life – a lifetime of stress and a declining brain and heart – are related.

Dr. Vaccarino and her colleagues are raising the limits of sophistication for measuring the stress response system in the laboratory. They do this by measuring multiple organ system responses over long periods of time (twelve years) under a range of conditions and stressors in a large sample, at least half of whom have a stress-related chronic condition.

So measuring stress is possible, and it is difficult to do well, and it is costly. It can also be done outside the laboratory. Studies that collect data on stressors and stress responses during everyday life, like the SHINE study using momentary assessment methods recording a week or two of sample days and nights, like Ted was doing, achieve a similar level of sophistication and comprehensiveness of measurement.

The Problem with Slices of Time

Before we dig into the technical difficulties of measuring the stress response system in clinical settings where it can immediately guide a patient's treatment, we should remember that measurement in medicine is still young and insufficient. Most of the lab data we use to guide our treatments represent the equivalent of a few frame shots from which experts aim to guess at the whole movie of a current life.

That is, what we really care about for health and illness are the full range of daily variations over many months in our blood pressure or glucose or heart rate or mood, and we care about how all of these vary together. How well does the whole stress response system and each of its subsystems adjust over time? How much do these demands strain the capacities of this person?

Those two high blood pressure readings in Dr. Good's office that triggered the prescription for Mrs. B's third blood pressure medication were just a couple of frame shots in the long movie of her blood pressure before and after the bleed into her eye. These readings offer the best guess any doctor can do for now, but what we really care about is that movie of how her blood pressure has fluctuated day and night during heavy traffic, nightmares, and an argument with her sister.

If that sounds like too much data, you're right. Among the current barriers to that ideal level of monitoring are the challenges of collecting and analyzing that much "big data" in ways that are useful for the regular patient we doctors see every day in our exam rooms. However, those kinds of big data advances are developing rapidly enough that such a monitoring scenario will surely soon become a reality for selected healthcare systems.

Wearables such as Fitbits and Apple Watches are only the beginning. The key point to keep in mind is how our current approach to monitoring the functioning of the stress response system captures only the tiniest fraction of the relevant data. Our current definitions of clinically meaningful hypertension or diabetes or depression rely on insufficient slices of data, and will surely be revised when we can watch the whole movie.

The Problem with Stressful Events

A few exceptionally well-funded research scientists measure stress in most of its dimensions for short intervals, but the rest of the clinical world waits, or looks the other way. Why is it so difficult to measure stress?

The difficulties are rooted in our many definitions of stress. Since the 1990s Scott Monroe, PhD, a professor of clinical psychology at Notre Dame, has been studying how we measure stress. Early in his career Dr. Monroe wondered how we do on what is perhaps the easiest aspect of stress to measure, stressful life events. He discovered that our recall of stressful life events is not as good as we pretend. In fact, it's often embarrassingly poor.

To appreciate the extent of this problem, think about the last stressful life events questionnaire you saw. Most of the initial efforts to formally assess stress focused on self-report questionnaires about events (reporting them), as opposed to your responses (how you reacted) to those events.[3] They asked what kinds of stressful events you have been exposed to and, for each exposure, how severely affected you were: death of a family member, job loss, promotion, wedding, car accident, for example.

Dr. Monroe and colleagues interviewed samples of people who had responded to these questionnaires and learned some sobering facts about their answers.

First, respondents commonly endorsed items that later proved not to match the questionnaire's threshold for a stressful event. These false positives resulted from the questionnaires not specifying thresholds of severity and from wide variations in the ways we appraise what is stressful to each of us.

Is a fender bender a stressful event, or must it be a car accident that leads to car damage or injury or results in a driving phobia? And false negatives are also a problem. Checklists often fail to

capture what later prove in interviews to be valid stressful events. Multiple studies have found that even the best self-report measures of stressful life events capture less than half of the valid events identified by interview.

We forget, we deny, we misinterpret the questions, we distort our answers to please our imagined raters, and we change our responses with time and prompting.

These early shortcomings in the measurement of stress are forgivable if we understand that the measurement of stress focused only on self-reports of stressful events, because that was the easy and cheap way to collect stress data on large samples. The reports on stress were unreliable and hard to interpret, sloppy science – the mismeasure of stress exposures. And they ignored the rest of the stress experience, as we will see next.

One barrier to measuring stress is that the cheap and easy way, the self-report questionnaires about stressful events, is inherently unreliable if used alone. Interviews help to obtain useful measures of exposures, but extensive interviews are not practical for large samples of people or hurried primary care practitioners.

The Problem with Stress Responses

Measuring exposures to stressful life events is only one part of the stress measurement task. If the event is the stimulus, what is the response? Four main types of responses are important to distinguish, because they don't always work in concert: cognitive, emotional, behavioral, and physiologic responses.

In the 1970s and 1980s Richard Lazarus and Susan Folkman, both PhDs at the University of California at Berkeley, made the case for expanding the concept and measurement of stress to include how we respond to the stressful event.[4] They argued that at least as important as what we are exposed to is how we perceive

the exposure, because that's what determines how we respond in every way.

Consistently, pessimists and optimists tend to look at the same events differently. And you might even react to the same event quite differently when feverish or frightened than when you are healthy and well rested and feeling safe.

One of the key distinctions we make when we appraise a demanding event is the difference between a challenge and a threat. To help us draw the line between stress responses that make us stronger and stress responses that harm us, Drs. Lazarus and Folkman examined how we look at the demands of a task in relationship to how we judge our resources.

When we think our resources exceed the demand (fit enough for volleyball, quick enough for trivia), we tend to view a task as challenging and feel uplifted by meeting that challenge. However, when we see that our resources don't meet the demand – we lack the money to pay the tax collector, lack the knowledge to pass the test, lack the brute strength to lift the car off the pinned child – we see the task as a threat.

The subjective experience of stress responses is harder to measure than stress exposures, and, relatively speaking, there has been less research on how we perceive or evaluate stress than on the more measurable exposures to life events.

The most widely used, best-studied, and easiest to administer measure of stress appraisal is the Perceived Stress Scale (PSS), first published in 1983.[5] It's a ten-item self-report form that asks you to rate on a five-point scale your perceptions over the past month of how upset you have been, how often you felt unable to control the important things in your life, and how confident you felt about your ability to handle personal problems. It takes no more than a few minutes to complete.

The authors of the PSS have shown that mental and emotional appraisals of stress have a different impact on illness than exposures

to life events. Both aspects of the stress experience are important and influential, but distinguishable in their effects on illness. This becomes useful when thinking about how the stress response system influences illness, and ultimately which treatments to try.

For example, Mrs. B may ruminate more about the stress in her life and score higher on the PSS than her sister. Mrs. B has always viewed their world as a more threatening place than her sister has, though they grew up exposed to roughly the same events and currently live in the same neighborhood. Mrs. B spends more time on high alert and more energy coping with threats each day and each night than her sister does.

Cognitive therapy could help Mrs. B reduce and manage her daily perceptions of threats and may reduce her vulnerability to illness more than changing the number of stressful events she is exposed to, though both approaches would help.

Related to and overlapping with appraisals of stress are how we look inward and how aware we are of our emotions and thoughts (are we feeling anxious or depressed, for example), which determines what we report as stressful. This, too, is a psychological skill that some people do better than others.

Stress and Resilience

As we saw earlier, the risk for illness rises as the stress burden rises, and it declines as resilience increases. People facing high levels of stressors may do well if they also can sustain high levels of resilience. Over the past half-century the measurement of resilience has lagged behind the measurement of stress, so we have fewer good measures of resilience, and we know less about their strengths and weaknesses.

Further complicating the measurement of stress responses and resilience is the fact that, in addition to life events and our

perceptions of our responses to these events, we must consider the body's responses that all too often escape our awareness.

Just as today's temperature doesn't tell us about global warming, today's blood pressure or cortisol level does not tell us about our cumulative risk for illness. We can't hook everyone up to Dr. Vaccarino's lab wires and tubes. Even the three monitoring devices plus saliva, blood, and urine collections can be endured only for a few days by Ted Daley and the most willing and forgiving volunteers. The complexity of the stress response system – its social, psychological, and biological dimensions – and its variations over a lifetime make for a thorny measurement dilemma.

If toxic stress matters in chronic illness, then the measurement of toxic stress matters. The difficulty of any task is not a good reason to avoid trying, and the efforts of stress researchers in this area have contributed to substantial recent progress in measuring stress. The road to understanding other complex systems, such as the global climate, the human genome, stellar space, and the human experience of pain has always run through incremental advances in methods of measurement.

Making Stress Visible

When Ted Daley completed his final visit in the SHINE study, he met with one of the investigators, and she briefly reviewed his experience and handed him a sheet that summarized some of his data.

Several months later when I asked him what he had gained from participating in this study, he said one of the best parts was the half hour he spent by himself later that day looking over his data. It included the ranges of his heart rate and his blood pressure over the four days of recording. He felt reassured to notice that his heart rate varied between 58 and 96 beats per minute and stayed mostly in the 70s. He didn't see any alarming spikes in his heart rate or

blood pressure and concluded that his recorded week had been uneventful.

When Ted and I reviewed his data summary sheet, he started to notice a few patterns. His blood pressure graph on workdays was notably higher than on weekends. And the summary of his blood pressure showed an average blood pressure when he was awake of 167/97 and asleep of 148/91. That's 79 blood pressure readings, taken about every hour over four days, and it included his relatively lower blood pressures during the weekend. By any definition, these readings add up to high blood pressure (hypertension), at least during his workdays and nights.[6] And yet at the time of the study no doctor or nurse had ever recorded a high blood pressure reading on Ted Daley, as far as he knew. Six months after the study, however, he had had several high blood pressure readings at his doctor's office.

He thinks about his brother who died of a heart attack at thirty-eight and his sister who is overweight, maybe prediabetic. His own BMI is 35, though he doesn't think of himself as obese. According to his doctor, he had not yet needed any treatment for his blood pressure, but he thought he might share this data summary with his doctor next time.

Is work stress driving Ted Daley to hypertension? Measurement at this level of detail can begin to answer such a question. This simple graph and numerical summary of his blood pressure made visible to Ted both his pattern of work stress and the possibility of his developing hypertension.

Does Measurement Help?

One final point in favor of bothering to measure stress, before we look at the best measures. After years in the trenches of clinical care, I am so convinced of the therapeutic value of monitoring

that I often spend a significant chunk of my early sessions with a new patient exploring ways to track our progress or the lack of it, like with Teresa or like Dr. Good with Mrs. B. This approach also makes it clear that it's okay to discuss whether what we're doing is effective or not. Transparency about effectiveness is usually beneficial. And it implies that there are alternatives if we're not making progress.

Perhaps the most dramatic demonstration of the therapeutic value of measurement in clinical settings comes to us from the UK National Health Service's program called Improving Access to Psychological Therapies.[7] In 2008, when this project launched its first pilot, depression and anxiety were widespread (15 percent of all visits) in the UK but only 10 percent of those afflicted received therapy, and half of those lucky few got substandard or ineffective treatment.

To address this problem of insufficient supply of psychological services, a massive training and distribution of therapists to primary care health centers throughout the UK took place, raising the access to psychological therapies to 16 percent, and aiming for 25 percent by 2021.

But David Clark, PhD, the project's director, first had to tackle the problem of how to prove that all this training and services would be worth the money invested. In his first two pilot sites, one site collected outcome data on 54 percent of the people seen, the other site on just 6 percent. Missing data were traced to those patients who left treatment before their expected completion date.

So as a next step, to make sure they collected a final measure on everyone, Dr. Clark rigged the system so that at every visit the patient would complete a symptom measure for depression, anxiety, and functioning. It took about five minutes in the waiting room each time, and, surprisingly, only a few patients objected. The data were automatically entered into the NHS chart and could be displayed graphically for review with the doctor.

By addressing his need for transparent outcome data to fund his program, Dr. Clark inadvertently also contributed to a dramatic rise in demonstrable remission rates. In 2008, when the program started collecting these data, remission rates for depression hovered around 20 percent. That is, one in five people treated for depression in this program achieved full recovery. Within two years that rate doubled, and it has gradually risen to around 50 percent in the subsequent years. That's as good as anywhere in the world, though few other countries can boast such a data set to prove it.

On the whole, around two-thirds of all depression patients in this UK program showed significant improvement. Measurement has been good not only for the patients but for the therapists, who now have numbers to back their confidence and raise their value. This step toward transparent measurement has proven therapeutic in several ways.

In the process of identifying people for whom toxic stress may be contributing to stress-related illnesses, we begin with the simple approaches, single measures that screen for toxic stress, and we build as needed to more complex measures. In the next chapter we will look at some specific measures and what it takes to create a stress profile.

10

. . . . .

A Peek Inside the Black Box of Stress

Modern medicine is flush with profiles. The medical assistant who ushers you into your annual checkup is collecting a profile of your vital signs: weight, height, blood pressure, heart rate, and temperature. These vital signs offer a crude picture of how you're doing on a few selected physical measures, a starting point for your conversation with your doctor.

That questionnaire you just filled out in the waiting room provides another profile of your current symptoms. It will find its way into your medical record along with the medical history taken by your astute doctor. That history leads to her revising your problem list, which is also a profile of possible priorities for your treatment plan.

The problem list of Ted Daley, the PR and marketing man at Carnegie Mellon whom we met earlier, and who was taking part in the SHINE study, is short: sleep apnea and overweight. The problem list of Teresa Langford, the disabled veteran, is long: hypertension,

obesity, low back pain, diabetes, ADHD, obstructive sleep apnea, abdominal hernia, and alcohol use disorder in remission. Those are two very different and useful profiles that guide the planning of treatment.

Both patients are likely to stop at the lab on the way out to give blood for a comprehensive metabolic panel, another profile that will sketch the state of their livers, kidneys, bones, and pancreases through a list of numbers and ranges of normal. Somewhere in her chart Teresa might have a number for her Framingham Heart Index, a profile of her already moderate risk for coronary heart disease based on her age, gender, lipid levels, blood pressure, glucose levels, and smoking.

Modern medicine values these profiles because they help healthcare providers see patterns across several organ systems – a skill that relies on art, science, and a wise doctor's experience and intuition. Each profile provides a different lens trained on a different focal point to answer a specific set of questions.

But where's the profile that captures patterns of toxic stress? Most primary care docs will tell you they don't know of such a profile, much less one they routinely use in practice.

The absence of a standard stress profile contributes to the invisibility of the stress response system. Our difficulty "seeing" this part of our bodies is a reminder that not so long ago it was also difficult for us to see specific types of mental impairment, such as dyslexia, learning disabilities, early dementia, and attention deficit disorder, at a level that could guide treatment.

Profiling the Brain

One of the more useful profiles in medicine is a battery of tests to assess how the mind and brain are working. For example, a young woman struggles with staying organized at home and at work and

her boss is threatening to fire her. She had a traumatic brain injury from a car accident two years ago, but she has also coped with ADHD and severe anxiety since her teens. Are her current troubles a part of her brain injury, her attention disorder, her anxiety, or some combination of all three?

For her, testing can help identify what is interfering with her memory, attention, and problem solving. It can also point to treatment approaches that may help her keep her job. Primary care doctors use neuropsychological testing to help assess the mental capacities of a patient with traumatic brain injury, stroke, dementia, learning problems, autism, Parkinson's disease, and other neurologic or psychiatric conditions.

Obtaining a neuropsychological profile can be expensive in time (six to twelve hours) and money ($1,600 to $3,000) for a psychologist to complete this battery of tests over several half-day testing sessions. The battery includes measures of IQ, perceptual acuity, short-term memory, immediate recall, attention, spatial orientation, and problem solving, to name a few. The menu of tests varies depending on the questions that need to be answered, but it can include twenty to thirty different tests.

The report summarizing this battery of tests can take a few weeks for the specialist to prepare, and often the report is four to five pages long, single-spaced, including the assessment and recommendations. This report provides a useful profile of the patient's cognitive functioning in relation to behavior and emotions – usually worth the time and money.

Today, most major medical centers in the US keep a neuropsychological testing service busy full-time. But this profile of brain functioning is a recent advance, the product of the mushrooming discipline of cognitive neuroscience.

In the 1980s neuropsychological testing services were rare, even in large medical centers. No wonder we knew so little then about the various types of intellectual disability, attention deficit disorder,

traumatic brain injury, stroke, autism spectrum issues, and the "software" problems imposed by psychiatric disorders like depression and bipolar disorder.[1]

As complex as the brain is, the stress response system is even more complex because it consists not only of the central nervous system but most of the other major organ systems (endocrine, immune, cardiovascular, as we have discussed). Perhaps it's not surprising then that no such profile for the stress response system exists yet in clinical practice.

The field of stress neuroscience today may be similar in its development to the field of neuropsychology fifty years ago. Then, neuropsychologists had lots of measures of cognitive function but no standards of practice, no consensus on the essential elements of a comprehensive neuropsychological assessment, and few norms for interpreting results.

In the last chapter we looked at some of the reasons for the current gap between the science of stress and the clinical practice of stress assessments. In this chapter we look at the ways that a stress profile could become a useful part of your next doctor visit. It does not have to be expensive, intrusive, or exhaustive to be useful. But it should strive to be comprehensive, blending some essential components of all stress profiles with some measures that are specific to needs of the individual patient.

Building the Stress Profile

We can organize the stress profile into four groups of measures, each of which overlaps with the others: subjective distress, cumulative life stress exposures and responses, physiologic stress measures, and social determinants of health. The Distress Thermometer summarizes this process by listing some options for selecting measures in each of these groups.

The assessment of toxic stress begins with measures of subjective distress – the psychological dimension of the process of adapting to high demands. The logic of this starting point rests partly in the importance of current distress as a motivator for behavior change.

People are most motivated to change high-risk health behaviors when they believe those changes could relieve their distress. A clear understanding of the patterns of discomfort over the recent months can indicate the need for a plan to reduce the distress, and this pattern can readily be assessed with a visit to a primary care doctor. The Distress Thermometer combines your overall estimate of distress with some guesses about the sources of the distress, which are often social factors like financial problems or unemployment or lack of childcare.

In 1997 the National Cancer Center Network adopted a guideline for the systematic assessment of distress at every visit, using

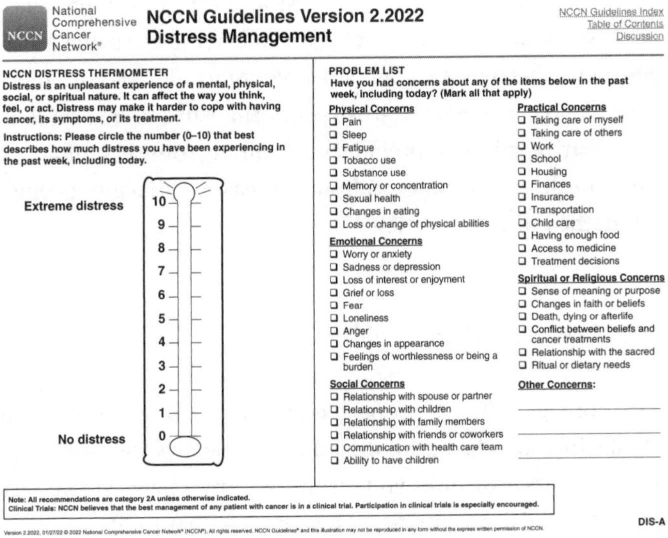
National Comprehensive Cancer Network®

NCCN Guidelines Version 2.2022
Distress Management

NCCN Guidelines Index
Table of Contents
Discussion

NCCN DISTRESS THERMOMETER

Distress is an unpleasant experience of a mental, physical, social, or spiritual nature. It can affect the way you think, feel, or act. Distress may make it harder to cope with having cancer, its symptoms, or its treatment.

Instructions: Please circle the number (0–10) that best describes how much distress you have been experiencing in the past week, including today.

Extreme distress 10
9
8
7
6
5
4
3
2
1
No distress 0

PROBLEM LIST

Have you had concerns about any of the items below in the past week, including today? (Mark all that apply)

Physical Concerns
- Pain
- Sleep
- Fatigue
- Tobacco use
- Substance use
- Memory or concentration
- Sexual health
- Changes in eating
- Loss or change of physical abilities

Emotional Concerns
- Worry or anxiety
- Sadness or depression
- Loss of interest or enjoyment
- Grief or loss
- Fear
- Loneliness
- Anger
- Changes in appearance
- Feelings of worthlessness or being a burden

Social Concerns
- Relationship with spouse or partner
- Relationship with children
- Relationship with family members
- Relationship with friends or coworkers
- Communication with health care team
- Ability to have children

Practical Concerns
- Taking care of myself
- Taking care of others
- Work
- School
- Housing
- Finances
- Insurance
- Transportation
- Child care
- Having enough food
- Access to medicine
- Treatment decisions

Spiritual or Religious Concerns
- Sense of meaning or purpose
- Changes in faith or beliefs
- Death, dying or afterlife
- Conflict between beliefs and cancer treatments
- Relationship with the sacred
- Ritual or dietary needs

Other Concerns:

Note: All recommendations are category 2A unless otherwise indicated.
Clinical Trials: NCCN believes that the best management of any patient with cancer is in a clinical trial. Participation in clinical trials is especially encouraged.

DIS-A

Figure 10.1 The distress thermometer.

the Distress Thermometer. The NCCN has published guidelines for patients and doctors over the years on the measurement and management of *distress*, a term they define simply as "an unpleasant experience of a mental, physical, social, or spiritual nature."

The NCCN use of the term *distress* is broad and includes mental and emotional responses to stress exposures of any kind. Think of the thermometer as rating your stress responses over the past week and the Problem List as identifying some possible types of exposures to stressful events or threats or social determinants of health.

The impact of the Distress Thermometer on the care of cancer patients has been helpful in some specific ways. In one recent study the cancer centers that followed the screening protocols for the Distress Thermometer reported 18 percent fewer emergency department visits and 19 percent fewer hospitalizations during the two months after the distress screening, suggesting better care and lower costs.

In primary care settings the benefits and barriers to routine screening for distress are likely to be similar to those in cancer centers. However, the proven benefits of this simplest of all stress measures make it the place to start. For those who screen positive by scoring over 4 on several successive assessments, the Distress Thermometer initiates the conversation on what's going on with you. In other words, it's not just the knee pain but the worry about not being able to get around.

This is particularly helpful for those with severe and persistent distress over six months. The Distress Thermometer provides the sensitive first step to identifying those in greatest need, which is one of the key roles of primary care. It points the way to the second step for those who screen positive: referral to a health psychology service that selects and collects the data from more specific measures for the remainder of the stress profile.

Measures of distress may also include brief self-report inventories of symptoms of depression or anxiety, along with a measure

of resilience, such as the Brief Resilience Scale.[2] These symptom measures can identify the patients who are in need of a full stress profile.

Cumulative Life Stress

What more would a patient and doctor want to know about risks for illness if a screening measure such as the Distress Thermometer suggested a high risk for illness? As we saw in the last chapter, a meaningful measure of stress should include both the events we've been exposed to and our responses to those exposures. And any period less than the person's full lifespan captures only a fraction of the toll on the stress response system.

The Adverse Childhood Experiences (ACE) Scale. One measure that captures part of the process (exposures) over part of the lifespan (childhood) is worth mentioning again because it has had an impact on recent clinical practice, at least in the US. Ten years after the first ACE study report was published in 1998, Nadine Burke Harris, MD, discovered that report when a psychologist she had hired to work in her fledgling pediatrics clinic recommended she read it.

Reading that report turned on a lightbulb that shifted her approach to patients with complex illnesses in her practice. She realized she needed a clinical procedure that her mentors at Stanford had not known about or taught her: a profile for the impact of childhood trauma on health and illness. She discovered the power of applying arithmetic to childhood adversity experiences.

The ACE consists of ten items about possible adverse experiences in childhood. The items include some common experiences, such as divorce or living with a relative who was a problem drinker or had a mental illness, and some less common experiences, such as the threat of sexual or physical injury. No single question alone would be considered unusual in a routine pediatric evaluation.

Adverse Childhood Experiences (ACE) Questionnaire
Finding Your ACE Score

While you were growing up, during your first 18 years of life:

1. Did a parent or other adult in the household **often** . . .
   Swear at you, insult you, put you down, or humiliate you?
   or
   Act in a way that made you afraid that you might be physically hurt?
   Yes No   If yes enter 1 _____

2. Did a parent or other adult in the household **often** . . .
   Push, grab, slap, or throw something at you?
   or
   Ever hit you so hard that you had marks or were injured?
   Yes No   If yes enter 1 _____

3. Did an adult or person at least 5 years older than you **ever** . . .
   Touch or fondle you or have you touch their body in a sexual way?
   or
   Try to or actually have oral, anal, or vaginal sex with you?
   Yes No   If yes enter 1 _____

4. Did you **often** feel that . . .
   No one in your family loved you or thought you were important or special?
   or
   Your family didn't look out for each other, feel close to each other, or support each other?
   Yes No   If yes enter 1 _____

5. Did you **often** feel that. . .
   You didn't have enough to eat, had to wear dirty clothes, and had no one to protect you?
   or
   Your parents were too drunk or high to take care of you or take you to the doctor if you needed it?
   Yes No   If yes enter 1 _____

6. Were your parents **ever** separated or divorced?
   Yes No   If yes enter 1 _____

7. Was your mother or stepmother:
   Often pushed, grabbed, slapped, or had something thrown at her?
   or
   Sometimes or often kicked, bitten, hit with a fist, or hit with something hard?
   or
   Ever repeatedly hit over at least a few minutes or threatened with a gun or knife?
   Yes No   If yes enter 1 _____

8. Did you live with anyone who was a problem drinker or alcoholic or who used street drugs?
   Yes No   If yes enter 1 _____

9. Was a household member depressed or mentally ill or did a household member attempt suicide?
   Yes No   If yes enter 1 _____

10. Did a household member go to prison?
    Yes No   If yes enter 1 _____

Now add up your "Yes" answers: _____ This is your ACE Score.

Figure 10.2 The ACE Questionnaire.

What is novel and powerful about this scale is the collecting of scores on these ten items tapping abuse, neglect, or dysfunction in the family, adding up the scores, and using the sum of these childhood exposures to estimate risks for later illness.

Imagine how this simple questionnaire could have identified childhood experiences with Mrs. B and with Teresa Langford?

In 2018, another ten years after her realization about the impact of childhood adversity on health, Dr. Harris and selected colleagues in the region adopted this scale as a standard screening measure. She and her foundation, the Center for Youth Wellness, have collaborated with colleagues in the Bay Area through the PEARLS study to examine the impact of systematic ACE screening in primary care on health outcomes. Since 2014, her vocal advocacy for screening for adverse childhood experiences in primary care pediatric populations has earned her the attention of her mayor, Gavin Newsome, who, as the newly elected governor of California in 2019, promptly appointed her the state's first Surgeon General.

As an early screening step in the process of building a stress profile, the ACE scale offers a promising complement to the Distress Thermometer. The ACE screens for past childhood stress *exposures*, while the Distress Thermometer reflects current adult stress *responses*.

There are plenty of measurement shortcomings in the ACE scale. It does not specify the age of exposure or quantify the frequency or severity of these exposures. It does not ask about the severity of the person's responses to them. It gives equal weight to parental separations, sexual abuse, and not feeling loved. Yet in spite of these psychometric shortcomings, responses to this list of exposures have proven to predict many of our most important public health outcomes in adults, not only in the initial Kaiser sample in San Diego, but also in twenty-five states around the country.[3]

Aside from age, no other risk factor can claim such predictive power. The secret of this power lies in part in its simple addition. It

recognizes that each of us has a limit to the burdens we can manage during the formative stages of our childhood.

The Life Stress Test. Questionnaires about cumulative life stress tend to be affordable but long, whereas interviews are expensive and often longer. Ideally, we need a way to combine the best of both methods for collecting information about cumulative life stress.

In one of the more innovative efforts to combine the convenience of questionnaires with the validity and depth of interviews, George Slavich, PhD, and his team at UCLA have spent over a decade creating an interactive online assessment of stress exposures and responses called the STRAIN or the Life Stress Test.[4] After developing this measure through over a hundred studies in research settings, the researchers have recently begun looking at how the Life Stress Test can be adopted into clinical practice.

The Life Stress Test is an easy measure to complete, but to make sense of the results you need a clinician who is certified to interpret the results. You can try it at www.lifestresstest.com. It will take you twenty to thirty minutes, and it generates four sets of results to help you and the certified clinician make sense of your cumulative stress level: number of stressors, severity of stressors, stress exposure by life domain, and resilience.

Why is the Life Stress Test one of the better measures among the few available for assessing cumulative exposures and responses in the doctor's office? It asks not only about the number and types of events, but when they happened, how frequently, at what ages, and how you responded. It can collect a lot of relevant data on both stress exposures and responses in a relatively short time because it selects questions according to the answers provided to stem items. For example, it avoids asking a thirty-year-old unmarried male about retirement and grandchildren.

The Life Stress Test provides an immediate tally of your stress data in a form that is easy to read as a profile that charts your lifetime stress levels across nine domains relative to other people of

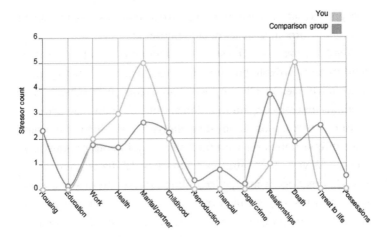

Figure 10.3 Lifetime stress exposures by domain.

your age and gender. These features make it attractive for use in clinical practice.

Compared to a neuropsychology test battery or a colonoscopy, the Life Stress Test is quick, cheap, and easy. And a lot less stressful. In a short time at low cost with minimal effort invested by professionals, the therapist and patient can obtain a stress profile that is both specific and measurable. The Life Stress Test can help you and your doctor focus your stress reduction treatments on the specific domains of the stress profile that are of greatest risk to your future health, whether it's sleep, time management, risky relationships, or unhealthy habits.

The Body Keeps the Score

But something is still missing from this stress profile. In addition to subjective measures of current distress and a profile of cumulative life stress, doctors and patients need to know what's going on in the body.

My friend and colleague Bessel van der Kolk, MD, has made a strong case in his popular book *The Body Keeps the Score: Brain, Mind, and Body in the Healing of Trauma* for attending to the signals from the body when assessing the impact of trauma over the lifespan. Ideally, physical measures of stress should be a part of anyone's profile.

In a haphazard way we already pay attention to some indirect measures of stress when we focus on weight, blood pressure, hours of sleep per night, and pain or fatigue levels. But a useful complement to our psychosocial measures of the cumulative toll of stress is a measure of the cumulative toll on our body's stress response systems. If it's true that the body keeps the score and chronic stress accelerates aging, is there a way to measure that toll?

Among those who have explored this question, the most vocal and persuasive voice has been that of Bruce McEwen, a neuroendocrinologist who spent his career at the Rockefeller Institute in New York conducting research on various aspects of the stress response system.

Since 2000, he has published at least twenty-four scientific articles with the term *allostatic load* in the title, and has talked at length about stress and health on PBS, CBS, NBC, NPR, and other popular media.

The elusive allostatic load. Dr. McEwen, in the company of other esteemed scientists such as Teresa Seeman, PhD, at UCLA, ventured into the troubled waters of stress measurement in the late 1990s with a proposal for an allostatic load index based on these ten biomarkers, which they proposed could capture the cumulative toll of lifetime stress:[5]

1. Systolic blood pressure (the first number in a normal blood pressure of 120/80)
2. Diastolic blood pressure (the bottom number)
3. Waist–hip ratio
4. Total cholesterol

5. HDL (high density lipoprotein)
6. Hemoglobin A1C (a measure of glucose levels over three months)
7. Dehydroepiandrosterone (DHEA, an adrenal steroid that counters cortisol)
8. Cortisol
9. Epinephrine
10. Norepinephrine.

Dr. McEwen's concept of an allostatic load index was potent and promising enough that it generated lots of studies that aimed to replicate or improve on the original proposal. Like generativity in nature, generativity in science can be both fruitful and wild. The offspring stray from home. In a recent analysis of many studies of allostatic load in the workplace,[6] the reviewers found that, in summary, the concept of allostatic load has proven both robust and unruly.

One of the practical issues limiting the use of the allostatic load index in clinical practice is the problem of how to collect the data necessary to calculate the index. A definition of allostatic load that requires collecting only a thimble-full of blood is more likely to be used in primary care than one that requires a thimble-full of blood plus twelve hours of urine plus measuring the person's waist and hip circumferences with a tape measure.

Dr. McEwen's original ten biomarkers require all three sources of data (the DHEA, cortisol, epinephrine, and norepinephrine come from urine collection). Then someone has to enter the data on all ten biomarkers and calculate the index according to an algorithm that generates the allostatic load index, a number from 0 to 1 that can be used to estimate cumulative physiologic stress and risk for illness.

Primary care clinics usually don't hire people to crunch numbers like this. They count on laboratories to deliver such a service and the number, and so far no commercial laboratory offers such a service for allostatic load.

Another issue that has limited the use of allostatic load in the clinic for estimating risk is the unresolved debate about which combination of biomarkers offers the best predictive power at the least cost. We know that multiple measures of allostatic load predict poor health better than any single measure, but do fifteen biomarkers predict health outcomes better than ten or five? That question has not been answered yet. Five would be better (cheaper, easier), but which five work best for all populations? Good scientists are studying the question.[7]

Another important limitation to the original list of biomarkers proposed by McEwen and his colleagues has spurred experimentation with new biomarkers. The original list does not include measures of two of the important physiologic systems that we saw in earlier chapters play major roles in acute and chronic stress responses: the immune system and the autonomic nervous system.

What we need but don't yet have is a measure of allostatic load that combines the single best cumulative measures of each of the five main organ systems of the stress response system in a way that is easy to collect and calculate as an index that predicts risk for future illness. Better still, if this measure improves with effective toxic stress reduction and worsens with toxic stress events, it would be a useful guide for monitoring the effectiveness of intensive stress management. That kind of measure will raise the visibility of toxic stress for both patient and clinician.

Biological aging. What if your doctor were able to take a sample of your blood and tell you how old your body is, in contrast to how old you may actually be? We're not too far off.

In a variation on the concept of allostatic load, a group of investigators from Duke University, King's College London, and the University of Otago in Dunedin, New Zealand, have examined a measure of composite physiologic measures, which they call biological aging, in contrast to the person's chronological age.[8]

From the prospective longitudinal Dunedin study, this team has been able to identify a composite of seventeen physiologic measures of biological aging, five of which overlap with the original measures of McEwen's allostatic load. With this composite measure of biological age collected at three time points before the age of thirty-eight, the researchers found that biological age correlated with physical functioning, self-reported health, and mental decline.

A recent review found that biological aging may be a better measure for predicting risk than other measures,[9] but biological aging is not yet ready for use in primary care.

Recently investigators have found that a more accurate measure of biological aging is the amount of methyl molecules that have accumulated on our DNA, dubbed the DNA methylation process or epigenetic aging because the rate of DNA methylation varies with the epigenetic changes that accelerate the aging process.[10]

This measure suggests the appealing promise of providing the patient and doctor a summary number for a person's biological age, calculated from one blood sample to compare with the chronological age.

Imagine how you would react if, during your routine checkup at age forty, your doctor told you that your biological age was already fifty-three and accelerating? And when you return at forty-five, your biological age is now closer to sixty-five. How would that grab you?

We need a lot of science to fill in the blanks before we can make this kind of conversation a reality, but we already have some promising new ways of seeing the biology of our stress response systems as they slip into trouble.

Telomere lengths. All your life your chromosomes have been slowly fraying at the ends, like the aglets (keep this word handy for Wordle) on your shoelaces, those tightly wrapped tips that begin to fray with the wear and tear of life. And all your life the enzyme telomerase has been trying to repair your fraying aglets.

As discussed earlier, cumulative stress and the normal aging process are intertwined at every level. Telomeres are the DNA strands at the ends of chromosomes, and telomere length is a measure of biological aging that is also sensitive to cumulative stress loads, including the stress of certain chronic illnesses.

Chronic stress generally inhibits telomerase, and in that way can accelerate cellular aging and cellular death. When telomeres reach a certain shortness, the cell dies. So, the cellular aging process varies with stress exposures and the environment.[11]

Telomere length can be assessed from white blood cells taken from any blood sample. In general, the higher the cumulative stress load, the shorter the telomere length, if you adjust for age.

Telomere length tests are just beginning to be used in clinical settings to guide treatment, but there are at least ten ways to assess telomere length, and the methods differ in their variability and costs, which range from $100 to $400 per sample. Commercial labs that offer telomere tests are not currently regulated by the government, so it can be hard to know what their reports mean.

And once again, although the science is good and the concept is sound, the logistics of collecting and testing and interpreting telomere lengths still need to be refined. This test is also not yet ready for you to ask your doctor about.

This absence of a good measure of the cumulative toll on the stress response system, one that is useful for primary care doctors at your regular physical exam, remains a high priority for the translation of stress neuroscience into clinical practice.[12]

Social Determinants of Health

If we are going to measure psychological and biological factors affecting the stress response system, shouldn't we also measure social factors?

The Institute of Medicine proposed in 2014 a method of estimating risk for common chronic conditions by collecting social and behavioral data through electronic health records.[13] Recognizing that the burden of collecting new information in primary care settings can be prohibitive, this report recommends focusing on twelve measures that either are routinely a part of the medical history-taking process, or could be easily added as specific new items:

1. Alcohol use — 3 questions
2. Tobacco use — 2
3. Race and ethnicity — 2
4. Residential address — 1 (geocoded)
5. Census tract median income — 1 (geocoded)
6. Education — 2
7. Financial resource strain — 1
8. Depression — 2
9. Stress — 1
10. Intimate partner violence — 4
11. Physical activity — 2
12. Social connections and isolation — 4

By calling for all healthcare systems with electronic health records to join in collecting these uniform data at prescribed frequencies, this report recognizes the need for a social profile to measure a common set of exposures to demanding social conditions.[14] Though some of the items tap physiological conditions, such as smoking and physical activity, and others tap psychological conditions, such as depression and perceived stress, this list creates a profile of the social demands on the stress response system.

This social profile may be as effective as the psychological or physiological profiles in estimating a person's risk for developing illness, but that question, too, needs to be studied.

Stress Testing the Heart

Consider also the role of challenge tests. The most common stress test in clinical practice is the treadmill. This test has become so routine in primary care and cardiology that it is what most doctors assume you're talking about if you mention taking a stress test.

The graded exercise tolerance test assesses how well your heart tolerates increasing or "graded" amounts of exercise on a treadmill up to a brisk walk or slow jog, which usually raises heart rates up to 150 beats per minute or more.[15] The measure of tolerance or the fitness of your heart is the ST segment of the EKG that records your heart activity while you're huffing on the treadmill.

If that ST segment drops down a certain amount, it's a signal that your heart is straining against a dwindling supply of oxygen. It is poetically referred to in the trade as "ST depression" – the prelude to myocardial ischemia, the signature mechanism of heart attacks.

The catch here, and the key to the value of this test in clinical practice, is that most of us don't feel our ST depressions at rest or during exercise. And when we're lying on our backs during a resting EKG, our tracings may look normal. But under the demands of exercise, well before our heart disease causes us shortness of breath or chest pressure or angina, these silent ST depressions, if we're lucky enough to have them measured soon enough, signal the early stages of coronary heart disease, when it's easier to treat and possible to *prevent* heart attacks.

If the modest physical demands of walking on a treadmill and doubling your heart rate can expose the vulnerabilities of early heart disease, what about mental stress?

Since many of us who live in relative physical comfort are more frequently exposed to mental stress than physical stress, wouldn't it be helpful to know how our hearts respond to mental stress?

Dr. Vaccarino and her team at Emory University have been exploring this question with a focus on women. She wondered if women with heart disease might be more prone to "silent" ischemia (narrowing of arteries) in their hearts during physical and mental stress.

The standard protocol for mental stress – induced myocardial ischemia – is about as simple as walking on a treadmill, but it requires a lab setting. While a six-lead EKG records heart activity, the person performs either a timed arithmetic test or a two-minute speech to strangers in lab coats. This has proved to be sufficiently stressful for most people to trigger measurable and meaningful responses across a variety of mental and physical stress response measures, including measures of transient ischemia or ST depressions on the EKG.

Dr. Vaccarino and others have found that women with coronary heart disease are nearly 40 percent more likely to have mental stress-induced ischemia than men with coronary heart disease. And the difference is more pronounced in women under fifty who have heart attacks.[16]

Why are younger women with heart disease more likely to have silent ischemia under mental stress? Dr. Vaccarino notes that women in general report more mental stress of all kinds (trauma, mental illness, poverty, work stress, discrimination, among others) than men, and the mechanism of their silent ischemia is still unclear.

Dr. Vaccarino's group has also shown in the largest and most rigorous study of its kind that mental stress-induced ischemia is a more powerful predictor of worsening heart disease than physical stress.[17] The cardiologist's traditional stress test on the treadmill may have focused over the last fifty years on the less predictive kind of stress. It's time now to add mental stress tests to the physical stress tests that identify those most at risk for heart attacks.

Studies like these of mental stress-induced ischemia are making the case for adding this kind of stress measurement to the routine assessments of heart disease.[18] They remind us of how much we don't know. Wouldn't you like to know what your road rage or those too frequent arguments with your spouse are doing to your heart? If you have high blood pressure or Crohn's disease or diabetes, wouldn't you like to know if your mental stress is aggravating your condition?

For now, this kind of challenge test is not readily available to doctors to order for their patients when assessing a stress profile, and then there are the barriers of technology, cost, and data interpretation.

The Stress Profile Service

In primary care, the first step is to identify those people with severe and persistent distress. For those who screen positive for distress, the next step requires deciding who needs what kinds of help: who may need the help of a social worker for housing or financial problems, who needs a mental health specialist for managing a mental disorder, and who may benefit more from a regimen of exercise, sleep management, and meditation.

This second step requires a more in-depth assessment of stress exposures and responses, specific trouble spots, and which social situations causing the current problems could be modified.

As we'll see in the next few chapters, guidance about stress measurement depends on the patient's stress profile, and this process works best when the primary care provider is guided by a mental health specialist, such as a health psychologist, who knows how to keep it simple and useful for each patient.

Given the complexity of the assessment process and the clinical judgment required to translate the findings into recommendations

for treatment, the creation of the stress profile should be the responsibility of a certified health psychologist. Similar to the neuropsychology testing report, the stress profile could be generated by the standard consultation process for patients with known stress-related conditions or with high risks for developing stress-related conditions.

Copies of the stress profile would go to the patient and the primary care doctor or the specialist who requested the consultation, to be placed in the patient's medical record. Because health psychologists are also the specialists who deliver most of the stress management interventions, these reports will be written in terms that translate readily into treatment plans.

Although this seems like a logical process that would follow traditional consultation procedures, it is still rare that any large medical center in the US provides a health psychology consultation service for these kinds of stress profiles.

Peering into the Well

Nadine Burke Harris reminds us in *The Deepest Well* of a few lessons about the measurement of stress that she has learned since her eyes were opened to the role of childhood trauma and adversity in health and illness.

Dr. Harris makes the point that our current understanding of how toxic stress in childhood dysregulates the stress response system is comparable to the understanding of infections in the nineteenth century before germ theory. At that time the leading theories about how infections operate focused on poisonous vapors and the "miasmas," but these were just guesses.

The observations of John Snow about cholera around the London water pump and Joseph Lister about the impact of hand-washing to reduce infection rates during surgery came long before the confirmation that certain microbes were the culprits.

Early in the course of changing the way medicine understands complex processes such as infection or toxic stress, any measure that improves vision advances the field: the thermometer, the microscope, the blood pressure cuff. And I will add the ACE scale as one measurement tool that has improved our ability to recognize a toxic combination of stress exposures in early life that predict later poor health outcomes.

Consider the advances in our understanding of cancer and its treatments over the past half-century. In 1966 during my ninth-grade year, Craig, one of our forty-five classmates, died of Hodgkin's lymphoma. Two years later another of our classmates, Peter, died of acute lymphoblastic leukemia (ALL). In those days, half of patients with ALL died within six months of the diagnosis; my friend was one of the lucky ones to last two years. Now 85 percent of children with ALL are cured.

These advances in childhood cancer over the last half-century have required unprecedented collaborative research networks and funding from basic science to the bedside across many cancer centers worldwide.

This example of progress in treating a complex set of processes shows the way forward for the 15 to 20 percent of us who live with persistent toxic stress. Though our current level of understanding of the dysregulation of the stress response system may resemble our basic understanding of cancer in the 1960s, nonetheless the stress measures we currently have can guide the next steps in that journey and help us offer effective treatments. That requires facing two tough questions: How can we treat a dysregulated stress response system? And how much does it improve the course of a chronic illness to relieve distress and reduce the psychosocial risks for that illness?

Part IV

Treatment

Part IV

Treatment

Boot Camps for Our Stress Response Systems

The good news Donna could no longer bear to hear was "normal neurologic exam." She'd heard this good news four times in the past six months since her knees first buckled at their May faculty meeting. Just like that, she dropped to the floor. Such a mess and such a fuss.

The ambulance really wasn't necessary. It was nothing at the time, yet looking back now it seems that fall in front of her colleagues was the beginning of the end. Two more falls at home later that week, and the shaking spells came on in both hands.

"No stroke," Dr. Philpot told her each time. "Normal neuro exam, aside from these tremors." But he sent her anyway to see first one neurologist, then another, with her husband, Mike, doing all the driving, bless his heart, while keeping an eye on things at home.

By the time Donna saw the second neurologist, summer had passed, and she'd gone from the cane to the walker, and the

shakings had worked their way from her legs up to both arms and into her neck. Now the rocking of her head had become such a fright she couldn't bear to be seen in public, much less the classroom.

How could that doctor say normal neurologic exam with her in such a state? And you could hardly blame her superintendent for inquiring each month when she could return to duty in the classroom. They were, after all, her duty, her sixth-grade class, all twenty-eight of them, and, of course, her son, Nick, at home at age thirty-four.

What does it take to retrain the stress response system after a stress-related illness has developed? Is Donna's illness stress related? We're looking for treatments with effects strong enough to change the course of functional tremor disorders like Donna's, or heart disease, diabetes, depression, and the mother of all stress disorders, PTSD.

I could just as well choose obesity, hypertension, metabolic syndrome, or your other favorite stress-related conditions to make the point. In this chapter, let's look in detail at five programs that focus on specific groups of illnesses, all programs that use similar methods.

I can go on about the theoretical understanding of how severe and persistent stress exposures lead to illness, as I have in earlier chapters, but none of this matters unless you are the patient, and you and your doctor are convinced you can do something about it.

In fact, most of us don't care how an illness starts or a treatment works as long as the treatment relieves our suffering or cures our illness. Six months into feeling robbed of her legs, her coordination, and her roles in her family and community, Donna and her husband cared less than her doctors did about her diagnosis. Donna urgently needed to know whether she could do anything to get her life back.

But if we're trying to understand how an illness progresses and how we can stop it or slow it down, studies of effective treatments often expose the driving forces of these illnesses. Understanding these mechanisms of illness is often key to designing effective treatments.

As you will see, the most effective treatments across this range of stress-related disorders share some blend of counseling (individual or group), physical therapy or exercise, medication that dampens hyperarousal while restoring autonomic balance in the nervous system, and the daily self-management of work–play rhythms, restful sleep, mood regulation, limiting worrying habits, and relaxation or meditation.

And then there's the management of social contacts and the immediate environment. Combinations of these treatment approaches appear to work better than any single approach alone.

Keys to Effective Treatment Plans for Stress-Related Conditions

Essential components include

- Weekly counseling (expert-led support group or individual therapy)
- Daily self-management regimens
- Physical exercise program
- Medication as needed
- Daily treatment for four to five months.

The routines that work for most stress-related conditions require many months of practice. They're worth understanding because they're effective on the level of the group, the individual, the organ, the cell, and the gene. And you don't have to be a health fanatic or a Marine to make these regimens work for you. Most people who start and make it through the third session in well-planned programs rise to the challenge and keep on doing them. Dean Ornish has discovered why.

Undo It: Reversing Coronary Heart Disease

If you sign up for the Ornish Reversal Program,[1] you sign up for eighteen four-hour sessions with a small group of six to nine people, all of whom have coronary heart disease. For four to five months you meet every weekend for a full morning or afternoon with a trained group leader, and between sessions you practice daily what you learn on the weekends. This format has proven to be as effective as, and more accessible than, the intensive month-long retreat at a hotel that Ornish first provided in the 1980s, as I described earlier.

People with full-time jobs and family obligations can accommodate this weekend workshop schedule for five months. For those who are eligible, the Ornish Reversal Program is now paid for by Medicare, which tells you it has passed a level of scientific scrutiny and has proven its cost-effectiveness.

The four key elements of this Lifestyle Medicine approach are eat well, move more, stress less, and love well. That is, by attending daily to nutrition, fitness, stress management, and social support for five months, you can change your lifestyle enough to widen the passageways of your coronary arteries. It's not magic. It's sensible habits delivered in a tight package: the small group meeting every week with daily practice between meetings. You change how you eat (vegetarian), how you move (gently and often), how you think and feel (worry less), and how you relate (close and safe).

And it's not just the coronary arteries that improve. Chest pains, blood pressure, inflammation, overweight, worrying, anxiety, insomnia – the range of improvements can be measured in many organ systems. These broad-ranging improvements are the payoff for achieving more consistent regulation of your stress response system in multiple ways over many months.

You spend much of the four hours of each weekend session learning and practicing various approaches to stress management: yoga, meditation, stretching, exercise followed by relaxation, cognitive therapy techniques to reduce worrying and rumination, time management, toxic relationship management, and the safe expression of feelings. Your daily monitoring of these efforts between sessions and your reporting each week to your small group builds the changes in habits that sustain the improvements.

The effect of the social support that develops in the small group is strong enough that over 80 percent of the participants voluntarily continue meeting with each other after the required eighteen sessions are over. They continue because they like it, and it works! The effort pays for itself with results. And they know they need this group to keep the routine going in the early months and years.

This treatment starts out as work, but it soon feels so good you don't want to stop. You change habits that don't feel so good in favor of new habits that feel irresistibly good, life-savingly good. This program gives most participants the experience of power over their lives, which they like better than pills. That's the kind of treatment that people don't quit. And it requires no prescription. Once you've mastered the habits, it costs almost nothing from your wallet.

How can this be? How can a weekend boot camp so dramatically improve the health of people who have faced repeated heart attacks, some of whom have been given a diagnosis of terminal heart disease?

The list of health measures improved by this program is long: less chest pain, wider coronary arteries, lower blood pressure, better heart rate variability, lower cholesterol, better control of blood sugar, lower inflammatory markers, weight control, improvements in telomere length, better quality of life even at work, and lower risk of death.[2] Any set of interventions that results in sustained improved functioning of the cardiovascular system, the metabolic system, the inflammatory activity in coronary arteries, and the endocrine

system is operating at a deep level, simultaneously re-regulating many components of the stress response system toward finer harmony and greater efficiency.

These are the ingredients for longevity found in the Blue Zones communities described by Dan Buettner, where it's more common to age into the nineties without chronic illness. As effective as the Ornish Reversal Program (and the new name, the Undo It with Ornish program) has been, there are many regions of the country, like my own, where there are no Undo It programs and doctors have never heard of Dean Ornish.

Is It Possible to Prevent Diabetes?

The process of developing diabetes, the kind that comes usually with weight gain in adults, is gradual. If you look for it, it's often possible to identify early warning signs of diabetes months or years before the diagnosis – a phase called prediabetes. Persistent mild elevations of blood sugars (fasting blood sugars in the 100 to 125 mg/dl range, or hemoglobin A1C in the 5.7 to 6.4 range) define this phase of prediabetes. It's a sign that your insulin and insulin receptors are not working as they should, a condition called insulin resistance.[3]

You still produce the insulin, but receptors on your cells don't let the insulin efficiently move the glucose from your bloodstream into your cells where it can be stored or burned. Age, genes, weight gain, abdominal fat, red meat, sweetened drinks, and physical inactivity are some of the factors that hasten this process of insulin resistance or prediabetes. Once you're in this phase, your risk of soon developing the diagnosis of diabetes rises dramatically. It's time to act, but what can you do?

Listen to Rena Wing, PhD. Since the 1990s, the champion for diabetes prevention in this country has been Dr. Wing, a sociologist

and a professor in the department of psychiatry and human behavior at Brown University. She has devoted her long career to understanding what makes losing weight so difficult, especially for those at risk for diabetes. This is a tough question that has frustrated many good scientists, partly because it requires such a thorough study of the physiology, the psychology, and the sociology of weight gain and obesity.

One of the triumphs of Rena Wing's career, and a triumphant milestone for Lifestyle Medicine, came with the completion of the Diabetes Prevention Program in 2002, a major multicenter NIH-funded trial with 5,000 adults at high risk for diabetes. The study was stopped early because the preliminary results were so dramatically good that it was deemed unethical to continue the study. It was time to tell the world.

In this randomized trial lasting one year for each participant, one group took a placebo (a medicine with no active ingredient), another took metformin (a common diabetes medication known to be effective at improving glucose metabolism, also called glucophage), and the third group participated in a lifestyle intervention.

This lifestyle intervention consisted of weekly small group meetings for six months (then monthly for six months) with a focus on establishing routines for diet and exercise, regular meetings with a one-on-one coach, and daily practice of diet and exercise. They aimed for two and a half hours a week of gentle exercise and a modest weight loss goal of 5 to 7 percent (about 10 to 14 pounds for most people) over a year.

About 40 percent of those who took the placebo went on to get a diagnosis of diabetes within the year. This was the control group that would represent those who did nothing about their condition.

About 30 percent of those who took metformin converted to diabetes. Better but also, not good.

Drum roll. And just 20 percent of those in the lifestyle intervention group converted to diabetes. Any intervention that prevents a major illness and reduces the risk by half is worth celebrating.

The Diabetes Prevention Program is now available nationwide, and an outcomes study continues to monitor its effectiveness. Reducing your weight by 5 to 7 percent and adding 150 minutes a week of exercise has led to a 58 percent reduction in risk for diabetes in this program.[4]

This Diabetes Prevention Program is remarkable in the same way that the Ornish Reversal Program is remarkable. Both show us that, in large numbers of people, consistent behavioral change in the form of eating well and moving more and connecting more intimately with people who come to care about you often reverses the course of two common chronic illnesses within six to twelve months. One program focuses on retraining the cardiovascular system, the other on retraining the endocrine system, but both are most likely re-regulating the whole stress response system.

During each treatment process, the inflammation in the coronary arteries subsides for those who have coronary disease, and insulin resistance fades in those who have prediabetes. These effects seem to last: for participants, ten years after completing the Diabetes Prevention Program, the risk of converting to diabetes was still lowered by a third for those who completed the lifestyle intervention.

One offshoot of this trial is the National Diabetes Prevention Program,[5] organized by the Centers for Disease Control and Prevention. Within fifty miles of where I live, there are now twenty-six sites that offer this program.

I wondered why the Diabetes Prevention Program packages its intervention without drawing attention to the stress management component, so I visited a DPP class taught by ten-year veteran teacher, Christine Zerges. We met in one of the exercise rooms upstairs at the Lindner Y in Norwood, an urban setting near

downtown Cincinnati, for what was session two of the twenty-five in a yearlong program. Five group members, all overweight and apparently between thirty and fifty, and all with high blood sugars but not yet diabetes, settled in around the tables, with Christine at the head.

The early sessions of the DPP curriculum focus on basic information about food, calories, exercise, and energy metabolism. Christine began this session, titled in their course binders as "Be a Fat Detective," with a weigh-in.

One woman grumbled at her number, "Disgusting!"

The woman across from her came back with, "Don't say that. We're in this together."

They talked about the essentials of monitoring behaviors, and as they worked their way through the basic skills of identifying fat content and reading food labels, one woman said she has trouble finding the time to walk. Another said she couldn't just eat a few chips, she has to eat the whole bag. They talked about eating too fast, and what happens if you slow down. They talked about the games we play to fool ourselves.

The heaviest woman confessed she chops a stick of butter into small pieces so she doesn't eat so much, then dumps all the pieces into the frying pan. Big howls of laughter. This was only their second meeting, and they were already making the group work. I sensed the same healing force that makes AA meetings work – unconditional acceptance.

After the meeting, Christine and Janella Straw, a lifestyle coach and the director of the DPP for the Cincinnati region, talked through the DPP curriculum with me. Each group meets weekly for sixteen sessions, and then sessions seventeen through twenty-five are spaced out over the next six to eight months.

The last half of the weekly curriculum is all about the psychology of habit changing and self-management. These sessions are titled Take Charge, Problem Solving, Talking Back to Negative Thoughts,

the Slippery Slope of Lifestyle Changes, Social Cues, You Can Manage Stress, and Ways to Stay Motivated. That sounds like two months focused on the basics of stress management.

To stay in the program for the full length, the group members have to complete the first four sessions. After that hurdle, the completion rates are high, and Christine told me that it's rare – not even close to the national rate of 20 percent – that a group member develops diabetes during the course of that year. So that's an impressive local success record for a program designed to prevent the development of diabetes in a high-risk group.

On a national level, any program that can reduce the risk of a devastating illness like diabetes by 58 percent should be provided everywhere for everyone at risk. Yet in the first decade of the Diabetes Prevention Program (2010–2020), less than 1 percent of the 84 million people with prediabetes have attempted the program. Only one in ten were even told by their physician they had the condition – another sad reminder that good science is not enough to change practice patterns.

The Dysfunction in Functional Disorders

How can Donna find treatment for the crippling functional tremors that have shrunk her life over the past six months? She is unlikely to take comfort from the successes of those who participate in Ornish's intensive cardiac rehabilitation or CDC's diabetes prevention programs. She has no problems with her heart or her pancreas. For her, it's her muscles and nerves that have betrayed her and robbed her of the life she intended to lead.

In her navigations through the healthcare system, she eventually found her way to Alberto Espay, MD, who is now professor of neurology and director of the movement disorders center at the University of Cincinnati. At the time she met him in 2011, Dr. Espay

was starting his academic career by launching a study that aimed to examine in more detail than ever before the neurological and psychological responses to a twelve-session cognitive behavioral therapy (CBT) intervention designed to reduce or resolve functional tremors. Specifically, he planned to watch what happened to the brains of his patients through fMRI scans, the video version of structural MRI brain scans.

He wanted to know what parts of the brain, if any, were activated by these functional tremors like Donna's, and whether CBT changed their brain functioning as well as their tremors. Remember that the justification for the use of the term *functional* is that it's a euphemism that confesses we don't know what the underlying disease process is.

To conduct this study, Dr. Espay did something few neurologists bother with – he learned to do CBT, a technique in the realm of psychiatry and psychology. After his neurology training in the early years of his academic life, he spent several years learning to be a mental health therapist so he could understand the process and deliver some of the CBT to the fifteen patients enrolled in the treatment arm of his study, collaborating with a therapist who specializes in CBT, which helps people modify problematic habits of thinking in ways that improve how they feel and behave.

Following the model of a protocol for treating certain types of seizures (not epilepsy) with CBT,[6] the therapy focused first on helping the person learn to monitor for a few weeks the situations, thoughts, and feelings that influence the daily onset of their tremors, and what makes them worse or better. This led to identifying some ways of understanding and controlling the tremors, which then led to practicing both physical and psychological techniques for reducing, managing, and preventing tremors. Eventually, the therapy focused on regaining the physical and social functioning that had been so impaired by the tremors.

For Donna one nuance that stood out to Dr. Espay early in the evaluation was her talent for identifying what others were feeling, in contrast to her avoidance of identifying what she was feeling. At sixty-two she still often looked puzzled when asked how she felt. She would respond with an observation about others, or an opinion about the situation.

It turned out that she was born the first of five siblings, three of whom were now on disability, and she described two of her sisters as hypochondriacs. She remembers her mother being over-whelmed by five children within seven years, and Donna learned early to give a helping hand.

During the study, when asked to monitor the severity of her tremors during the course of each day, she was startled to learn that her tremors were not constant. They varied widely, usually in the 3 to 8 out of 10 range, and she had three to five spells of tremors a day, with some hours totally tremor-free. The tremors worsened around other people and when she worried about her responsibilities.

At the third CBT session she described the hospitalization the previous April of her son, who still lived at home with them, for yet another episode of suicidal threats and behaviors. She described the hospitalization as routine, the eighth such hospitalization since he had to move back home at the age of twenty-eight.

When she was asked if Nick had a mental illness, she said, "He's not right mentally." Her husband added, "He has schizoaffective disorder. Donna has a thing she says, 'I have to be the strong one.'"

Donna assumed she had to be the caregiver, strong for everyone all the time, yet she sensed she could not do enough for her son. Was the toxic stress of these demands making her sick, and making her hands and feet tremble?

When Donna and Dr. Espay figured out that she could exert some control over the frequency and severity of her tremors, often by changing her patterns of thinking (the CBT at work) and her activities, the tremors started to diminish. By two months into the

weekly treatment, she was walking without a cane and had only three tremor spells during the week, just one moderate, and two mild.

In Dr. Espay's study, by the end of the three to four months of CBT, nine of the fifteen people who participated in the intervention had achieved full remission, including Donna – no tremors, no impaired functioning. Another two achieved 75 percent improvement completely separate from any other health issues or mental concerns. Younger people had higher response rates.

These are impressive results for a group of patients who had not responded to multiple other treatments, but this is a small pilot study on a highly motivated group of self-selected people.[7]

Perhaps the most interesting and promising findings of the study came from the imaging data. Those with functional tremors started the study with abnormally high activity in a region of the brain that regulates emotions, located deep in the forebrain above the eyes. With CBT, the high activity in this region came down as the tremors lessened or went away, suggesting that CBT may help regulate the way people with functional tremors process emotions.

The baseline data also showed decreased connectivity in two areas that regulate sensorimotor integration, or the ways that sensations guide movements. By the end of the protocol, however, CBT appeared to have corrected some or all of this decreased connectivity, allowing for better motor coordination and fewer or no tremors.

This study suggests that CBT may re-regulate key circuits to correct a combination of impaired emotion processing and impaired sensorimotor integration. In the process, the tremors go away. Of course larger, more rigorous (and more expensive) studies will be needed to elaborate on this possibility before this brand of CBT can be anointed the treatment of choice for functional tremors.

Meanwhile, in Copenhagen at Aarhus University, for more than a decade Per Fink, MD, PhD, DMSc, and his team have been

treating people like Donna together with people who on the surface have troubles that don't look at all like hers.

Some have chronic fatigue syndrome; others have irritable bowel syndrome; some have chronic unusual chest pains; some have seizures complicated by pseudo-seizures; others have multiple chemical sensitivities; others have what mental health specialists call somatic symptom disorder (that is, distressing physical symptoms that disrupt daily life for many months, such as hypochondria).

Fink established the practice at Aarhus of treating people with any of ten specified conditions under the single umbrella term *functional somatic syndromes* (and later *bodily distress syndromes*) in the same clinic, where they all participate in the same treatment.

The treatment was originally designed for a randomized controlled trial of an intervention developed for a study called STReSS, a loose acronym for Specialized Treatment for Severe Bodily Distress Syndromes.[8] This study provided this specialized treatment to fifty-four patients, in comparison to forty-seven patients who received "enhanced" usual care, which meant that the primary care doctors received the assessment but handled the care on their own as they usually would.

Patients in both groups were selected for having moderate to severe symptoms in at least three different organ groups for at least two years, with moderate to severe impairment of functioning. The specialized treatment was delivered in groups of nine patients by two therapists during nine modules of 3.5 hours each over a sixteen-week period. Each patient was assigned a contact therapist with whom to design and develop individual treatment plans.

These sessions, conducted in small groups, focus on habit change, self-monitoring, regular gentle exercise, relaxation training, and daily practice of new habits.

Sound familiar? It's the Ornish boot camp (minus the diet) delivered to a different population of impaired people. Isn't this the essence of the Diabetes Prevention Program as well? No drugs,

no surgery, but intensive talk and physical therapy and training in self-management.

What was the outcome? At the end of the sixteen weeks, compared to the usual care group, the intervention group reported marked improvements in physical health, less severe physical symptoms, improved mental health, lower levels of anxiety and depression, less worry about illness, and enhanced ability to be social. These gains were sustained or increased at forty and sixty-four weeks. These broad improvements in outcomes suggest wide-ranging changes in stress response system functioning, though the study did not include physical measures of stress. Eight other studies have shown similar benefits.[9]

This is a promising start that sets an example for the rest of the world outside of Denmark to consider studying and possibly changing the way we take care of these patients with bodily distress disorders.

The argument is growing stronger that the dysfunction in functional disorders lies deep in the obscure workings of the stress response system. The presenting symptom, initially seemingly confined to one organ, may be just the most visible sign of persistent dysregulation in the whole system. Much remains to be learned about how toxic stress transforms into these disabling disorders and about the mechanisms by which these treatments relieve suffering and bodily dysfunction.

More Than One: TEAMcare and COMPASS

We clinicians like to talk about treating single chronic illnesses, but we don't usually see them alone. More often we see people who have multiple chronic conditions and long problem lists. It's almost a cliché in the VA primary care clinics that the men in their sixties who have diabetes also have high blood pressure, obesity,

and coronary heart disease. Or if they have chronic back pain, they also have depression, substance abuse, and degenerative joint disease.

In the US a quarter of the general population has more than one chronic condition, and that rate rises to over 50 percent of those age forty-five to sixty-five and over 80 percent in those over sixty-five.[10] These are just numbers, unless that patient is you or someone you love.

The sheer number and complexity of multiple chronic conditions can overwhelm patients, their families, and sometimes their doctors. The task of treating all these conditions becomes easier to manage when we recognize that some of these conditions come in clusters and represent the multiple faces of a common process.

Let me give you an example. A man who struggles with chronic depression in his twenties and thirties may overeat and gain weight to manage the evening carbohydrate cravings that come with his depression. He comes to believe a bag of cookies and a six-pack is the key to falling asleep. He gains enough of a beer belly to constrain his exercise – think of all the overweight former athletes you know who now look like they're eight months pregnant – and this weight hangs heavily on his lumbar disks in his back.

By the time he's a young grandfather and semiretired from laying tile, his joints have worn down to the point of bone-on-bone chronic pain, which may drive him to more alcohol use or narcotic pain relievers. His heavy consumption of sweets each evening has worn down his pancreas and his insulin receptors. Eventually this man has depression, obesity, degenerative joint disease, chronic pain, substance abuse, and finally diabetes – six problems sharing a common source.

The difficulty for this sixty-year-old now is that the source of his six problems began forty years ago or more, and by now the momentum of his daily habits has the force of a locomotive. How can he change his ways?

The good news is that for some clusters of chronic conditions, the treatment that works for one condition may indirectly improve the others. What's good for the brain is often good for the heart and the pancreas.

Wayne Katon, MD, spent most of his career as a psychiatrist at the University of Washington working in primary care settings. Because in the US more mental illness is treated in primary care than in specialty mental health, and mental illness comes first to the primary care clinician, Dr. Katon was convinced that the best place to identify and treat the most common mental illnesses (depression, anxiety, and substance abuse) was in primary care clinics.

He spent much of his considerable research energy and talents developing the most effective way to treat depression in primary care. After ten years of studies of interventions that did not improve outcomes for depression in primary care, he and his team finally published in 1995 a study that did improve these outcomes. The intervention not only improved outcomes for depression, it was also a cost-effective intervention. This proved to be a breakthrough study, opening the way for Dr. Katon to spend the rest of his career building the collaborative care model for depression in primary care.[11]

Dr. Katon knew that depression rarely travels alone. Combinations of health problems are the rule in primary care. His final major study, the TEAMcare study published in 2010, applied the collaborative care model to the treatment of depression in primary care patients who also had coronary heart disease or diabetes.[12] This intervention provided the eligible patients with nurse care managers who either met with or called the patients two to three times a month until the patient met improvement targets, and then monthly for maintenance visits up to a year.

The nurse care managers worked with the patients and their primary care physicians to identify goals and develop individualized treatment plans for their depression and diabetes or heart disease. They educated the patients about their illnesses and used

motivational interviewing, behavioral activation,[13] and problem-solving therapy (a form of CBT for depression in primary care) to help each patient develop a daily self-management plan for both the depression and the diabetes or heart disease.

These daily regimens involved such activities as improving adherence to medications; practicing regular exercise and relaxation; scheduling pleasurable social contacts; monitoring blood pressure, blood sugar, and mood; and adjusting diet.

Using an electronic patient registry, the nurse care managers tracked each patient's progress on multiple measures over the course of their year in the study. This registry formed the basis for weekly systematic case reviews by the care manager with the primary care physicians and the supervising psychiatrist and any other consulting clinicians.

These case reviews refined the treatment plans toward treatment guidelines and symptom targets. Once patients achieved targets for depression symptoms, blood sugar control, reduction in cholesterol levels, and blood pressure control, they shifted the focus of their efforts to maintaining these gains and preventing relapse, with the help of the care manager.

If you read between these lines, you see that this set of interventions designed to bring about relief for major depression and reduce the severity of diabetes or coronary heart disease contains most of the elements of the Ornish Reversal Program, the Diabetes Prevention Program, and the Aarhus program for bodily distress disorders.

Minus the group meetings that are an important part of the other three programs, the Katon collaborative care intervention included the weekly coaching on daily self-management habits, the cognitive therapy aimed at solving problems related to each illness, the focus on exercise and diet plans that can be sustained, the close monitoring of progress toward goals, the cultivation of team and patient responsibility for meeting these goals, and the gradual reduction of

intensity of treatment contacts as the patient establishes the capacity to maintain the gains with a self-management regimen.

Like the other interventions – each of them the product of separate specialties in our medical culture – Dr. Katon's collaborative care intervention puts these patients through a boot camp level of intense retraining in the ways these patients take care of themselves day and night. And the retraining lasts a full year. The experience transforms most people who go through it, and the effect lasts well beyond the duration of the intervention.

The payoff for the TEAMcare trial came when the federal government, in the form of the Substance Abuse and Mental Health Services Administration (SAMHSA), poured millions of dollars into a demonstration project called COMPASS. SAMHSA was willing to invest such funding because the TEAMcare study offered one of the few interventions that met the triple aims of healthcare reform: improved outcomes through better quality care at a lower cost. And the intervention had made a sizable dent in three of our most common and costly chronic conditions: depression, diabetes, and heart disease.

Dr. Katon and his good friend, colleague, and coinvestigator Jurgen Unutzer lobbied effectively to persuade SAMHSA to disseminate the TEAMcare model to healthcare systems and primary care clinics across eight states. From 2013 to 2015 the COMPASS project showed that this model could be adapted to a wide range of settings at various levels of intensity, depending on the available resources. And the outcomes varied in proportion to the intensity of the interventions. The more intense the treatments, the better the outcomes.[14] That's true of most boot camps, up to a limit.

Treating PTSD the VA Way

If you want to understand how toxic stress dysregulates the stress response system in the extreme, there's no better field lab than

239

programs that treat posttraumatic stress disorder or PTSD. And no healthcare system in the US has devoted more research and resources to the treatment of PTSD than the US Department of Veterans Affairs or VA. When it comes to retraining a broken stress response system, the VA knows something about running effective boot camps.

If you served in the military, what happens when you're ready to get help with severe PTSD?

The first step is for you and your VA doctor to prove yourself eligible for intensive treatment. Often that process begins with your primary care doctor identifying high levels of anxiety associated with your exposure to some major traumatic event that happened recently, or sometimes many years before but now triggered by a recent stressor, such as an accident, illness, divorce, or retirement.

You're more likely to qualify for PTSD treatment if you've completed the PCL-5, the VA's checklist screening measure that assesses the severity of your PTSD symptoms.[15] If you score over 40 on the PCL-5, you have a high likelihood of meeting the diagnostic criteria for PTSD.

The PTSD triage clinician you talk to on the phone may ask you to identify the trauma you experienced in general terms and your PCL-5 score. Then you'll be invited to attend one of the orientation sessions held each week, and after you spend an hour in a room with other veterans hearing about the options, you schedule an evaluation appointment with a clinical psychologist, which will last sixty to ninety minutes and will include a thorough medical and psychiatric history and a review of your specific PTSD symptoms and the course of your illness. You leave that session with recommendations about your best treatment options.

Why is this like signing up for Army basic training boot camp? Experience has proven that this kind of treatment for PTSD requires a motivated participating patient, not a passive or reluctant one. In

both the inpatient and the outpatient PTSD programs, the patient works for six to eight hours a day, sometimes more, five to seven days a week for at least seven weeks to get started. Three months is the usual length of treatment. These are expensive treatments because they require high levels of face-to-face services by highly trained professional clinicians.

Cognitive Processing Therapy is the backbone of the VA approach to PTSD, a brand of CBT tailored to the intensive treatment of PTSD in individual and group settings. Education and psychotherapy – group, individual, family, and couples therapy – are the main focus, and medication is at the bottom of a long list of services that also includes virtual reality and anger coping skills.

To retrain a stress response system whose central nervous system is in the habit of false alarms, overreactions, numbing shutdowns, fragmentations of memory, and dissociations from cues about reality requires daily practice, with the help of both fellow sufferers and trained professionals. Medications can help temper the storms of PTSD in ways that facilitate full engagement in the therapy, but too much or the wrong kinds of medications can undermine or sabotage the retraining process.

A week or two of intensive treatment is rarely enough, but two to three months is often sufficient to get the retraining process established and launch the maintenance phase of treatment in less specialized and less intensive settings, such as primary care or weekly therapy in the mental health clinic.

The VA approach to PTSD leans heavily on psychological and social experiences to retrain the stress response system. Other experts – notably Bessel van der Kolk, MD, founder of the Trauma Center at the Justice Resource Institute in Boston, and author of *The Body Keeps the Score* – emphasize adding physical therapies, such as yoga, dance, theater, and neurofeedback to facilitate the reintegration of the conscious and unconscious physical functions with thoughts and emotions during the recovery process.

In this respect, comprehensive PTSD treatment looks similar to comprehensive coronary heart disease reversal treatment in the Ornish program. One focuses more on reaping benefits for the brain, and the other focuses more on benefits for the heart, but the essence of the content, structure, intensity, and duration of the treatment programs follows the same principles for retraining the stress response system.

The urgent need for greater access by many to more of these kinds of programs grows painfully clear when we look closer at Teresa Langford's long journey to recovery. And there are lessons her journey can teach us.

12

• • • • •

Yes, You Can Retrain the Brain

In the real world of the primary care clinic, life is a juggling contest, especially if you're Teresa Langford, my patient whom we met in earlier chapters. In this chapter we will follow Teresa through her long but ultimately helpful journey through a wide range of approaches to retraining her stress response system, though neither she nor her doctors thought of this journey that way.

We will also look at other options in the toolkit for retraining dysregulated stress response systems. We end with four lessons learned about the treatment of stress-related disorders.

When you're juggling six chronic conditions while recovering from a near-death bout of pancreatitis, you can't focus on one goal for very long. After Teresa's first appointment with a psychologist who worked down the hall from me in September 2011 to discuss the possibility of applying for disability, she didn't return to the psychologist until five months later when she was concerned about her

persistently foggy brain: just couldn't concentrate, get organized, or get motivated.

Neuropsychological testing at the time confirmed decreased mental efficiency, and difficulty with verbal learning and word retrieval, and it led to the recommendation of cognitive rehabilitation through speech therapy, which she did with some modest benefit.

By the next fall, however, she was back in the psychologist's office with a new phobia for the shower. Like many phobias, this one made no sense, but it was troubling enough to prompt a more careful exploration of her past traumas and her childhood. I had seen her a few times by then to monitor and adjust her antidepressant, which had been started during her hospital stay the year before. Recovering from a phobia requires some daily practice of relaxation techniques and monitoring of your anxiety as you work your way up a hierarchy of challenging situations. Teresa was not doing much practicing.

On the chance that depression was sabotaging her efforts to practice managing her anxiety, we added a second antidepressant, and she started meeting every other week with her psychologist. Within a couple of months Teresa shifted from focusing on the oddities of her shower phobia to talking about the military sexual trauma she had experienced in Korea at age twenty-one, and then to the other stressors of her childhood.

For several months she attended individual therapy in the PTSD program, but after seven sessions she hit a wall. They agreed to stop. Teresa was not engaged, and the therapist was not impressed with what she had chosen as her index trauma, which technically did not meet strict criteria for PTSD. However, to Teresa's relief the shower phobia had gradually gone away.

About a year later, in March 2014, she came back to me frustrated by her inability to regain her earlier level of energetic functioning. In fact, it had been over ten years since she had functioned

well on the job as a production manager. Was she still depressed? Her symptoms didn't add up. We talked about her frustrating but ultimately rewarding experiences in grade school, high school, and college. We talked about the jobs where she thrived and the ones where she foundered.

What emerged from that appointment was the possibility of undiagnosed adult ADD (Attention Deficit Disorder), masked by an impressive work ethic. She had revealed her lifelong inability to sustain concentration when sitting, her easy distractibility and forgetfulness, and a habit of using coffee and Mountain Dew to improve her mental performance under pressure. On a standard inventory for ADD symptoms in adults, she scored positive for twelve of the eighteen criteria, well above the threshold of six needed for diagnosis. All this suggested she may have ADD, overlooked for her adult life and maybe during her childhood too.

What clinched the diagnosis for both of us was her response to a trial of methylphenidate or Ritalin. She and her partner noticed a quick shift for the better in her ability to attend to conversations, concentrate, organize her daily life, and finish tasks while taking medication twice a day. Equally impressive was how quickly she reverted to her foggy brain when the medication wore off after four hours.

Although the identification and treatment of her ADD felt like a breakthrough for her, it did not turn out to be the breakthrough she hoped for. That breakthrough came nine months later when she was referred by her psychologist to both the pain clinic and the MOVE programs at the same time.

Now at age fifty, the chronic pain in her knees and lower back was screaming at her, partly the product of the extra weight she'd been carrying mostly in her belly for thirty years. None of her efforts over the past two years had budged her BMI below 38.

MOVE was the VA's weight management program, combining individual meetings with nutritionists and weekly group meetings with others trying to lose weight.

The pain clinic was the main vehicle for the Cincinnati VA to transition patients from chronic opiates to non-opiate regimens. Patients attended several times a week to build a treatment plan that combined physical therapy, acupuncture, medication management, group cognitive therapy, and patient education about chronic pain and options for better management. At its best, people came out of this boot camp doing more with better pain management on less pain medicine. But you had to work at it to get the benefit.

Teresa took to both programs like a soldier to boot camp. She rediscovered her zeal for learning. She could concentrate and organize herself and her daily activities. She practiced daily at home between sessions in the program. She felt alive and on her game again.

By May 2015 she was volunteering fifteen hours a week as a peer coach for the Healthy U program, an educational service that focuses on helping veterans develop self-management habits that can prevent or manage common chronic illnesses. Today Teresa wonders what allowed her to finally turn the corner.

"I don't know. Maybe time. I found out I could do what I needed to in the MOVE and pain clinic programs. I could do the work and later I could teach it. That's the teacher in me," she said.

The structure of the volunteer work proved to be just right for helping her get out of the house and show up every day, and come home feeling she had served her mission. She felt she was living a life of purpose again. It took her six months of this kind of daily practice to feel confident she had changed her habits and could hold on to them.

Other Tools in the Toolkit

Teresa Langford's turnaround and the similarities across these proven programs for the treatment of coronary heart disease, diabetes prevention, functional disorders, depression, and PTSD

underline the shared pathways through these stress-related chronic conditions. However, it is equally important to emphasize that each disorder also requires its specific treatments to achieve optimal outcomes.

Cholesterol-lowering drugs and statins will improve coronary heart disease but will do little for high blood sugar or suicidal thoughts. In the depressed mother with diabetes, antidepressants and CBT may dramatically reduce depressive symptoms without dramatically reducing her hemoglobin A1C. It's important to understand which treatments improve specific outcomes and which improve the more general outcomes. And what do these various tools in the toolkit tell us about the treatment of toxic stress?

Meditation. Some form of meditation or relaxation practice plays a role in many of these effective treatment programs because meditation improves a broad range of outcomes. Meditation is attractive partly because, relative to medications and surgery and some forms of exercise, meditation is relatively easy, cheap, adaptable, and free of side effects. And for many people meditation feels good quickly, reduces their symptoms, and improves their functioning. Hard to argue with that.

But how is it possible that meditation can have helpful effects on such a wide range of health measures as early risk for death, pain, insomnia, coronary heart disease, the prevention of major depression, obesity, loneliness, metabolic syndrome, immune function, high blood glucose, high blood pressure, high heart rate, stress-related gene expression, and telomere length? Is there one mechanism in meditation affecting all these outcomes, or are there many mechanisms? And is one kind of meditation better than another for improving health outcomes?

The research on the health benefits of meditation has only recently started to achieve a rigor that persuades skeptics, so consequently there is plenty of debate about all these questions,

including how meditation works, and if it works at all.[1] The best evidence may be for meditation's effects on depression, anxiety, and pain. But the strength of the evidence is limited by the wide range of definitions of meditation, the frequent lack of good control groups, and the absence of attention to the possible negative effects of meditation. More rigorously designed studies should clarify the remaining questions about how meditation might work to improve our health.

Part of the problem for researchers who try to answer these questions is how to define what meditation is. Consider just some of the ways meditation has been branded in my lifetime: transcendental meditation, the relaxation response, mindfulness-based stress reduction (MBSR), resilience training, SMART training, yoga, prayer, mindfulness-based cognitive therapy.

The best studied of these brands have been the relaxation response and MBSR. Herbert Benson tells us the essential component of the relaxation response is the regular practicing of a quiet alertness, the resting state of the autonomic nervous system with low sympathetic activity and high parasympathetic activity, as indicated by low resting heart rates and respiratory rates.

Jon Kabat-Zinn tells us that the hallmark of MBSR is attention to a nonjudgmental awareness of the mind, a practice of attending to the present. How either the quiet alertness or the attention to your mind in the present leads to better health outcomes has not been well established. And there's no consensus on how to verify that a person is in the prescribed state of quiet alertness or mindfulness, nor how long that state is sustained.

One potential mechanism that explains how most brands of meditation improve health is that all of these forms of meditation either intentionally or as a by-product reduce sympathetic activity and increase parasympathetic activity during the meditation session. Through scheduled physical rest and the pausing of our critical thoughts, these practices dampen our overstimulated brains

and increase our autonomic balance for a period of fifteen to thirty minutes once or twice a day.

In this way these practices are retraining the overactive autonomic nervous system toward a healthier balance of sympathetic and parasympathetic tone. Dr. Kabat-Zinn's mantra to attend to your mind in the present delivers a strong message to try pausing your daily worrying habits. Attend to the content of your thoughts and then let them go. Skip the judging part. Adopt a curious detachment.

To do this with regularity for fifteen to thirty minutes once or twice a day, you have to practice believing a few other messages: It's safe to do nothing for this time, nothing but counting your breaths. Nothing bad will happen if you pause your worrying and your doing and your connecting. It's safe not to concentrate or ruminate or solve problems for a short while. For a few minutes every day it's safe to avoid judgment, decision-making, hurrying. It's safe to feel anything and then let it go. It's safe to be quiet and still for a while.

In cognitive therapy terms, meditation amounts to practicing automatic thoughts that reduce our attention to threats. Meditation asks us to practice internally the same sort of unconditional love and support that AA asks us to practice in the best of home group meetings.

Meditation is practicing the assertion several times a day that we can choose to some extent how and when to be anxious or calm, when to feel threatened or safe. These messages and this ritual behavior require a level of acceptance that, at its best, usually brings about a pleasurable calmness, a state that is meaningfully different from a nap or watching TV while slouching on the couch. Meditation is a way of practicing stress response reduction every day.

Since the full benefits of regular meditation accumulate over several months of daily practice, it's likely that meditation eventually

helps adjust the set points of the whole stress response system closer to their homeostatic levels. Seasoned meditators who have practiced for years generally have lower resting heart rates and respiratory rates than the rest of us, even when they're not meditating. They also tend to have lower stress reactivity in response to challenges and faster stress recovery rates. And they harbor less low-grade inflammation.[2]

For some people, these kinds of meditative mind games don't work; they only increase the anxiety and make the person squirm. For them, walking or slow dancing or chanting or gentle drumming or yoga may provide better ways to achieve the same retraining of the stress response system through actions rather than through thoughts. The effect on the autonomic nervous system and health outcomes may be equally strong for these forms of relaxation in motion.

The payoff of some kind of meditation or relaxation practice comes with improved attention control, emotion regulation, and self-awareness, all of which are good for the stress response system and for health.

Purpose-built communities. Along the spectrum of treatment targets from the individual to society, meditation represents one approach to stress management at the inner individual end of this spectrum. At the opposite end are the broad social interventions that aim to make environments less stressful and healthier. The argument for broad social interventions is that, though they require a greater initial investment, the payoff in public health improvements is greater for a larger number of people. If you make an environment favor healthy behaviors, many individuals adopt new habits without individual training.

For example, Dan Buettner's Blue Zones communities aim to build neighborhoods in the US and elsewhere based on the principles that contribute to longevity and relative freedom from the afflictions of chronic illness, the "Blue Zones Power 9." As we saw

in an earlier chapter, these nine lessons include such mantras as "move naturally," "belong," "purpose," "down shift," "loved ones first," and "plant slant" (or adopt a plant-based diet).[3]

It's no accident that these Blue Zones lessons overlap with and echo the messages embedded in the Ornish Reversal Program, the Diabetes Prevention Program, and the STReSS intervention for bodily distress disorders.

In the span of three to ten years, these Blue Zones community redesign projects have revamped city streets, public gathering spaces, schools, and grocery stores in small rural towns like Albert Lea, Minnesota, large cities like Fort Worth, Texas, and middle-class beach cities in Southern California, like Redondo Beach.

The results for these purpose-built communities appear promising, according to claims on the Blue Zones website: "Double digit drops in obesity, smoking, and BMI (body mass index). Millions of dollars of savings in healthcare costs. Measurable drops in employee absenteeism."

The lesson through these demonstration projects may be that the fastest way to improve the health of large numbers of people is through large-scale environmental interventions that drive individual behavior changes in the direction of better health.

Redesigning streets to make it safe and inviting for people to walk or ride bikes has a rapid beneficial effect on their physical activity levels and their frequency of social contacts, with no individual costs for a gym or health coach. Providing tasty vegetarian meals at school has a rapid effect on children's body mass index measures and their eating habits during formative stages of development. Smoking rates drop. Healthcare costs drop. Work productivity improves. At least that's the promise from these few examples.

The nonprofit organization Purpose Built Communities offers consulting to communities aiming for this kind of renewal. The town of East Lake, outside of Atlanta, is their most developed project,

with measurable health improvement in obesity and asthma rates during the first ten years.[4] The aims of this organization include rescuing some of the most distressed neighborhoods. These projects prove that to some extent community structure and function can drive lifestyle in the direction of better health outcomes.

Lifestyle Medicine works at the middle and upper ends of the socioeconomic ladder. Does it work at the low end where stresses are greater for longer and the choices fewer? And does it require overhauling the whole community? Gregory Miller and Edith Chen have shown that social interventions can also work in a select high-risk group without changing the whole community.

In a low socioeconomic sample from rural Georgia, they delivered a seven-week family-oriented intervention to over 600 mother–child pairs. The intervention was designed to enhance parenting, strengthen family relationships, and foster competencies in eleven-year-olds. The results showed that this intense and targeted family intervention can have measurable and lasting beneficial effects on six inflammatory markers assessed eight years later, when the young teens were now nineteen. The key factor was improved parenting by the mothers.[5] This study shows one way that effective mothering can provide powerful buffers against the health effects of chronic stress in rural poverty.

The Miller and Chen team also studied the effects of a resilience intervention called Shift and Persist in several low socioeconomic samples, and found it effective at improving inflammation in adolescents with asthma. This team has also found that the resilient teenagers in poorer neighborhoods who do well also pay a price for their better adjustment with higher allostatic loads than their less competent peers. Poverty is not destiny, but success comes at a price, usually a price we don't learn about until many years later.

Are the most mistreated children beyond the reach of stress management? A group led by Mary Dozier, PhD, of the University of Delaware designed an active parenting intervention called

Attachment and Behavioral Catch-up for mothers of four- to five-year-olds referred to child protective services for allegations of neglect.[6]

In this randomized controlled trial, a trained parent coach delivered the intervention in ten weekly sessions in the home with the child and mother. The intervention coached the mothers on increasing nurturance to the child in distress, increasing the mother's responsiveness in communications, and decreasing frightening parental behaviors. The children in the intervention group, compared to a group that only received parental education about child development, showed significantly improved cortisol levels three months after the intervention and again three years later.

These findings suggest that effective parenting interventions in high-risk families can have lasting beneficial effects on the stress hormone cortisol levels in the affected child when the intervention happens while the child is young.

It is possible to retrain certain hormones in the brain of even the most distressed children through retraining the primary caregiving relationship, the chief source of both stress and security for a four-year-old. More studies with longer follow-ups will be needed to assess how these interventions affect their risks for stress-related illness in adulthood.

Oxytocin. The power of these social interventions to protect us from disease raises the question of how this could be. Why should bolstering our social networks translate into less physical illness now or many years later? Some species, such as wolves, and some people seem to prefer to navigate life alone, but most of us do better with others by our side, either literally or psychologically.

We feel safer in a group or a family than alone. We humans are also guided by our inborn levels of oxytocin, a hormone produced in the brain and released into the bloodstream, and how these levels rise and fall. The evolution of the limbic system and its capacity for love is part of what allowed mammals to triumph over dinosaurs.

Oxytocin does more than make breast milk flow. In children, men, and women who are not breastfeeding, oxytocin also sharpens our attention to social cues, buffers our fight-or-flight response, and generally has a calming effect that helps us connect to others. Low levels of oxytocin, on the other hand, are found in people who are socially isolated or lonely or short on empathy, such as people with autism spectrum disorder.

Could extra oxytocin provide a way to buffer toxic stress? In laboratory studies, repeated doses of oxytocin lower blood pressure and cortisol levels, raise trust and endorphin levels, and reduce the release of norepinephrine, a key driver of sympathetic nervous system reactivity.

So why don't we all take oxytocin with daily vitamins? Its chemical properties do not lend themselves to being taken as a pill, at least not yet. But consider the ways we can raise oxytocin levels.

Consensual physical contact, from handshakes to intercourse, raises oxytocin. Contact with pets can do it too. Dog owners have better survival rates after heart attacks than non-dog owners. The longer a mother breastfeeds, the lower the mother's risk of later developing diabetes or heart disease, possibly through the stress-buffering effects of oxytocin.

Coaching a frustrated mother of a misbehaving toddler to shift to a close, firm, and affirming response is likely to boost oxytocin levels in both the child and the mother. Exercise and eating, particularly if done in good company, may also raise oxytocin levels.[7] This is the chemistry of affection that prolongs life.

Biofeedback. Because most of us are poor readers of all but the most extreme messages from our internal organs – I often confuse fatigue with hunger – the retraining of the stress response system is more efficient when guided by a few measures of our physical responses to stress.

Since the 1990s the science of biofeedback has grown quietly in the background during the emergence of stress neuroscience.

Biofeedback is now the basis for the booming industry of "wearables," these monitoring devices like the Apple Watch that have become fashionable in the fitness world. They come as wristbands, armbands, headbands, belts, and vests. The technological innovation that has moved biofeedback from the lab to the fashion and fitness markets is the development of apps that store and display the data on our phones in ways that make sense to us.

Though we would have a hard time explaining how we do it, most of us can learn in a half-hour how to raise the temperature in our left hands, guided by a thermometer taped to our left index finger. That's our capacity to achieve selective local vasodilation (the widening of blood vessels). Without the thermometer we're much less likely to achieve that warming. It's useful for training people with the cold hands of Raynaud's disease, an autoimmune condition of reduction of blood flow in the hands and feet.

We can also raise and lower our resting heart rates or blood pressures when given a monitor that shows us the current numbers. Some people can learn to manage their hypertension with biofeedback alone. We can reduce gastric acid secretion when given the feedback about stomach acid levels, which can be useful for people with ulcers or esophageal reflux.

Although we usually assume that we have little control over these autonomic functions, biofeedback has shown us that we can influence them in the desired directions with a little information and consistent practice. In this way it's possible to retrain our stress response systems, organ by organ.

If biofeedback works by telling us what's going on in our arteries, hearts, stomachs, and muscles, can it tell us anything about what's going on in our brains?

The first claims I heard for neurofeedback came in the early 1970s from the guru Maharishi Mahesh Yogi when I was initiated into the movement of transcendental meditation (TM). I learned then that alpha brain waves on the electroencephalogram (EEG)

are associated with relaxation, that state of restful alertness that is the aim of TM.

Alpha waves on the EEG were one of Herbert Benson's key outcome measures for the relaxation response studies he did at Harvard in the 1970s to explain the workings of TM. Masters of TM proved adept at generating alpha waves. Neurofeedback devices, which display the relative proportions of alpha, beta, delta, and theta waves (some more reliably than others), help people to train themselves to generate alpha waves at will. This approach has been used to treat PTSD and ADHD and to enhance the performance of professional soccer teams and musicians.[8]

Rollin McCraty, PhD, one of the leaders in the development of stress-related biofeedback approaches, has been working at the HeartMath Institute since 1991. Using a concept he dubbed heart coherence, he has conducted studies that examine our capacity to improve our heart rate variability with the help of training and biofeedback.

In general, the more a heart can vary its rate to meet the varying demands of daily life, the more healthy that heart is. Within certain limits, high heart rate variability is good heart health.

Building on the work of Stephen Porges, the author of *The Polyvagal Theory*, and Bruce McEwen's concepts of allostasis and homeostasis introduced earlier in this book, Dr. McCraty proposed that heart coherence represents a pattern of heart rate variability that matches the brain's emotional state; it is proposed to be most efficient and consistent with heart health.

For example, a recent study of seventy-one professional and family caregivers of patients with dementia reported impressive improvements in the heart rate variability of both the professionals and family caregivers within three months of weekly training and practice.

Using a technique called heart-focused breathing, similar to common meditation techniques, coupled with feedback about

heart rate variability, the percentage of each group demonstrating high heart coherence ratings (think brain, heart, lungs synchrony) jumped from 9 percent to 86 percent in the first three months. After training and biofeedback was over, high heart coherence ratings remained above 80 percent after six months, suggesting that the skill persists without the biofeedback device.[9]

Dr. McCraty has tested this approach in a variety of people undergoing high stress conditions. The concept of coherence extends to the whole stress response system, to relationships between two people, and to the degree of physiologic harmony among members of a group.[10] However, the intriguing concept of heart coherence remains to be replicated by independent investigators.

So if you're trying to figure out whether meditation or walking or doing crosswords or petting your poodle is reducing your stress response levels, instead of guessing effectiveness only by how much or little stress you feel, try measuring effectiveness also with several carefully selected biofeedback measures such as apps on your Apple Watch or Fitbit or any number of similar wearables. The best ones add a more reliable measurable dimension to the process.

We're so good at fooling ourselves and so inconsistent in how we gauge progress along complex subjective metrics such as pain, tension, fatigue, nausea, anxiety, and stress. Knowing how many steps you walked today or how many times you woke up in the night or what your lowest resting heart rate was during meditation helps you train yourself. It keeps you honest about what works and what doesn't.

Why has biofeedback been so little used in chronic disease management?

A partial answer is rooted in the economics of medicine. Compared to most medical machines, biofeedback devices are relatively simple and cheap. Once you buy one, you don't need to buy another. Unlike the pharmaceutical companies that make big

money with pills because we have to buy them over and over, the companies that make biofeedback devices never make big money by selling these products. So the devices and their use have not been promoted. And only a few devices are covered by insurance, a major disincentive for many patients.

Until recently the collection, management, and display of the data for the more complex devices were cumbersome enough that they had to be managed through a lab. Now that apps make the data useful for any smartphone owner, the role of biofeedback in stress retraining is likely to turn into new methods that will be increasingly helpful as we figure out the optimal uses of these devices and their data.

We will all be smarter stress managers once we can learn which behaviors in our daily lives lower our heart rates or improve our heart rate variability or make our sleep more efficient and restful.

Neuromodulation. If monitoring the brain's alpha wave activity can help people cultivate the skill of relaxation and restful alertness, can stimulating the brain in certain ways also help reduce stress and increase resilience?

Brain stimulation or neuromodulation as a medical treatment takes a range of forms. The most global form is electroconvulsive therapy (ECT), which stimulates the whole brain for a few seconds under general anesthesia over a series of eight to ten treatments delivered during several weeks. ECT is the most effective treatment for severe major depression, achieving remission rates as high as 80 percent in some of the best studies.

At the other end of the spectrum, the most focal form of neuromodulation is deep brain stimulation, which delivers a stimulus to a very small region around a probe surgically implanted in a specific nerve tract or brain circuit. The frequency and intensity of this stimulus can be varied by adjusting the settings on the program that delivers the stimulus from the regulator implanted under the collarbone.

Deep brain stimulation is effective for the treatment of Parkinson's and has proven promising for some forms of major depression. Between the extremes of ECT and deep brain stimulation are two other approaches: transcranial magnetic stimulation and vagus nerve stimulation, both of which try to bring about changes in the brain through initially stimulating either the cortex or the limbic system via the vagus nerve. These forms of brain stimulation are being explored for their usefulness in a range of neurologic and psychiatric disorders.

Chronic back pain that is not helped with pain meds can be treated with another kind of neurostimulator, the TENS unit, which reduces the experience of pain by stimulating competing nerve fibers in the spinal cord. This is a bit like creating a sense of quiet though the generation of white noise where one signal drowns out the other.

More germane to the task of retraining the stress response system is the experimental device called the portable neuromodulation stimulator, or PoNS™, as described by Norman Doidge in *The Brain's Way of Healing*.

Since 2005, Yuri Danilov, PhD, at the University of Wisconsin, has led the development of the PoNS, a lollipop-sized device now manufactured by Helius Medical Technologies. The PoNS delivers low-level stimulation through 143 electrodes on the surface of the device as it lies on the person's tongue. The stimulation is mild enough to avoid being unpleasant but strong enough to deliver stimulation to the brain stem, which sits right behind the tongue and to which the tongue has rich connections via the trigeminal and facial nerves.

The PoNS is based on the principle that neuromodulation fosters neuroplasticity, or the reactivation of dormant circuits, and in some cases the regeneration of new circuits in the area of the brain stem that regulates much of the autonomic nervous system and motor coordination in the cerebellum. As an aid to

rehabilitation, this kind of neuromodulation has led to promising results for patients with traumatic brain injury, multiple sclerosis, and stroke.[11]

Its potential use for assisting with retraining the stress response system in people with stress-related disorders is also promising in a number of cases, but large systematic studies have not yet been published.

Another approach to retraining the stress response system that may be considered a form of neuromodulation is the use of eye-movement desensitization and reprocessing (EMDR) to enhance the psychotherapeutic treatment of PTSD. This approach takes advantage of the observation that rhythmically alternating stimulation – the movement of the eyes from side to side ("follow my finger") or a sound that moves from one ear to the other or a tactile stimulus from left to right and back – facilitates a person's access to repressed memories.

How we access these memories and what we make of them depends on the skill of the therapist, but the benefits of this technique in the hands of skilled therapists have been well described and studied.[12]

Can pills work? The debate about the role of medications in stress management boils down to the one sound answer to most complex questions, "It depends." In part, it depends on the key contributing factors to the toxic stress.

When the source of toxic stress is a major mental illness that requires medication to manage the illness, such as severe depression or bipolar disorder, there's no question that effective medication can play a powerful role in reducing the burden of stress on the risk for physical illnesses. The same applies to the effective medication management of physical illnesses. Any illness exacts a toll on the stress response system, and the sooner that toll is relieved by effective management, with or without medications, the better.

If the damage from toxic stress can be traced in part to autonomic imbalance, is there evidence that correcting excessive sympathetic activity is good for health? Jennifer Knight, MD, at the Medical College of Wisconsin, was curious about the data showing that chronic stress increases the risk for spread in some forms of cancer. In a multicenter placebo-controlled randomized treatment trial, she and her co-investigators have shown that the beta-blocker propranolol, which reduces sympathetic activity throughout the central and peripheral nervous system, also reduces metastases and improves survival in patients with the blood cancer multiple myeloma.[13]

She and Steven Cole, PhD, at UCLA, have shown that beta-blockers like propranolol have measurable beneficial effects on CTRA gene expression, a collection of genes that regulate the stress response system.[14]

More studies are needed to examine how effective this approach could be in other cancers, but these initial studies have shown the value of the concept.

On the other hand, a number of studies of the treatment of depression in people with heart disease have shown that depression treatments – mostly antidepressant medications and psychotherapy – that improve the depression and the person's quality of life do not measurably improve the course of the heart disease.[15] The follow-up for these studies has usually been short, three to six months, and these clinical trials of antidepressant medications rarely include other treatments, such as intensive exercise, diet, meditation, or group support. This is likely to be a case of too little, too late.

This disappointing set of studies confirms what these other more effective treatments have taught us: for a complex chronic illness like coronary heart disease, one medication is not enough. Retraining the dysregulated stress response system to reverse heart disease requires multiple types of treatments over many months.

The telomere effect. In their book *The Telomere Effect*, Elizabeth Blackburn and Elissa Epel describe multiple ways to improve the chances of lengthening life by lengthening telomeres, or at least reducing the rate at which telomeres shorten with aging.

You may recall my earlier discussion of telomeres and their shortening as a risk for illness. The essence of their prescriptions reads like a manual for stress management, or like the Ornish Reversal Program, or like the Diabetes Prevention Program.[16] Their unmistakable message is that the key to longevity and long telomeres is a Blue Zones lifestyle: move more, love more, balance work and play and rest, eat well, stress less, sleep well, have fun, make contact, live with purpose. A modest purpose is good enough as long as it's meaningful to you.

Most of us find it hard to achieve even a few of these lifestyle habits, so any neighborhood or program or set of relationships that make any of these behavior changes easier is likely to favor longer lives with less chronic illness. *The Telomere Effect* reminds us that these Blue Zones habits penetrate to the cellular level and translate into more resilient epigenetic events and behaviors.

Lessons Learned

From a distance, this collection of treatments for toxic stress may look too varied and messy for scientific rigor and simple lessons. There's nothing neat and simple about the treatments required to reverse a dysregulated stress response system. And that will always be true because the stress response system will always be complicated, whether regulated or dysregulated, and chronic illness will always be messy.

But there are a few lessons to keep in mind as we think about how to care better and smarter for those on these fast tracks to dying young.

Lessons Learned

- Explore boot camps, not Band-Aids.
- Changing behaviors takes practice.
- Find programs that work in clinical practice.
- Plan to prevent relapses.

First, Band-Aids don't work for toxic stress – not for the patient and not for the public health of our society. That is, treating a fifty-five-year-old man's coronary heart disease with stents to open blocked blood vessels or a bypass graft to replace the damaged vessels rescues him from the immediate crisis of chest pains but does nothing for the process that first clogged his arteries and will continue to clog them.

Boot camp level retraining works, and it works for a wide range of people when smartly designed for easy access and long-term participation. And it only works if continued for six to twelve months. This is partly because retraining multiple systems (brain, heart, immune, endocrine, digestive, musculoskeletal) to regain a coherent set of rhythms works in a cascade, with one system change facilitating the others. Achieving coherence requires layers and layers of retraining.

The good news is that a wide range of methods for retraining the stress response system have achieved sustainable results.[17] Individual tailoring of treatment plans is not only possible but more effective than the one-size-fits-all approach.

Second, we can't retrain our stress response systems without changing our behavior. A drug or a stent or a surgical implant can't retrain our stress response systems, but the consistent practice of selected behaviors such as meditation and healthy eating can. The list of these behaviors is long and familiar to us, and a variety of combinations seem to be good enough for most people most of the

time. But the intensity of the practice needed to retrain our systems is something few of us can imagine until we've done it.

One of the most pressing enigmas facing those who aim to improve our approaches to chronic illness and the cost of health-care in the US is why it's so hard for most of us to change our high-risk health behaviors. To address this problem, NIH is funding a project called the Science of Behavior Change.[18] This funding mechanism supports research on measures and mechanisms of behavior change.

For example, Alison Miller, PhD, at the University of Michigan, is currently exploring through her ABC Brain Games Study whether four interventions can improve children's ability to regulate their emotions, their food biases, and other behaviors related to obesity.

Judson Brewer, MD, PhD, director of research and innovation at the Center for Mindfulness, Brown University, recognizes self-management of chronic illness as the third leg of treatment, along with surgery and medicine.

"The next wave of innovation in medicine is digital therapeutics," he told me. He was working on the first of several apps, Eat Right Now, which helps impulsive eaters reduce their cravings and intake with ten minutes of mindfulness-based stress reduction daily.

Digital therapeutics have ushered stress neuroscience into the era of big data, offering the possibility of changing high-risk behaviors by monitoring the stress response system during daily life, which is the equivalent of shifting from still photography to movies. Once we can see our stress response systems in motion, then we'll begin to understand how they really work. Then we have a better chance to change toxic habits.

These kinds of innovations in digital therapeutics are contributing to the science of behavior change in ways that could readily translate into better health outcomes for large numbers of people.

Third, most of these advances in the treatment of stress to achieve better outcomes of chronic illness have earned their credibility initially through randomized controlled trials, the current standard for scientific rigor. But controlled trials rarely change clinical practice. And by definition, controlled trials can only answer a few narrow questions for a limited sample of patients in the wide array of questions about the factors that drive the development and progression of most chronic conditions.

In addition to clinical trials, most of the effective stress management approaches described in these chapters have found their way into practice through large dissemination projects over many years. The Ornish Reversal Program, the National Diabetes Prevention Program, the COMPASS project, and the VA PTSD programs began as randomized controlled trials.

These interventions have now been tested in real-world clinical settings and found to be feasible, affordable, and effective. In fact, these approaches are starting to change the culture of healthcare for those who adopt them.

Finally, as promising as these interventions are for retraining the stress response system, the possibility of relapse to the old ways is a fact of life for all who test that question in their daily lives. Especially in the early years after retraining and recovery, slacking off on the regimen that achieved the recovery often leads to a return of the toxic habits and symptoms.

When Teresa quit her job as a peer coach to take care of their soon-to-be-adopted son, she lost her daily contact with her support team at the hospital, she had to walk less, and she could eat whenever and whatever she wanted with less accountability than when she was coaching most days of the week. Depression returned and her weight started climbing.

Once again, she had to figure out how to regain the strategy that had worked for her. Now that her son is approaching preschool, she knows she has what it takes to return to work. So relapse

prevention usually requires some way of maintaining the essential components of the routine, such as sticking with your vegetarian diet, walking three times a week, and meeting with your group once a month. For each of us, the trick is finding and maintaining the lifestyle we need to keep our stress response systems playing like a symphony.

13

· · · · ·

Talking about Stress with Your Doctor

How does discussing toxic stress work best when you're sitting in an exam room with your primary care doctor? Is it possible for you and your doctor to weave stress measurement and treatment into the hurry of the standard fifteen-minute primary care appointment? Sandwiched in between blood pressure readings and indigestion?

Here are three ways Dr. Good and Mrs. B might approach treatment with attention to the role of stress in her life, depending on three ways she might have responded to his first visit with her, as I introduced in an earlier chapter. We can learn some lessons here.

Scenario A: Watchful Waiting

The surprises of his first visit with Mrs. B had put Dr. Good on notice to enter the exam room a month later for her second visit with low expectations. Her priority had been to drive again so she could tend

to her grandbaby. His priorities had been for better blood pressure and blood sugar control, and to help her take better care of herself, though he was not yet sure how to engage her in that process.

Now he found her sitting in the chair next to his doctor's stool in her hot pink jumpsuit, nails glittering, hair freshly braided and beaded, and smiling. She might be one who dresses up for her doctor appointments, he thought. Before he had a chance to ask her how she's doing, she said, "Fine. Just fine, Dr. Good."

"Really?" he said. "Last time I saw you that floater had you plenty upset."

He glanced at the Distress Thermometer sheet his assistant had left on the counter. Mrs. B had circled the 2 and checked the boxes for health and finances. Last time she'd circled the 6.

She said, "Last time I had the fever, Doc. Now I'm cool." She laughed.

"Tell me what you've done since I saw you a month ago to feel so fine now. You drove yourself today?"

"I'm back on the road. Done everything you told me – almost. I saw the eye doctor – nice lady. She didn't waste any words on me, but she told me that floater was already shrinking and should be gone by the time my grandbaby comes, if I mind my diet."

"Really? Tell me what that means."

"That means I cut out my night snacks – no snacking after eight. That's all there is to it, Doc. I don't like it, but I only drink diet now. Tastes nasty, but cutting down might even save me a dollar a day."

"I see your weight's already down a couple of pounds. Can you feel a difference?"

"I'm on the road, Doc. My neighbor fell and broke her hip, so she asked me could I walk her dog. I don't mind. We go out half an hour in the morning and half an hour after dinner. If I forget, she calls me up. Instead of snacking in the evening, I'm walking her dog and talking to all those other dogs out there. Everybody loves dog talk."

He said, "Your neighbor did you a favor, got you out of the house. Sleeping any better?"

"Her bad luck is my blessing. I guess I am sleeping some now. Not so shifty."

"Your blood pressure's below 90, your diastolic I mean. That's good. You okay with staying on these three medications for now? If you keep walking and dieting and sleeping like this, we may be able to cut back on one of these blood pressure pills someday."

He picked up her ACE scale and noted she'd scored a 3, one each for divorce, mental illness in the family, and alcohol in the family. "Did my assistant tell you why we asked you to fill this out?" He ushered her up onto the examining table while grabbing the ophthalmoscope.

"She told me you'd explain. You trying to find out if I'm some kind of trouble? Christine's already told you I'm trouble, right?"

He chuckled. "No, in fact she never told me anything about you. I was surprised to learn you were sisters. No, this questionnaire is something we ask all my new patients to fill out because these kinds of troubles in childhood can raise your risks for illness as an adult. Your score of 3 is not high, but it's not low either. Tell me about these three things. Now keep your eyes on that clock behind me." He zeroed in with the ophthalmoscope to get a look at the remnants of her floater.

"Christine's my half-sister. She's old enough to be my mother. Her daddy left our mama when she was pregnant with our brother. Just disappeared one day and wrote from California he wasn't coming back. After Pete was born, Mama took to the bed for a while, a long while, and that made Christine grow up fast, ten years old and four little kids under her and Mama who couldn't pull herself out of bed. I tell Christine she can thank her misfortune. That's how she came to be a school principal, minding all us kids!"

"You mentioned mental illness and alcohol," said Dr. Good, moving his fingers swiftly from her carotid to her radial to her pedal pulses.

"When Mama married my daddy, I was already in the oven. He'd moved up here from Miami, spoke French, dressed nice, drove a gold Buick, and ran his own taxi service. When he moved into our house, so did his brother Uncle Binkie. Uncle Binkie stayed on the third floor, but he was not right. He had to take a lot of medications, and when no one else was around, he talked creepy to me about sex and animals. I was afraid of Uncle Binkie all those years, thinking he was going to do something. They left me with him. Nobody believed me. I never felt safe. He never touched me, but he talked so creepy I grew up sure some day he'd do something and nobody would believe me."

"Did anyone in your family ever harm you or threaten to harm you?"

"Not that bad. I was a scared little girl, but nobody hurt me like that."

"Your mother couldn't help you? Your older siblings?"

"They were mostly gone to jobs or college or the military. Mama had her eye on Daddy. He played too much, drank too much. Not mean, just rowdy. You just had to stay away from him when he got like that. He got a DUI twice, lost his license, and then he quit. I was a teenager by then. I never did like his drinking, but I got my playboy genes from him. I found other ways to have my fun."

Dr. Good said, "You've done a good job getting your weight and blood pressure under better control, but your mother and your other half-sister having diabetes and your being heavy so many years and your hemoglobin A1C of 6.1 – it all puts you in the prediabetes range. Your history of high stress in childhood adds to that risk. I'm going to ask my assistant to come back in and talk with you about the Diabetes Prevention Program, which is designed to help people like you avoid or delay developing diabetes. Interested?"

"How's a program going to keep that octopus out of my eye?"

"That depends on how hard you work your program. If you can avoid diabetes, your eyes won't bleed. Give it a try. I'll see you back in three months. Bring me pictures of your grandbaby. And call sooner if your weight or your blood pressure or your distress level starts climbing again."

"I can try."

Three months later Mrs. B came back with pictures of baby Janelle and news that she now had a rescue dog of her own to walk and sleep with. She was a month into her Diabetes Prevention Program at the Y and had no plans to drop out. Her weight, blood pressure, blood sugar, and distress scores were all improving.

Dr. Good had spent twelve and then eight minutes in each of these two appointments, and each confirmed the value of his watchful waiting approach to managing her distress. Good outcomes were achievable with a few precious professional resources (attentive primary care, timely eye consultation, patient education by his assistant, and referral to the Diabetes Prevention Program).

Without belaboring the questions, doctor and patient were able to establish early what she wanted from the appointments, from the treatment, and from life (her sense of purpose). Screening with the Distress Thermometer and the ACE scale alerted them both to a moderate level of risk for stress-related conditions.

By the second visit Mrs. B had been able to make the specific changes needed to affect the key indicators of trouble in her stress response system: high distress, insomnia, high blood pressure, high blood sugar. Simple and repeated measures over four months of her central nervous system (using the Distress Thermometer), cardiovascular system (blood pressure and heart rate), and metabolic system (blood sugar levels, hemoglobin A1C, BMI) outlined a pattern of relatively better regulation across all these organ systems since that first visit with the floater in her eye. Mrs. B's orchestra was playing with a conductor again. But things don't often go so well so fast.

Watchful Waiting Works

- A few timely measures can define risks.
- Many people will rise to the challenge to meet goals.
- Clarifying risks can bring about behavior changes that meet goals.

Scenario B: Starting Treatment

Shall we rewind the tape? Dr. Good found Mrs. B sitting in the chair next to his doctor's stool in her hot pink jumpsuit, nails glittering, hair freshly braided and beaded, and sipping her supersized drink through a straw. She might be one who dresses up for her doctor appointments no matter how she feels, he thought, but this supersized cup is probably not a promising sign. She eyed him, and he eyed her.

Taking his place on the stool, he asked her, "So how're you doing since I saw you last?"

She said, "Fine," sipping loudly.

"Really?" he said, recalling how quickly she had said "fine" when he first met her with a floater in her eye, and she'd said it again. But today she said "fine" just once and looked away. He glanced at the Distress Thermometer sheet his assistant had left on the counter. Mrs. B had circled the 5 and checked the boxes for health and finances and mood and family. Last time she had circled the 6.

"How's that floater?"

"I don't know. Some better, I guess. I had to get a cab today. I can't be leaning on Christine for everything."

"Were you able to make that appointment with the eye doctor a couple of weeks ago?"

She paused. "It's scheduled for next month."

"What happened with that appointment we made for you two weeks ago?"

"I couldn't make it."

"Couldn't make it? What got in the way?"

She paused again. "I couldn't make it out of bed, Doc. It was an eight o'clock appointment. I didn't sleep much that night – couldn't stop thinking about what they might find. I'm sorry you went to all that trouble. I'll be there next time, I promise."

"You'll make it if you can sleep the night before," he said. He wrapped the blood pressure cuff around her upper arm and rested her forearm on his. Her aroma was powdery and moist. Her breath had the acrid edge of anxiety. "Your sleep hasn't gotten any better? And your distress rating is still up there near where it was last time. You checked your mood on this problem list, and your family. That's new."

"I just don't see myself ready to take care of my grandbaby. I can't do that to my daughter. She moved up from Miami to have this baby here so I could help her out. She can't quit her job. Christine told her, 'Don't count on your mama,' but she came anyway."

Tears welled up. She tried sipping her drink, but put it back down. "I can't be like this. She delivers next month."

He ushered her up onto the examining table and quickly ran his stethoscope through his routine positions, front and back. "Your mood's down but you're holding your own with your blood pressure, still around 90, your diastolic I mean. And your weight's the same. How many days in the week do you have trouble getting out of bed?" He grabbed the ophthalmoscope from the wall behind him and zeroed in to get a look at the remnants of her floater.

"[long pause] Most days, I guess. Some days I don't get out of my bedclothes till noon."

"Your floater's half the size it was a month ago. That's no octopus anymore. I think you should start driving again."

She looked at him, incredulous, and said nothing. He stood by her, his right hand lingering on her shoulder. She heaved with a sigh, and he then moved both hands swiftly over her pulses from

her neck to her wrists to her feet. Then fluttering his fingers high and low at arm's length in front of her, he checked the visual fields of both eyes to make sure he wasn't jumping the gun.

He said, "You've got a lot of work to do, and you might need a car to do some of it. The season's about to start and you're late for spring training."

A half-smile cracked across her face. "I walked my neighbor's dog for a while."

"When was that? How'd you like it?"

"Right after I saw you last time. She fell and broke her hip, so she asked me could I walk her dog. I walked that dog around the block and down to the park and every which way. That puppy got a crush on me." She winked at him, then her gaze dropped to her hands. "Then it rained, and a few times I forgot, so I guess she called her daughter to walk her dog. I guess that's best."

He helped her down to the chair, moved to the desk, opened her chart, and set up the orders section. "For now we're going to raise that new blood pressure medicine, metoprolol, up a notch. So pick up your prescription for the higher dose. That dog gets you walking and you like it. You could call up your neighbor and offer to help again. What else can you do to get ready to watch a baby eight hours a day?"

She was silent, apparently stuck with her eyes in her lap. He handed her a laminated sheet with a questionnaire on it and a dry marker. He said, "These are some common symptoms people experience with depression. Circle how frequently each of these has bothered you over the past two weeks. It may help us decide a few next steps."

He entered her Distress Thermometer score into the chart, typed some notes, and when she handed him the laminated PHQ 9 form, he entered her score of 14.

"This tells us you're struggling with a moderate level of depressive symptoms. Could be worse. You're not thinking about suicide,

and you have some good days, right? But most days you're bothered by poor sleep and fatigue and low mood and no interest or pleasure in much of anything, right?"

The tears welled up again and she wiped them away.

He said, "Let's see what we can do to get you more restful sleep and lift your depression so you can get ready for your grandbaby. What do you think about raising the dose of that antidepressant you were on last year, citalopram, to 20 mg each morning? And any night you can't fall asleep in half an hour, take this medication, trazodone 50 mg. It should help you get some restful sleep through the night. You can take it every night if you want for the first month. We'll call you in a couple of weeks to make sure you're okay with these medication changes and check on any side effects. I want to see you again in four weeks."

She blew her nose and started packing her purse. He was already late for his next appointment, and he knew it was stretching his luck to add a new item to her treatment plan, but he also knew she would need more than a phone call in two weeks to keep up any momentum generated by this visit.

He said, "You've got some catching up to do and you're already doing some of it. So I'm going to ask my assistant to come back in. She's going to give you another short questionnaire, the ACE scale, about your childhood, and talk with you about the Diabetes Prevention Program, which is designed to help people like you avoid or delay developing diabetes. Once a week group meetings and a coach. Interested?"

"How's that going to keep that octopus out of my eye, Dr. Good?" She was standing now, her purse dangling from one arm and a fistful of tissues in the other hand.

"That depends on how hard you work your program." He reached down and handed her the cup from behind the leg of her chair.

"That's my Dr Pepper. He's cheaper and easier than you are. I see him many times each day," she said, patting her belly.

"If you work this program, you might be able to cut back on some of your medications and see less of Dr Pepper. If you can avoid developing diabetes like your sister and your mama, you'll have a better chance of avoiding floaters and all the other nasty things that come with that disease and make it hard to take care of a baby. Would you do that for your grandbaby?"

"If you pay me," she said, with a wink, sitting back down. He winked back at her and left the room. She has a good point, he thought to himself. If we paid our patients to participate in these lifestyle interventions, more would do it. $100, $500, $1,000? What's the right price for prevention? Who should pay? After twelve minutes with her he was only five minutes late for checking on the teenage mother in room 7 whose labor had stalled. So far, this was a good day.

When Mrs. B came back a month later for her third visit, Dr. Good walked into the room knowing from a chat with his assistant that her weight was down two pounds, her diastolic was under 85 on two readings, her distress rating was down from 5 last time to a 2, her PHQ 9 score was down to a 10 from 14, and her ACE scale score from last time was 3. The report from the ophthalmologist had confirmed resolution of the floater with no evidence of diabetic retinopathy. And she'd brought baby pictures.

Mrs. B flashed her phone at him with the bundled infant filling the frame. "Janelle came a week early, Doc. Ready or not, I'm on the job when my daughter goes back to work."

"Congratulations. How'd you do it?"

"I didn't do nothing. My daughter did all the work!"

"I mean how did you get so ready? You're looking good and all your numbers are looking good."

"Is that right? You think I'm going to make it?"

"If you can keep doing whatever you're doing. What's your secret?"

She smiled. "I got no secret. I just take my medication. And a few weeks ago I started that class at the Y she told me about. Had the third one yesterday. It's not too bad."

"What's the chance you'll go next week?"

"I paid my money, I better show up. They lock you in that way."

"How much?"

"$429 for a year. My daughter paid half, so what choice do I have? That buys me a membership at the Y, and her too. We might need their childcare someday if I can't haul my ass out of bed."

"How much has that been a problem since I saw you last? You reported on your PHQ 9 that you're sleeping better, not so tired?"

"I took that white pill every night for a while. Knocked me over the fence, so after a couple of weeks of sleeping like mud, I said enough of that. A night's rest is the Lord's medicine."

They talked about her ACE scale score, and she told him about her playboy daddy and Uncle Binkie and her lifelong weight problem. After ten minutes he said to her, "Mrs. B, it's been a long road, and now you're on the road to recovery. Can you feel it? We've got a plan that seems to be working if you can keep it going. You're sleeping at night and walking your neighbor's dog again. All your numbers are moving in the right direction. And you've got yourself into a program that can help you start moving and losing in ways that will lower your chance of diabetes."

"You gonna get rid of me now, Doc?" she said with a laugh.

"No getting rid of you. We're just getting started. We'll be at this a few years. My assistant's going to call you each month to check on how you're doing and get a few numbers. Just a five-minute phone call to make sure you're making progress and to answer any of your questions. I'll see you in three months."

This scenario required a more complex set of assessments and negotiations about treatment than Scenario A to manage the depression that was undermining her progress. A combination of medicine (metoprolol, citalopram, and trazodone), social (the DPP

referral), and psychologic interventions (supportive counseling by her primary care doctor) were guided by a combination of physical and psychological measures. Her Distress Thermometer scores led to a series of PHQ 9 scores and an ACE scale that quickly, in the context of measures of her weight, blood pressure, blood sugar, vision, floater size, and retinal pathology, helped Dr. Good place the current moderate depressive episode in the framework of her life story.

They started the process of building a self-management plan that could give her a chance to beat the odds against her, and possibly to prevent or delay diabetes. And the self-management for her diabetes served well for her depression. This particular blend of medications, counseling, and behavior change over several months helped her recover her capacity to regulate her stress response system, which she experienced as regaining the resilience to tend to her grandbaby.

Complexities in Primary Care

- Initial stages of toxic stress are best managed in primary care.
- Blend counseling, medications, and behavior change.
- Daily self-management plans are an essential part of retraining the stress response system.
- Monitoring progress builds hope and effort.

Everyone loves it when treatment works, and it's especially gratifying when, in spite of the frustration of her initial efforts, now everyone – patient, doctor, assistant, daughter, DPP group, and consulting ophthalmologist – is engaged in a plan that works. But what do we do when the revised plan does not work? These are the people and the processes that cost time and money and effort for everyone involved.

Scenario C: Collaborative Care?

Rewind yet again. When Mrs. B came back a month later for her third visit, Dr. Good walked into the exam room knowing from a chat with his assistant that her weight was up four pounds, her diastolic was 90 and 94 on two readings, her distress rating was still at 5, her PHQ 9 score was 15 today, and her ACE scale score from last time was 3.

The report from the ophthalmologist had confirmed resolution of the floater with no evidence of diabetic retinopathy. Christine sat in the corner chair with a book in her lap, and Mrs. B sat in the chair next to his stool and desk. The energy in the room was so low he just settled onto his stool and said, "Tell me how you've been."

After a long pause and a glance at her sister, Mrs. B said, "I wasn't going to make it today, until my chauffeur came to get me out of my bedclothes."

Christine gave me a knowing look and returned to the book in her lap.

He said, "So it's still a struggle getting out of bed? How's your daughter?"

"She's all right. She had her baby a week early. Baby's all right too. Nice girl, she fusses a lot."

"Her name?"

"Janelle."

"Are you still planning on helping out with Janelle when your daughter goes back to work?"

"If she'll let me."

"You don't know?"

"We haven't talked."

"Are you taking the citalopram and trazodone?"

"One in the morning, one at night."

The downward pressure in the room seemed to pull harder with each utterance, as though there was a sinkhole in the floor draining the life from each of them. Dr. Good stood up, feeling a shade

279

heavier himself, and ushered her up to the examining table. With one hand on her left shoulder and the other pressing his stethoscope over her aortic valve, he escaped into the thrum of her chest, lingering longer than usual while he rehearsed their options: hospitalization, specialty referral, or collaborative care?

With his two hands he held the inert heaviness of her slumping shoulder while absorbing the frantic rush of her heartbeats, estimating them at about 96 beats per minute with occasional skips. This soundtrack added to his sense of urgency.

"Give me some deep breaths," he whispered, and he noted as she drew in that he, too, drew in a long one. He caught himself stalling, his attention drifting away to the Indian wedding ceremony he had attended last weekend. He pulled his stethoscope off his ears and helped her back down to the chair.

"We need to do more for you," he said, moving to the desk and opening her chart. "Let's see if we can get Heidi Baker to step in here for a moment to meet you. She's our diabetes care manager and she knows a lot about depression too. She runs our Diapression program and works in the Resilience Center." He paused to tap a text message on his phone.

"The other thing we checked on after your last visit was your thyroid. Your TSH was a bit high, 14 – not too bad but you may have hypothyroidism. Low thyroid activity might explain part of why you've had a hard time getting back on your feet."

Christine chimed in, "Mama had low thyroid. Took medication for it many years."

"It can run in families, sometimes mistaken for depression. We'll add Synthroid to help you get your pep back. It's not the whole story, but maybe a part."

Christine said, "Tell him the other part."

Mrs. B dropped her gaze to the floor again and waited. "My daughter never said anything about it, but when Janelle came early, they found cocaine in her urine. How can that be, Doc? How can

she act so normal and work her job 9 to 5 and be taking crack all that time and none of us know? How can I take care of a crack baby, fussing day and night? What if they take Janelle away to foster care?"

He felt that downward drag again, now with the edge of Mrs. B's anger. They all sat immobile when the knuckle hit the door and in walked Heidi Baker, RN. Sensing the interruption, she stopped with just one foot forward and glanced at Dr. Good, who waved her in.

After introductions he said, "Mrs. B's granddaughter was born just last week. Mrs. B is planning on helping with childcare, but she's struggling with getting out of bed and low motivation all around. She's feeling pressure to prove to the county that she can take care of her grandbaby if her daughter goes into rehab for cocaine. I think her A1C of 6.1 and her PHQ 9 of 15 qualify her for our Diapression program, right?"

"Right." She looked at Dr. Good and then at Christine and back at Mrs. B again. They all seemed to be begging her to fill the void. "Mrs. B, could you stay for another fifteen minutes after you finish with Dr. Good? I can wrap up this other visit and come back here to talk with you about how we can get you started in the program."

Dr. Good spelled out the key parts of the program: Weekly appointments here with the care manager, Heidi Baker, either in person or on the phone. Weekly appointments next door at the Resilience Center with the clinical psychologist for counseling for depression and education about how depression affects diabetes. Learning how to do daily monitoring of moods, activities, and calories. A home visit by the nutritionist and the psychologist. Transportation vouchers for the DPP classes. And monthly case reviews by her team to make sure she's progressing with both her prediabetes and her depression.

"Seems like a lot?" he said. "It's a part-time job, and it doesn't pay right away. You up for it?"

Mrs. B glanced at Christine, who gave her a firm look.

"What's it gonna cost me?"

"Time and effort mostly. Your insurance should cover the appointments, but it will mean more copays."

Christine said, "We can help with that part."

Mrs. B looked up to the ceiling, squeezed her eyes shut, blew a long breath out, and said, "I can try."

A Stepped Care

- Poor or partial response to primary care leads to collaborations with specialty care.
- Decisions about next steps are most efficient when guided by systematic monitoring.
- Scarce resources for specialty care are best allocated to those who don't respond to primary care.

This visit took no longer than the Scenario B visits because the measures of Mrs. B's distress quickly gave Dr. Good a clear picture of her lack of response to his initial efforts to treat her. Her demeanor and the presence of her sister immediately spelled difficulties, the specifics of which he was quickly able to elicit in a way that led to their negotiating a plan for intensifying her treatment through the collaborative care Diapression program and the Resilience Center next door.

This efficiency about complex psychosocial problems is only possible in settings where stress measurement is a routine part of the practice culture, easily documented in the chart, and supported by resources for managing severe stressors, in this case recurrent depression and an addiction in the family. The medical assistant, nurse, and physician conversed as easily about distress, clinical depression, and childhood adversities as they did about hypertension, diabetes, and thyroid disease.

This efficiency in the management of stress-related conditions depends on the availability of resources to address complex health

issues that exist at the same time, such as Mrs. B's hypertension, hypothyroidism, depression, obesity, and prediabetes. Without these resources, these conversations don't happen as readily or with such good outcomes.

The proximity and readiness of the Diapression program and the Resilience Center in the same building made Dr. Good's appointment shorter and more effective than if he had had to patch together a plan on his own. And for Mrs. B, expanding the treatment team to the care manager and the Resilience Center allowed her to build her plan on her relationship with Dr. Good and to keep the depression treatment tied in with her diabetes prevention.

These specific scenarios illustrate a few key points for effective conversations between doctors and their patients about toxic stress. Alternate scenarios with different people, symptoms, problems, goals, resources, and resistances to treatment could illustrate these points just as well. At each level of complexity the same principles drive the treatment planning process.

First, these scenarios begin with efforts to clarify what the patient wants. What are her goals (a) for this appointment, (b) for this course of treatment, and (c) for life? What gives her a sense of purpose?

Sometimes this is a short conversation, and sometimes, when patients don't know what they want or the doctor and patient don't know each other well, it may take several visits or more to clarify these goals. Understanding the stress process begins with understanding the gaps between the goals and the current reality. Effective clinicians find ways to balance their own goals for the practice of good medicine with the goals of their patients, and then they narrow the gaps between the current reality and their shared goals.

Second, when the system of care is designed to identify patients with severe or persistent distress and stress-related conditions, brief screening measures help raise the signal for clinicians and

patients in timely ways. The patient's perception of distress is often a better predictor of poor health than the number or severity of stress exposures, but both are helpful for the big picture.

Third, for those who report high levels of distress, the next step is to start building the stress profile through simple self-report stress measures. For Mrs. B this was achieved by adding to her Distress Thermometer and ACE scale scores, a series of PHQ 9s to better describe the severity and progress of her depression. Her blood pressures, TSH, and hemoglobin A1Cs also clarified the state of her cardiovascular and endocrine systems. This first step toward a stress profile then guides risk stratification (low, medium, or high risk), the selection of targets for reducing the stress burden (depressive symptoms, sleep, transportation, and others), the selection of treatment methods for reducing the stress burden (antidepressant medication, counseling, exercise, and other tools), and the monitoring of the effectiveness of these treatment methods.

Fourth, the payoff for this approach to stress in chronic illness comes through the process of negotiating plans for reducing stress exposures or responses and for building resilience. The art of motivating people to engage in self-management for chronic conditions is one of the skills that differentiates the great clinicians from the good ones. It begins with understanding what a person wants in both the short and the long run and then requires helping them find the team of people that can join them in this project.

It often takes a village to manage a chronic condition. This process is best achieved in primary care through a series of fifteen- to thirty-minute appointments over a period of three to six months, sometimes years. In these appointments, stress management is consistently among the high-priority items on the agenda for patients with severe or persistent distress. Continuity of care with the same doctor or team is the vessel that floats this boat.

Written stress management plans that are an integral part of the overall treatment plan and are revised at each visit will guide

the conversations, the clinician's priorities, and the daily self-management efforts by the patient. These begin as simple plans in primary care and become more complex in the hands of mental health specialists. Variations on this process also take place in well-designed group programs, such as Ornish's Undo It program, the Diabetes Prevention Program, and the better weight management programs.

Across the spectrum, as the severity and complexity of stress profiles increases, the patient and clinician must expect that the number of clinicians contributing to the treatment plan and the range of expertise needed will also increase. This is behavioral medicine (or Lifestyle Medicine) at its most powerful, when it guides a person's overhaul of daily living habits by replacing toxic stress with greater resilience. The same approach works for many chronic conditions because the underlying "dis-ease" is being restored at the level of their common denominator, the stress response system, as well as the disease-specific problem. That's comprehensive care at its best.[1]

Of course, the Resilience Center does not exist today. Is there any promise that such a center will emerge soon near you? In the appendix, for those of you who are curious, I outline how a Resilience Center might work, and the current barriers to creating one. Until then, what do we do next to care for ourselves in the grip of toxic stress?

Part V

Our Next Frontier

14

· · · · ·

Next Steps for Our Next Frontier

In 2014 Bessel van der Kolk wrote in the epilogue of *The Body Keeps the Score*, "We are on the verge of becoming a trauma-conscious society." The truth of this observation is supported by his book remaining on the *New York Times* bestseller list nearly ten years later. And now the COVID-19 pandemic may have brought us to the verge of becoming a stress-conscious society, all around the globe, at least for a promising moment.

But consciousness is just one of the early steps toward culture change. Change (remember healthcare reform?) is sorely needed in the culture of modern medicine. As the last few chapters of this book have shown, some early adopters of effective ways of treating complex stress-related conditions have marked the way toward culture change, while the rest of modern medicine continues its more traditional and less effective approaches. This situation calls for equal measures of hope, action, and patience.

This book should give us hope that it is both possible and necessary for us to understand the stress response system in health and illness. We can learn to speak and think more clearly about stress exposures and stress responses. We can measure stress in ways that allow us to identify patterns of stress that are toxic and likely to lead to illness, long before the first heart attack or weight loss surgery. And through daily self-management plans, we can retrain our dysregulated stress response systems in ways that build resilience, whether we struggle with diabetes, chronic pain, depression, addictions, or disabling functional tremors.

To turn hope into health we need to take action on both a personal level and a social level by advocating for change in our healthcare systems. This kind of action begins in conversations with your primary care doctor about your conditions and how stress affects their course and the choices you have to make. In our doctors' offices we can insist on simple stress measures at first and more complex measures as needed.

Changing the course of any chronic condition is easier if we do it early, before the condition has advanced and turned complicated or become suddenly three conditions. And stress logs can clarify whether stress is having a measurable impact on the course of our conditions.

For most stress-related disorders, action will mean practice – most days practicing some habits that reduce your risks (dancing, calling a friend, meditating, counting your blessings, monitoring a key measure of your illness). Habits are hard to break and hard to make, so recruit a friend, a family member, or a pro to coach you in the early stages until these habits make your day.

And then keep going. For months, many months, and preferably for the long run, once you've found the combination that works to build your resilience against the conditions that threaten your health. You're retraining your stress response system, returning your conductor to your orchestra. Once you've recovered,

preventing the next episode becomes your priority, which is best achieved by continuing what led to your recovery.

It will also take action and advocacy to create the kinds of Resilience Centers that we need for people who have complex stress-related conditions. Like pain clinics and weight loss centers, these Resilience Centers (see the appendix) could concentrate experts, equipment, and programs in one location where people can develop comprehensive and intensive treatment plans.

We individuals can't create these centers alone. Some alliance of patient advocacy groups, committed clinician leaders, and health-care system administrators is likely to be necessary to build the momentum needed to create the model and then expand the numbers of Resilience Centers.

The seeds are already planted. There are at least seven guiding examples that come close in one way or another to the kind of Resilience Center we need.[1] Each of these praiseworthy examples represents an effort by teams of exceptional talent and vision to promote resilience in a select group of people at risk. None represents a standard of care either locally or nationally, and none aims to tackle the enormous problem of improving chronic illness care for a large number of people in their system or their region.

And since it is clear that large numbers of people are exposed to toxic levels of stress for long periods of time – about one in five of us – it's time to consider making toxic stress the focus of our next public health frontier.[2] In my lifetime the culture of medicine has changed dramatically for the better, due to public health campaigns against heart disease, smoking, and cancer. Now is the time for us to advocate for turning our public health resources to focus on the frontier of toxic stress and stress-related conditions. If not now in the wake of COVID, when?

Of course, all this hope and action requires much patience. In Dr. Harris's 2018 book *The Deepest Well* she imagines in her epilogue a future that includes "The Resilience Investment Act of 2020," a hope

that by that year the US government would have invested in large-scale funding for resilience efforts. Now several years later there is no sign yet of such an effort. But someday, somewhere, somehow....

In this book we have seen that the struggle that dysregulates our stress response systems is a long one, often many decades long. And the journey to recovery is also long, favoring the person with patience. Complex systems like our stress response system and our healthcare system take a long time and much care to improve. We now have what we need to improve them both.

Appendix

Imagining the Resilience Center

Though most of us, whether physicians or patients, may be able to appreciate the value of a Resilience Center for people like Mrs. B, as introduced as a resource for her treatment in the last scenario of chapter 13, we are not able to create such a resource. However, it's a useful thought exercise to imagine what it would take to create such a Resilience Center, because it shows us where we are and how we need to improve the ways we manage toxic stress.

Toxic stress is both an individual problem and a public health problem. Is there a way to approach toxic stress on a large scale?

The premise for this exercise is the premise of this book: that our most common and costly epidemics of chronic illness are often initiated and perpetuated by profound, persistent, and difficult-to-measure dysregulations of the stress response system. Specific types of dysregulation distinguish one disorder from another, but most chronic conditions share dysregulations in several parts of the stress response system.

As noted in the chapters on treatment, the shared features of the most effective regimens for reversing heart disease and diabetes are also effective for reversing depression, obesity, hypertension, functional neurological disorders, and PTSD. How effective these programs are for a broader range of conditions deserves to be studied.

Here's one way of sketching where we are currently: a sample of seven promising sites in the US that come close in one way or another to the kind of Resilience Center we need. Here's what they do and how they fall short of our needs:

- Columbia University in a partnership with West Point Academy runs a Resilience Center for Veterans and Families[1] under the direction of George Bonanno, PhD, one of the lead researchers on resilience. The laudable mission of this center is to help military veterans and their families develop resilience as they transition from active duty to civilian status, but it does not focus on the care of chronic illnesses for this niche of the military population.

- Harvard's Center for the Developing Child, located in the Harvard School of Public Health,[2] concentrates a range of disciplines on the dilemmas of childhood adversity, through research and community intervention projects. While this center supports projects that bolster resilience in children, it does not focus on reducing risks for chronic illness, and its scope is limited to children.

- UCLA's Nathanson Family Resilience Center[3] offers resiliency training for families facing challenges. Directed by Patricia Lester, MD, a child psychiatrist, this center provides clinical care for families and conducts research, but does not focus on reducing risks for chronic illness.

- The Veterans Administration provides at all its major medical centers the Primary Care Mental Health Integration Program (PCMHI),[4] a group of mental health specialists who provide mental health care for primary care patients, usually co-located in the same setting with the primary care clinicians. This service improves access to mental health services for primary care patients, but PCMHI has not yet been tasked by the VA to help improve chronic illness outcomes.

- The University of Washington's AIMS Center[5] has provided support for over a thousand organizations implementing various forms of

integrated care in primary care settings. Their TEAMcare model for improving outcomes for depression, diabetes, and heart disease best exemplifies one of the goals of the Resilience Center – namely, improving outcomes for a few specific common chronic illnesses. They are currently working on broadening that model to include a wider range of psychiatric and medical comorbidities.

- Ornish's intensive cardiac rehabilitation programs apply to people with established coronary artery disease. In their 2019 book, *Undo It!* Dean and Anne Ornish describe how their brand of Lifestyle Medicine programs has also prevented diabetes and prostate cancer in people at risk.[6] However, neither their book nor the website for the Preventive Medicine Research Institute identifies clinical practices that routinely provide these services for populations with these three conditions.

- The Benson-Henry Institute for Mind Body Medicine at Massachusetts General Hospital[7] aims to make mind body medicine and self-care an integral part of the MGH healthcare system. Central to its mission is the application of the relaxation response to the clinical care of complex illnesses. It serves as a referral resource while MGH primary care continues with usual care.

Each of these praiseworthy examples represents an effort by teams of exceptional talent and vision to promote resilience in a select group of people at risk. None represents a standard of care either locally or nationally, and none aims to tackle the enormous problem of improving chronic illness care for a large number of people in their system or their region.

Among these sites, the Veterans Administration has established the structures that could potentially deliver resilience services for chronic illness care to veterans on a national scale, the PCMHI programs, but so far the VA has remained focused on improving the process of care; it has not yet adopted at the primary care level incentives that reward better patient outcomes.

Purpose

The purpose of future Resilience Centers will be to provide clinical services and resilience training for people trying to reduce their burden of stress-related chronic illness in cost-effective ways. To be sustainable, the reduced burden must benefit both the patient and the healthcare system that delivers the care.

Funding

Initially, only healthcare systems that are accountable for a specific population that includes large numbers of people with chronic illness will invest in these services. That means that closed systems, such as the national healthcare systems in the UK, Canada, and most of Europe, and the Veterans Administration in the US, are more likely to invest in a service that will reduce their costs and improve their patient outcomes.

Who Gets What?

Because these services, as envisioned, would be complex and expensive, the business plan will often favor initially selecting those patients who use the most resources and cost the most to the system, because they may be the easiest group in which to show cost savings. In general, these Resilience Centers will target patients who meet three criteria:

1. Those with selected stress-related chronic conditions; or at high risk for developing those conditions
2. Those with evidence for severe and persistent distress; or high-risk lifetime stress profiles

3. Those with a demonstrated commitment to participate for six to nine months in a Lifestyle Medicine program.

Staff

The multidisciplinary staff working in Resilience Centers will be a blend of clinicians inclined toward integrated care that weaves mind and body into the same treatment plan. This blend includes nurse care managers, primary care clinicians, psychiatrists, psychologists, social workers, nutritionists, community health workers, peer coaches, data managers, and business managers – all with training and experience in models for delivering integrated care for chronic illness.

These types of clinicians are already scattered throughout large healthcare systems. The Resilience Center will gather them and train them to coordinate their services toward the goal of meeting the system's incentives for improving chronic illness care.

Services

The full menu of options may look like this. Because of local limitations in funding, space, personnel, and patient demands, no one center will provide all these services.

- Patient Education
- Personalized Health Plans
- Stress Screening, Stress Profiles, and Stress Monitoring
- Collaborative Care Management of Specific Conditions
- Stress Management Skills Training
- Group Support
- Individual Psychotherapy

- Psychiatric Care
- Social Work Services
- Personalized Health Data Management.

Whatever the combination of services provided, these services must be integrated into the patient's primary care treatment plan.

Incentives

These Resilience Centers will only emerge if they provide a more cost-effective way to deliver better care with better outcomes for an expensive group of patients. The US national health budget crisis is the big stick that drives competition in the US for more cost-effective models of care. Because chronic illness care is now the most costly item in the US healthcare budget,[8] the spotlight falls on our most costly patients – those with patterns of high utilization and those with multiple chronic conditions.

Healthcare that works is irresistible for most of us. Meaningful treatment invites heroic efforts, even from those with slim odds. That's a powerful incentive to invent the service that can provide a better way to manage chronic illnesses for those with severe and persistent distress, many of whom fill the ranks of the "refractory" or "treatment-resistant." At the very least we should give such people the option to choose between participating for six to nine months in a Resilience Center versus paying for another stent, bypass graft, or life on an insulin pump.

As healthcare reform in the US moves toward more fiscal restraints, it is likely that access to high-cost procedures will be further constrained. For example, access to cardiac bypass graft surgery could be limited to those who have completed a cardiac risk lifestyle change intervention for six to nine months. This is similar to the current restriction on bariatric weight loss surgery, which is

often restricted to people who have demonstrated the capacity to maintain a diet for six months. Access to liver transplantation is currently restricted in some settings to people who have demonstrated the capacity to abstain from alcohol for six months. The expansion of such restrictions for high-cost procedures will drive the demand for Resilience Centers that reduce risks at lower costs and provide a channel for access to scarce resources.

A further incentive comes from the recognition that our major epidemics since the 1990s (heart disease, HIV, obesity, diabetes, depression, ADHD, suicide, opiate addiction, and long COVID) all have well-described roots in severe and persistent distress. It is time to take a more systematic and efficient approach to these stress-related disorders and to those most affected.

Large-scale, early interventions to improve resilience to chronic illness among those at high risk represent an investment in health that is likely to eventually show up in a wide range of benefits across a wide range of costly illnesses. The challenge for services research remains figuring out the optimal timing of the optimal interventions for the optimal benefits. Those estimates will help Resilience Centers set reasonable goals and find sustainable resources.

Barriers

With these broad outlines in mind for the essential features of a Resilience Center, consider the reasons why we currently have no working models for such a comprehensive Resilience Center for chronic illness care. Understanding these barriers provides a platform for considering how to overcome them.

First, few healthcare systems in the US and other developed countries have rewarded their clinicians for good outcomes for chronic illness care. That is, most systems don't regularly collect data on which patients with a particular illness do well or poorly.

Nor do they collect data on which clinicians get better results for their patients with a particular illness. Nor do they pay bonuses to those clinicians with patterns of better outcomes, especially with the more severely ill patients.

As the number of accountable care organizations grows, however, this kind of outcome data is starting to influence small pockets of innovation. When healthcare systems and clinicians become accountable for their results, the incentives flip from rewarding the performance of more revenue-generating procedures to rewarding the prevention of the need for these procedures. When systems and clinicians save more money and make more money by achieving better health outcomes, clinicians change their behaviors to perpetuate these rewards. Finally, the patients become the true beneficiaries of the healthcare system.

Systematic tracking of specific illness outcomes is the first step toward laying this platform for establishing financial incentives for systems and their clinicians to improve care for high-cost patients, especially those with multiple chronic conditions. Currently, it literally does not pay in the US to provide more intensive and effective treatments for most chronic illnesses. No wonder healthcare systems have not invested in a Resilience Center whose mission would be to reduce the need for these revenue-generating procedures.

On the other hand, in a healthcare system that is paying for the procedures it performs, such as the VA or the UK National Health Service, if a Resilience Center could show that it reduced the number of cardiac stents and cardiac bypass grafts performed each year by just 10 percent, it could save a hospital system $1.5 million for every 100 patients who completed the intensive cardiac rehabilitation program. And that sum could pay for the annual salaries of roughly ten clinicians who work in the Resilience Center.[9] But until systems and their clinicians are rewarded for better health outcomes, the current economic incentives in healthcare will oppose the creation of Resilience Centers.

A second barrier to implementing Resilience Centers is the scarcity of the practice of using stress-related screening procedures to identify those at high risk for stress-related chronic illnesses before they develop. Early identification is the key to both primary and secondary prevention. Without systematic screening for toxic stress and a consultation service to generate stress profiles, as discussed in earlier chapters, it is not possible to intervene early on a large scale for those who would most benefit.

A third barrier to establishing Resilience Centers for chronic illness care is the traditional reluctance to engage in population-based primary care. That is, with the exception of a few notable specialty centers that focus on a single disorder, such as the Joslin Diabetes Center, most healthcare systems, and especially their primary care services, take all comers with all illnesses. A primary care clinic with thousands of patients will treat at least fifty common conditions and many rare ones. To establish population-based care within such a primary care clinic, the system has to be able to organize the data to compare care for all patients with the same condition.

Population-based care identifies specific patients with high-risk conditions, such as diabetes or hypertension, and follows them as a group with protocols to make sure they all get the basics of good care for that condition. If a patient misses one of the benchmarks of the protocol, the care manager shepherding those in that registry finds the missing patient and arranges for him or her to catch up on that benchmark of chronic illness care, such as a foot check for diabetes or a depression symptom check for the patient with major depression. Like outcomes-based pay, population-based care is one of the cornerstones needed to justify the creation of Resilience Centers for chronic illness care.

A fourth major barrier to the adoption of Resilience Centers may be the complexity of funding them. The junkheap of good ideas is filled with the unfundable. The question of who would

pay for a Resilience Center reveals the curse of the silo structure of modern medicine. Resilience Centers need to be staffed by many disciplines from many silos: primary care, psychology, psychiatry, physical therapy, social work, nutrition, pharmacy. This structural reality requires cooperation and funding across silos. It may ignite turf battles and leadership competitions and struggles over how the funds flow.

If better primary care for diabetes reduces the number of amputations required, do the savings go to the surgeons or to the primary care clinicians or to the patients in the form of reduced costs of health insurance? Which silo owns the Resilience Center? This is not a new problem. Pain centers and weight loss centers are multidisciplinary services that have struggled across the nation and over many years to establish sustainable business models. Resilience Centers will face the same difficulties.

Planners of Resilience Centers will have to persuade doubters that the evidence for their effectiveness justifies substantial investment. Is the services research data on the cost-effectiveness of these stress management services sufficient? Is the effect of intensive stress management on clinical improvements large enough to pay for itself?

Debates about the data will lead to calls for more definitive research studies. Designs of the definitive research study of the effectiveness of the Resilience Center will stumble over which government agency or private foundations would fund such a study. The answers are not obvious and the precedents are few.

How many randomized controlled trials for one stress-reducing intervention and one disorder will it take to demonstrate a substantial effect on prevention rates? And it will be difficult to generalize from the results of any meta-analysis of many trials of one intervention for one disorder to apply the lessons learned about that intervention to other populations with other disorders. It's complicated. The best we can hope for from services research is incremental

additions of smaller but rigorous studies, each a small brick in the growing behavioral medicine edifice.

The economic reality is that some healthcare systems will not wait for the data from services research or large demonstrations projects because they can't afford to wait. They will take the risk and invent the imagined Resilience Center, and, if it works to gain a competitive advantage in the marketplace, the Resilience Center will grow and multiply. If it fails, it will die. If enough systems prove the concept worthy of imitation, eventually the standard of care will adopt the Resilience Center for systems large enough to support them and benefit from them.

A final barrier to establishing Resilience Centers is stigma. Though stress is less stigmatized in our culture than mental illness, the two are closely related in our collective subconscious. The healthcare culture in the US is gradually improving its acceptance of mental illness, but stigma persists around the globe. The same inclination to dismiss or ignore mental illness contributes to our inclination to dismiss the role of toxic stress. Our reluctance to engage in systematic measurement and management of severe and persistent distress perpetuates both the mystery and the stigma.

Toxic stress is a painful topic – and messy to manage. If we can avoid it or delay attending to it, we will. Making persistent and severe stress more visible and clinically meaningful is one way to reduce the stigma that currently interferes with its management.

If toxic stress is a public health problem, it deserves some public health solutions. Imagining a Resilience Center is one way to think about services that reach large numbers of people.

Acknowledgments

To the countless unnamed people who have shared with me their stories over the years in the hope that I could help them, thanks for what you have shown me about the struggle for health.

And thanks to those who agreed to be interviewed for this book: at the University of Pittsburgh, Tom Kamarck; at the University of California San Francisco and the Preventive Medicine Research Institute, Dean Ornish; at the Cincinnati YMCA's Diabetes Prevention Program, Janella Straw and Christine Zerges; at the Cincinnati Veterans Administration Medical Center, Teresa Langford; at the Benson-Henry Institute, Massachusetts General Hospital, Herbert Benson, Sue Clough, Gregory Fricchione, and Darsan Mehta; at the UMass Memorial Health Center for Mindfulness, Judson Brewer, Diane Horgan, and Lynn Koerbel; at the Trauma Research Foundation, Bessel van der Kolk; at the University of Washington, Jurgen Unutzer; at the University of Cincinnati, James Herman; and at Emory University, Doug Bremner, Tene Lewis, Nancy Murrah, Arshed Quyyumi, and Viola Vaccarino.

For their help clarifying the issues related to measuring stress, thanks go to the members of the American Psychosomatic Society's Task Force on Stress in Primary Care: Beth Cohen, Brooke Jenkins, Lydia Roos, Sarah Sagui-Henson, Amit Shah, George Slavich, and Diana Wang.

My gratitude goes also to my editors at Cambridge University Press, Sarah Marsh and Kim Ingram, and to editor Sandra Wendel of Write On, Inc., as well as illustrator Sue Tyler, for shepherding this book with care.

For their help shepherding this book from conception to publication during the six years I worked on it, I thank the members of our monthly writers' group: Judy DaPolito, Greta Holt, Libby McCord, Don Schenk, Mary Ann Schenk, Ann Charles Watts, and Mary Thomas Watts.

Thanks also to colleagues and writer friends who have guided me during this project and read parts of the manuscript, including John Beardsley, Jim DeBrosse, Phil Diller, Joel Dimsdale, Alberto Espay, Gregory Fricchione, Julian Thayer, and John H. Wulsin Jr.

Special thanks to George E. Vaillant for his loyal mentorship during my career, for his love of the written word, for his talent for turning science into literature, for showing me how to think across the lifespan, and for his helpful attention to every chapter during early drafts.

And of course, my deepest thanks to my wife, Vic, for joining me on each turn of every journey, including this one, which surely started before this book.

Notes

Introduction: Your Body's Hidden Symphony

1 For a scientific review of the mortality associated with severe mental illness, see Walker, McGee, & Druss, 2015.

2 For more on race, discrimination, and mortality risks, see Lewis & Van Dyke, 2018.

3 For more on childhood trauma and risks for chronic illnesses, see www.cdc.gov/violenceprevention/aces/index.html.

4 For more on poverty, social rank, and mortality, see Marmot, 2015.

5 For more on the definition of chronic stress and its impact on physical health, see Epel et al., 2018 *Frontiers in Neuroendocrinology*.

6 For more on US rankings in healthcare, see www.who.int/healthinfo/paper30.pdf and www.commonwealthfund.org/publications/press-releases/2014/jun/us-health-system-ranks-last.

7 For more on the high costs and mediocre performance of the US healthcare system, see Starr, 2013.

1 Toxic Stress – You Won't See It Coming (Neither Will Your Doctor)

1 For more on Kamarck's stress research using ecological momentary assessment, see John-Henderson, Kamarck, Muldoon, & Manuck, 2016; Kamarck, Shiffman, Sutton-Tyrrell, Muldoon, & Tepper, 2012.

2 For more about this *Stress in America* survey, see www.apa.org/news/press/releases/stress/2021/decision-making-october-2021.pdf.

3 For more on stress across the life cycle, see Slavich & Shields, 2018 and www.uclastresslab.org/projects/strain-stress-and-adversity-inventory/.

4 For one example of rankings of countries by health indicators, see www.healthdata.org/research-analysis/health-by-location/profiles.

5 See also Desmond Tutu's *No Future without Forgiveness* (1999) and www.theforgivenessproject.com/.

6 For more on the Global Burden of Disease Study, see www.health data.org/gbd/2019.

7 For more on the data from the Behavioral Risk Factor Surveillance System, see www.cdc.gov/violenceprevention/childabuseandneglect/acestudy/ace-brfss.html.

8 For more on multiple chronic conditions, see Butorff, 2017.

9 For more on the global effects on chronic diseases during the pandemic, see www.healthdata.org/news-events/newsroom/news-releases/lancet-latest-global-disease-estimates-reveal-perfect-storm.

10 For more on US and global poverty rates, see https://blogs .worldbank.org/opendata/introducing-second-edition-world-banks-global-subnational-atlas-poverty.

11 For more on studies of chronic stress and mortality, see Kiecolt-Glaser, 1999; Rutters et al., 2014.

12 Doubters about progress in these areas should read Jeremy Rifkin's *The Empathic Civilization: The Race to Global Consciousness in a World in Crisis* (2009) and Stephen Pinker's *Enlightenment Now: The Case for Reason, Science, Humanism, and Progress* (2018).

13 For a theory about the role of persistent worrying in stress and illness, see Brosschot, Verkuil, & Thayer, 2017.

14 A well-designed study showed that although over 80 percent of smokers had tried to quit in the past year, less than 10 percent had been able to quit for six months. See Messer, Trinidad, Al-Delaimy, & Pierce, 2008.

2 The Mind Matters for Seeing Our Blind Spot

1 The most persuasive arguers for this evolutionary principle have been Hans Selye in *The Stress of Life* (1956) and Robert Sapolsky in *Why Zebras Don't Get Ulcers* (2004).

2 For more on the effect sizes of stress on common chronic illnesses, see Barth, Schumacher, & Herrmann-Lingen, 2004; Cohen, Janicki-Deverts, & Miller, 2007; Sgoifo, Montano, Esler, & Vaccarino, 2017.

3 For the AHA paper on depression as a risk factor for progression of coronary heart disease, see Lichtman et al., 2014. For the AHA paper on screening for depression in heart disease, see Lichtman et al., 2008.

4 For the TIMI risk estimation, see www.mdcalc.com/timi-risk-score-ua-nstemi. For the GRACE risk estimation, see www.mdcalc.com/grace-acs-risk-mortality-calculator. For the FRA risk estimator, see www.mdcalc.com/framingham-risk-score-hard-coronary-heart-disease.

5 For this review of the mortality of depression, see Wulsin, Vaillant, & Wells, 1999.

6 For more on stress as a contributor to declining life expectancy in the US, see Woolf & Schoomaker, 2019.

7 For more on the role of stress in depression, see Kendler, Thornton, & Gardner, 2000.

8 For the article on incremental medicine, see Gawande, 2017.

9 Recent guidelines for the treatment of heart attacks by clinicians in the US can be found in Goff et al., 2014. Guidelines for the treatment of diabetes can be found in American Diabetes, 2018.

10 For more biographical background on Dean Ornish, see Ornish, 2002.

11 For Ornish's first publication of the Lifestyle Heart Trial, see Ornish et al., 1983.

12 For more on adherence rates to the Ornish cardiac rehabilitation programs, see Silberman et al., 2010.

13 Ornish's most recent book *Undo It!* (2019) spells out the multiple pathways by which his programs reverse some chronic illnesses.

3 Before We Climb This Mountain

1 For more on the semantics of "stress," see Kagan, 2016; Koolhaas et al., 2011.

2 A scientific rationale for this definition of duration for chronic stress exposures and responses is provided in Epel et al., 2018 *Frontiers in Neuroendocrinology.*

3 For more on the health effects of earthquakes, see Ripoll Gallardo et al., 2018; Vlek, 2018.

4 For more on resilience, see Bonanno, 2004; Bonanno, Wortman, & Nesse, 2004.

5 For more on the effects of slow heart rate recovery on heart disease and mortality, see Cole, Blackstone, Pashkow, Snader, & Lauer, 1999; Okutucu, Karakulak, Aytemir, & Oto, 2011.

6 For more on allostatic load, see McEwen, 1998, 2017a.

7 For more on the effects of psychological and biological resilience on aging in healthy adults, see Harvanek, Fogelman, Xu, & Sinha, 2021.

8 For more on the barriers and promises of studying risks for multiple chronic conditions, see Suls, Green, & Davidson, 2016.

9 For an annotated repository of state-of-the art research measurements of stress, see https://stresscenter.ucsf.edu/.

10 For more on stress measures as targets for treatment in primary care, see https://aims.uw.edu/resource-library/measurement-based-treatment-target.

11 For this review of the mortality of depression, see Wulsin et al., 1999.

12 For this review of depression as a risk factor for the progression of coronary heart disease, see Lichtman et al., 2014.

13 For more on the current challenges facing behavioral medicine research, see Freedland, 2019.

4 Our Resilient Stress Response System

1 For more on Benson's early scientific publications about the relaxation response, see Benson, Rosner, Marzetta, & Klemchuk, 1974. And see Benson, Beary, & Carol, 1974.

2 For this excellent recent book on stress neuroscience, written for lay readers, see Fricchione, Ivkovic, & Yeung, 2016.

3 For more on the concept of coherence in the stress response system, see McCraty, 2017.

4 For more on these distinctions about good and bad stress, see McEwen, 2017b.

5 For more on Selye's definition of stress, see Selye, 1956:55.

6 For more on the general unsafety theory of stress, see Brosschot et al., 2017.

7 For more on the role of the vagus nerve in stress, attachments, and emotional regulation, see Porges, 2011.

8 For more on a systems approach to the stress response system, see Oken, Chamine, & Wakeland, 2015.

5 Symphony in 10-Flat by Usain Bolt

1 For more on neuroplasticity and neuromodulation techniques, see Doidge, 2015.

6 Resilience for Life – Yours

1 For more on this study of depression and heart attacks, see Galatzer-Levy & Bonanno, 2014.

2 For more examples of the benefits of positive psychology on the course of heart disease, see Kubzansky et al., 2018. A good measure of resilience in clinical studies since the 1990s is the Sense of Coherence Scale. For more on this measure, see Antonovsky, 1993; Madhu, Aslam, Siddiqui, Goyal, & Mishra, 2020.

3 For a summary of the Cigna survey on loneliness, see https://news room.thecignagroup.com/loneliness-in-america.

4 For the review of loneliness, social isolation, and mortality, see Holt-Lunstad, Smith, Baker, Harris, & Stephenson, 2015.

5 For Murthy's article on work and loneliness, see Murthy, 2017.

6 For the article citing the doubling of rates of loneliness, see www .nytimes.com/2016/12/22/upshot/how-social-isolation-is-kill ing-us.html#:~:text=Loneliness%20can%20accelerate%20cogni tive%20decline,after%20controlling%20for%20other%20factors.

7 Lichtman et al., 2014.

8 For more on the relationship between stress and depression, see Penninx, 2017.

9 For more on mortality in mental illness, see Olfson, Gerhard, Huang, Crystal, & Stroup, 2015; Walker et al., 2015.

10 For more on the effect of childhood maltreatment on cellular aging, see Tyrka et al., 2010. For more on telomeres and stress and aging, see Blackburn, Epel, & Lin, 2015; Epel & Prather, 2018.

11 For more on the measurement of biological aging to predict chronic disease, see Belsky et al., 2015.

12 For more on longevity studies and principles for longer living, see www.healthyat100.org and www.bluezonesproject.com.

7 Fast Tracks to Dying Young

1 For more on Cohen's studies of stress, the immune system, and health, see Cohen, 2021; Cohen, Tyrrell, & Smith, 1991; Cohen et al., 2012.

2 Other hormones in turmoil include insulin, glucagon, testosterone, LH and FSH, growth hormone, and oxytocin.

3 For more on the gene switching of epigenetics, see Nestler, 2011.

4 For more on the epigenetics of stress in humans, see Epel & Prather, 2018; Zannas & Chrousos, 2017. For a review of evidence from animal studies supporting epigenetic changes in chronic stress, see Stankiewicz, Swiergiel, & Lisowski, 2013.

5 For the study of childhood trauma, DNA methylation, and depression, see Peng et al., 2018.

6 For more on perinatal interventions that improve infant outcomes, see Norona-Zhou et al., 2022.

7 For an account of the struggle to popularize the ACE concept in the US, see Harris, 2018; for websites devoted to ACEs, see www .acestoohigh.com and www.pacesconnection.com.

8 For more on the effects of toxic relationships on health, see Bourassa, Ruiz, & Sbarra, 2019; Ditzen et al., 2019; Smith, 2019.

9 For more on this study of amygdala activity and cardiovascular events, see Tawakol et al., 2017. For the association between income and hippocampal volume, see Hanson, Chandra, Wolfe, & Pollak, 2011.

10 Complex systems find many ways to bend or eventually break down. The central nervous system and autonomic nervous system "bend" under persistent demands. Repeated interruptions of natural rhythms is one way to bend or break the central nervous system. Workers who switch shifts frequently have higher rates of absences, sick leave, and insurance claims for healthcare visits.

11 For more on Kevin Tracey and vagus nerve stimulation, see Tracey, 2015.

12 For more on atrophy of the hippocampus and amygdala during depression, see Cole, Costafreda, McGuffin, & Fu, 2011; Hamilton, Siemer, & Gotlib, 2008.

13 For more on blunted HPA responses to challenges in chronic illness, see www.sciencedirect.com/topics/medicine-and-dentistry/ dexamethasone-suppression-test.

14 For more on the associations between chronic inflammation and chronic illnesses, see Cohen et al., 2007; McEwen et al., 1997; Miller, Cohen, & Herbert, 1999.

15 For more on this study of the effects of improved parenting on inflammation, see Miller, Brody, Yu, & Chen, 2014.

16 For more on the effects of stress on cell-mediated immunity, see Dhabhar & McEwen, 1997.

8 Scan the Lifespan

1 For more on the Adverse Childhood Experiences Study, see www.cdc .gov/violenceprevention/aces/.

2 For the scientific paper in which we first presented this model, see Wulsin, Herman, & Thayer, 2018.

3 For more on the effects of stress on growth hormone, see chapter 6 of Sapolsky, 2004.

4 For a commentary on the status of the hypothesis about the fetal origins of adult disease, see Eriksson, 2005.

5 Thresholds for metabolic syndrome: BP >=130/85 mmHg; fasting glucose >=110 mg/dL; HDL-C <40 mg/dL (men), <50 (women); triglycerides >=150 mg/dL; waist > 40 in (men), 35 (women).

6 For more on the Diabetes Prevention Program, see www.cdc.gov/ diabetes/prevention/index.html. For more on the Lifestyle Medicine Program, see www.ornish.com.

9 Managing Begins with Measuring

1 For Rousmaniere's article "What your therapist doesn't know," see www.theatlantic.com/magazine/archive/2017/04/what-your-therapist-doesnt-know/517797/.

2 For more on the historical impact of the measurement of pain, see Noble et al., 2005.

3 For a comprehensive review of measures of stress, see Monroe, 2008.

4 For more on the appraisal of stress, see Lazarus, 1984.

5 For more on the Perceived Stress Scale, see Cohen, Kamarck, & Mermelstein, 1983; Cohen et al., 2007; Monroe, 2008.

6 When I reviewed these data with Dr. Kamarck, the principal investigator of the study, he cautioned that Suntech's monitor readings run high, and consequently at the study review Dr. Anderson did not interpret these values as alarming signs of hypertension that required urgent clinical evaluation. Several months later Ted Daley's physician began recording high blood pressure readings in the office visits, suggesting the study may have caught the early stages of his hypertension.

7 For more on the status of this project, see Clark, 2018; Clark et al., 2018.

10 A Peek Inside the Black Box of Stress

1 For more on the history of neuropsychological testing, see Casaletto & Heaton, 2017.

2 For more on resilience and the Brief Resilience Scale, see Smith, Epstein, Ortiz, Christopher, & Tooley, 2013.

3 For a CDC report on the impact of adverse childhood experiences on adult health outcomes in twenty-five states, see www.cdc.gov/media/releases/2019/p1105-prevent-aces.html.

4 For more on the STRAIN or the Life Stress Test, including the measures contained within it, see Slavich & Shields, 2018. How does the STRAIN assemble this profile? It draws on twelve measures: the Life Events and Difficulties Schedule (115 items), the Childhood Trauma Questionnaire (28 items), the Perceived Stress Scale (10 items), socioeconomic status, the Ten Item Personality Inventory, the Social Desirability Scale (17 items), the Positive and Negative Affect Scale (20 items), the Stroop test (of executive function), the Pittsburgh Sleep Quality Inventory (10 items), the Physical Health Questionnaire (14 items), the Psychological Distress Inventory (6 items), and a list of doctor-diagnosed disorders.

5 For more on the first proposal for a measure of allostatic load, see McEwen, 1998; Seeman, Singer, Rowe, Horwitz, & McEwen, 1997.

6 For more on this review of allostatic load measures in the workplace, see Mauss, Li, Schmidt, Angerer, & Jarczok, 2015.

7 For more on recent efforts to find a short form of the allostatic load index, see Mauss, Jarczok, & Fischer, 2015.

8 A promising variation on allostatic load is the more recent measure of "biological age" and the related measure "pace of biological aging," which are described in Belsky et al., 2015.

9 For more on the relative merits of biological aging, allostatic load, and the Framingham Heart Index as measures of risk for mortality, see Levine & Crimmins, 2014.

10 For more on DNA methylation as a measure of biologic aging, see Harvanek et al., 2021; Wang et al., 2022.

11 For more on the status of telomere research and its relationship to stress neuroscience, see Blackburn & Epel, 2017; Blackburn et al., 2015.

12 For more on barriers to assessing measures of stress in primary care, see Wulsin et al., 2022.

13 For the original IOM report (2014), see www.nap.edu/catalog/18951/capturing-social-and-behavioral-domains-and-measures-in-electronic-health-records.

14 For a report on the feasibility of collecting the recommended IOM measures of social determinants of health, see Giuse et al., 2017.

15 Another measure of physiologic stress response, heart rate recovery, is the time it takes at the end of the exercise tolerance test for the heart to return to its resting heart rate after reaching its peak heart rate during exercise. A healthy heart may take ten to fifteen minutes to drop from 160 to 75 beats per minute. A heart with advanced coronary heart disease might require forty-five minutes or more.

16 For more on mental stress-induced ischemia in young women, see Vaccarino et al., 2018.

17 For more on Vaccarino's study of mental stress-induced ischemia as a predictor of worsening coronary heart disease, see Vaccarino et al., 2021.

18 For a review of the current understanding of mental stress-induced ischemia in the larger context of risks for heart disease in women, see Vaccarino & Bremner, 2017.

11 Boot Camps for Our Stress Response Systems

1 For more on the specifics of the Ornish Reversal Program, see www.ornish.com/undo-it.

2 For more on the effects of the Ornish Reversal Program on specific health outcomes, see the collected research posted on www.ornish.com. Search under "research".

3 Insulin resistance is a different pathway to diabetes than the pathway to type 1 or juvenile-onset diabetes, which involves a deficiency in the synthesis of insulin.

4 For more on the NDPPOS outcomes study, see https://repository.niddk.nih.gov/studies/dppos/.

5 For more on the National Diabetes Prevention Program, see www.cdc.gov/diabetes/prevention/index.html.

6 For more on CBT for non-epileptic seizures, see LaFrance et al., 2009.

7 For the report on this pilot study, see Espay et al., 2019.

8 For more on the study of the treatment of bodily stress disorder at Aarhus University, see Schroder et al., 2012.

9 For this meta-analysis of treatments for medically unexplained symptoms, see Schroder, Sharpe, & Fink, 2015.

10 For more on the epidemiology of multiple chronic conditions, see Hajat & Stein, 2018.

11 For more on the development of the collaborative care model, see Katon, Unutzer, Wells, & Jones, 2010.

12 For more on the TEAMcare Study, see Katon, Lin et al., 2010; Katon et al., 2012.

13 An approach to changing high-risk health behaviors that focuses a person's readiness to change in steps that build toward lasting healthier habits. Behavioral activation focuses on practicing behaviors that improve a person's symptoms, such as daily walking to lift mood or reduce pain.

14 For more on the impact of the COMPASS project, see Rossom et al., 2017.

15 For more on the PCL-5 measure, see www.ptsd.va.gov/professional/assessment/adult-sr/ptsd-checklist.asp.

12 Yes, You Can Retrain the Brain

1 For a review of the state of research on meditation, see Stetka, 2017. For a review of the effect of mindfulness on cardiovascular disease risk, see Loucks et al., 2015. And for a recent academic critique of the state of the science of mindfulness research, see Van Dam et al., 2018 and the commentary in Davidson & Dahl, 2018.

2 For a review of the evidence for and against mindfulness-based stress reduction, see Creswell, 2017.

3 For more on the lessons from the Blue Zones Power 9, see www.bluezones.com/live-longer-better/#section-2.

4 For more on Purpose Built Communities and their health benefits, see https://purposebuiltcommunities.org/.

5 For more on the Miller and Chen family intervention study in rural Georgia, see Miller et al., 2014.

6 For more on the ABC Intervention for high-risk children, see Bernard, Hostinar, & Dozier, 2015.

7 For more on oxytocin and stress, see chapter 6 in Fricchione, Ivkovic, & Yeung, 2016.

8 For more on the science and clinical applications of neurofeedback, see chapter 19 in van der Kolk, 2014.

9 For more on the concept of heart coherence and this study of heart rate variability among dementia caregivers, see Sarabia-Cobo, 2015. For more on McCraty's research on heart rate variability biofeedback, see www.heartmath.org/research/.

10 For more on social coherence, see McCraty, 2017.

11 For more on the PoNS and neuromodulation, see Tyler et al., 2014, http://dx.doi.org/10.4236/jbbs.2014.43014, and https://heliusmedical.com/about-pons/.

12 For more on EMDR, see chapter 15 in van der Kolk, 2014.

13 For more on beta-blockers and cancer metastases, see Knight et al., 2016; Knight et al., 2018.

14 For more on CTRA stress genes, see Cole et al., 2015.

15 For more on clinical trials of depression treatments in heart disease, see Liu & Ziegelstein, 2010.

16 Sample chapter headings from *The Telomere Effect*: chapter 5, "Mind your telomeres: negative thinking, resilient thinking"; chapter 6, "Master tips for renewal: stress-reducing techniques shown to boost telomere maintenance"; chapter 7, "Training your telomeres: how much exercise is enough?"; chapter 10, "Food and telomeres: eating for optimal cell health."

17 For more examples of regimens that work, see (1) the In SHAPE Program at www.cdc.gov/prc/study-findings/research-briefs/inshape.htm, (2) the ACHIEVE Study at www.achievestudy.org/, and (3) the STRIDE Study at www.stride-study.org/.

18 For more on the Science of Behavior Change, see https://commonfund.nih.gov/behaviorchange/.

13 Talking about Stress with Your Doctor

1 One of the leading organizations promoting this approach is the American College of Lifestyle Medicine, founded in 2004 by a small group of fewer than 200 members. They now have over 3,000 members and host large annual meetings. For more on this organization's efforts to make Lifestyle Medicine the foundation of health and healthcare, see www.lifestylemedicine.org/.

14 Next Steps for Our Next Frontier

1 Seven guiding examples are the Resilience Center for Veterans and Families at Columbia University, see www.tc.columbia.edu/resiliencecenter/; the Center for the Developing Child at Harvard University, see https://developingchild.harvard.edu/; the Nathanson Family Resilience Center at UCLA, see https://nfrc.ucla.edu/; the Primary Care Mental Health Integration Program at the Veterans Administration, see www.patientcare.va.gov/primarycare/PCMHI .asp; the AIMS Center at the University of Washington, see https://aims.uw.edu/; Ornish Lifestyle Medicine programs, see www .ornish.com/undo-it/; the Benson-Henry Institute, see https:// bensonhenryinstitute.org/.

2 This is not a new idea. In 2014 Mental Health America commissioned a proposal authored by Andrea Blanch, PhD, David Shern, PhD, and Sarah Steverman, PhD, MSW, titled "Toxic stress, behavioral health, and the next public health era." For more on this proposal for a public health campaign on toxic stress, see Shern, Blanch, & Steverman, 2016.

Appendix

1 For more on the Resilience Center for Veterans and Families at Columbia University, see www.tc.columbia.edu/resiliencecenter/.

2 For more on the Center for the Developing Child at Harvard University, see https://developingchild.harvard.edu/.

3 For more on the Nathanson Family Resilience Center at UCLA, see https://nfrc.ucla.edu/.

4 For more on the Primary Care Mental Health Integration Program at the Veterans Administration, see www.patientcare.va.gov/primarycare/PCMHI.asp.

5 For more on the AIMS Center at the University of Washington, see https://aims.uw.edu/.

6 For more on Ornish Lifestyle Medicine programs, see www.ornish .com/undo-it/.

7 For the website of the Benson-Henry Institute, see https:// bensonhenryinstitute.org/.

8 The Centers for Disease Control (July 2020) estimated that 90 percent of US healthcare expenditures is spent on chronic diseases, see www.cdc.gov/chronicdisease/about/costs/index.htm.

9 This simplistic estimate is based on assuming a mean cost of a cardiac bypass graft is $150,000 and a mean salary for a clinician is $100,000. In any true case, the cost ranges will be wide and many other factors will influence the equation.

References

American Diabetes Association (2018). Improving care and promoting health in populations: standards of medical care in Diabetes – 2018. *Diabetes Care, 41*(Suppl. 1), S1–S12. doi:10.2337/dc18-Sint01

Antonovsky, A. (1993). The structure and properties of the sense of coherence scale. *Social Science and Medicine, 36*(6), 725–733. doi:10.1016/0277-9536(93)90033-z

Barth, J., Schumacher, M., & Herrmann-Lingen, C. (2004). Depression as a risk factor for mortality in patients with coronary heart disease: a meta-analysis. *Psychosomatic Medicine, 66*(6), 802–813. doi:10.1097/01.psy.0000146332.53619.b2

Belsky, D. W., Caspi, A., Houts, R., Cohen, H. J., Corcoran, D. L., Danese, A., ... Moffitt, T. E. (2015). Quantification of biological aging in young adults. *Proceedings of the National Academy of Sciences of the United States of America, 112*(30), E4104–E4110. doi:10.1073/pnas.1506264112

Benson, H., Beary, J. F., & Carol, M. P. (1974). The relaxation response. *Psychiatry, 37*(1), 37–46. www.ncbi.nlm.nih.gov/pubmed/4810622

Benson, H., & Klipper, M. (1976). *The Relaxation Response.* Mass Market Paperback.

Benson, H., Rosner, B. A., Marzetta, B. R., & Klemchuk, H. M. (1974). Decreased blood-pressure in pharmacologically treated hypertensive patients who regularly elicited the relaxation response. *Lancet, 1*(7852), 289–291. www.ncbi.nlm.nih.gov/pubmed/4130474

Bernard, K., Hostinar, C. E., & Dozier, M. (2015). Intervention effects on diurnal cortisol rhythms of Child Protective Services – referred infants in early childhood: preschool follow-up results of a randomized clinical trial. *JAMA Pediatrics, 169*(2), 112–119. doi:10.1001/jamapediatrics.2014.2369

Blackburn, E., & Epel, E. (2017). *The Telomere Effect: Living Younger, Healther, Longer.* Grand Central Publishing.

Blackburn, E. H., Epel, E. S., & Lin, J. (2015). Human telomere biology: a contributory and interactive factor in aging, disease risks, and protection. *Science, 350*(6265), 1193–1198. doi:10.1126/science.aab3389

Bonanno, G. A. (2004). Loss, trauma, and human resilience: have we underestimated the human capacity to thrive after extremely aversive events? *American Psychologist, 59*(1), 20–28. doi:10.1037/0003-066X.59.1.20

Bonanno, G. A., Wortman, C. B., & Nesse, R. M. (2004). Prospective patterns of resilience and maladjustment during widowhood. *Psychology and Aging, 19*(2), 260–271. doi:10.1037/0882-7974.19.2.260

Borysenko, J. (1988). *Minding the Body, Mending the Mind.* Bantam.

Bourassa, K. J., Ruiz, J. M., & Sbarra, D. A. (2019). The impact of physical proximity and attachment working models on cardiovascular reactivity: comparing mental activation and romantic partner presence. *Psychophysiology,* e13324. doi:10.1111/psyp.13324

Brosschot, J. F., Verkuil, B., & Thayer, J. F. (2017). Exposed to events that never happen: generalized unsafety, the default stress response, and prolonged autonomic activity. *Neuroscience and Biobehavioral Reviews, 74*(Pt B), 287–296. doi:10.1016/j.neubiorev.2016.07.019

Buettner, D. (2012). *The Blue Zones: 9 Lessons for Living Longer from the People Who've Lived the Longest.* National Geographic (second edition).

Butorff, C. (2017). *Multiple Chronic Conditions in the United States.* Rand Corporation.

Casaletto, K. B., & Heaton, R. K. (2017). Neuropsychological assessment: past and future. *Journal of the International Neuropsychological Society, 23*(9–10), 778–790. doi:10.1017/S1355617717001060

Clark, D. M. (2018). Realizing the mass public benefit of evidence-based psychological therapies: the IAPT Program. *Annual Review of Clinical Psychology, 14,* 159–183. doi:10.1146/annurev-clinpsy-050817-084833

Clark, D. M., Canvin, L., Green, J., Layard, R., Pilling, S., & Janecka, M. (2018). Transparency about the outcomes of mental health services (IAPT approach): an analysis of public data. *Lancet, 391*(10121), 679–686. doi:10.1016/S0140-6736(17)32133-5

Cohen, S. (2021). Psychosocial vulnerabilities to upper respiratory infectious illness: implications for susceptibility to Coronavirus Disease

2019 (COVID-19). *Perspectives on Psychological Science, 16*(1), 161–174. doi:10.1177/1745691620942516

Cohen, S., Janicki-Deverts, D., Doyle, W. J., Miller, G. E., Frank, E., Rabin, B. S., & Turner, R. B. (2012). Chronic stress, glucocorticoid receptor resistance, inflammation, and disease risk. *Proceedings of the National Academy of Sciences of the United States of America, 109*(16), 5995–5999. doi:10.1073/pnas.1118355109

Cohen, S., Janicki-Deverts, D., & Miller, G. E. (2007). Psychological stress and disease. *JAMA, 298*(14), 1685–1687. doi:10.1001/jama.298.14.1685

Cohen, S., Kamarck, T., & Mermelstein, R. (1983). A global measure of perceived stress. *Journal of Health and Social Behavior, 24*(4), 385–396. www.ncbi.nlm.nih.gov/pubmed/6668417

Cohen, S., Tyrrell, D. A., & Smith, A. P. (1991). Psychological stress and susceptibility to the common cold. *New England Journal of Medicine, 325*(9), 606–612. doi:10.1056/NEJM199108293250903

Cole, C. R., Blackstone, E. H., Pashkow, F. J., Snader, C. E., & Lauer, M. S. (1999). Heart-rate recovery immediately after exercise as a predictor of mortality. *New England Journal of Medicine, 341*(18), 1351–1357. doi:10.1056/NEJM199910283411804

Cole, J., Costafreda, S. G., McGuffin, P., & Fu, C. H. (2011). Hippocampal atrophy in first episode depression: a meta-analysis of magnetic resonance imaging studies. *Journal of Affective Disorders, 134*(1–3), 483–487. doi:10.1016/j.jad.2011.05.057

Cole, S. W., Levine, M. E., Arevalo, J. M., Ma, J., Weir, D. R., & Crimmins, E. M. (2015). Loneliness, eudaimonia, and the human conserved transcriptional response to adversity. *Psychoneuroendocrinology, 62*, 11–17. doi:10.1016/j.psyneuen.2015.07.001

Creswell, J. D. (2017). Mindfulness interventions. *Annual Review of Psychology, 68*, 491–516. doi:10.1146/annurev-psych-042716-051139

Davidson, R. J., & Dahl, C. J. (2018). Outstanding challenges in scientific research on mindfulness and meditation. *Perspectives on Psychological Science, 13*(1), 62–65. doi:10.1177/1745691617718358

Dhabhar, F. S., & McEwen, B. S. (1997). Acute stress enhances while chronic stress suppresses cell-mediated immunity in vivo: a potential role for leukocyte trafficking. *Brain, Behavior, and Immunity, 11*(4), 286–306. doi:10.1006/brbi.1997.0508

Ditzen, B., Germann, J., Meuwly, N., Bradbury, T. N., Bodenmann, G., & Heinrichs, M. (2019). Intimacy as related to cortisol reactivity and recovery in couples undergoing psychosocial stress. *Psychosomatic Medicine, 81*(1), 16–25. doi:10.1097/PSY.0000000000000633

Doidge, N. (2015). *The Brain's Way of Healing*. Viking.

Epel, E. S., Crosswell, A. D., Mayer, S. E., Prather, A. A., Slavich, G. M., Puterman, E., & Mendes, W. B. (2018). More than a feeling: a unified view of stress measurement for population science. *Frontiers in Neuroendocrinology, 49*, 146–169. doi:10.1016/j.yfrne.2018.03.001

Epel, E. S., & Prather, A. A. (2018). Stress, telomeres, and psychopathology: toward a deeper understanding of a triad of early aging. *Annual Review of Clinical Psychology, 14*, 371–397. doi:10.1146/annurev-clinpsy-032816-045054

Eriksson, J. G. (2005). The fetal origins hypothesis – 10 years on. *BMJ, 330*(7500), 1096–1097. doi:10.1136/bmj.330.7500.1096

Espay, A. J., Ries, S., Maloney, T., Vannest, J., Neefus, E., Dwivedi, A. K., … Szaflarski, J. P. (2019). Clinical and neural responses to cognitive behavioral therapy for functional tremor. *Neurology, 93*(19), e1787–e1798. doi:10.1212/WNL.0000000000008442

Freedland, K. E. (2019). The Behavioral Medicine Research Council: its origins, mission, and methods. *Health Psychology, 38*(4), 277–289. doi:10.1037/hea0000731

Fricchione, G., Ivkovic, A., & Yeung, A. S. (2016). *The Science of Stress: Living under Pressure*. University of Chicago Press.

Galatzer-Levy, I. R., & Bonanno, G. A. (2014). Optimism and death: predicting the course and consequences of depression trajectories in response to heart attack. *Psychological Science, 25*(12), 2177–2188. doi:10.1177/0956797614551750

Gawande, A. (2017). The heroism of incremental care. *The New Yorker*, January 23.

Giuse, N. B., Koonce, T. Y., Kusnoor, S. V., Prather, A. A., Gottlieb, L. M., Huang, L. C., … Stead, W. W. (2017). Institute of Medicine measures of social and behavioral determinants of health: a feasibility study. *American Journal of Preventive Medicine, 52*(2), 199–206. doi:10.1016/j.amepre.2016.07.033

Goff, D. C., Jr., Lloyd-Jones, D. M., Bennett, G., Coady, S., D'Agostino, R. B., Gibbons, R., … American College of Cardiology/American Heart Association Task Force on Practice (2014). 2013 ACC/AHA

guideline on the assessment of cardiovascular risk: a report of the American College of Cardiology/American Heart Association Task Force on Practice Guidelines. *Circulation, 129*(25 Suppl 2), S49–S73. doi:10.1161/01.cir.0000437741.48606.98

Hajat, C., & Stein, E. (2018). The global burden of multiple chronic conditions: a narrative review. *Preventive Medicine Reports, 12,* 284–293. doi:10.1016/j.pmedr.2018.10.008

Hamilton, J. P., Siemer, M., & Gotlib, I. H. (2008). Amygdala volume in major depressive disorder: a meta-analysis of magnetic resonance imaging studies. *Molecular Psychiatry, 13*(11), 993–1000. doi:10.1038/mp.2008.57

Hanson, J. L., Chandra, A., Wolfe, B. L., & Pollak, S. D. (2011). Association between income and the hippocampus. *PLoS One, 6*(5), e18712. doi:10.1371/journal.pone.0018712

Harris, N. B. (2018). *The Deepest Well: Healing the Long-Term Effects of Childhood Adversity.* Houghton Mifflin Harcourt.

Harvanek, Z. M., Fogelman, N., Xu, K., & Sinha, R. (2021). Psychological and biological resilience modulates the effects of stress on epigenetic aging. *Translational Psychiatry, 11*(1), 601. doi:10.1038/s41398-021-01735-7

Holt-Lunstad, J., Smith, T. B., Baker, M., Harris, T., & Stephenson, D. (2015). Loneliness and social isolation as risk factors for mortality: a meta-analytic review. *Perspectives on Psychological Science, 10*(2), 227–237. doi:10.1177/1745691614568352

John-Henderson, N. A., Kamarck, T. W., Muldoon, M. F., & Manuck, S. B. (2016). Early life family conflict, social interactions, and carotid artery intima-media thickness in adulthood. *Psychosomatic Medicine, 78*(3), 319–326. doi:10.1097/PSY.0000000000000259

Kagan, J. (2016). An overly permissive extension. *Perspectives on Psychological Science, 11*(4), 442–450. doi:10.1177/1745691616635593

Kamarck, T. W., Shiffman, S., Sutton-Tyrrell, K., Muldoon, M. F., & Tepper, P. (2012). Daily psychological demands are associated with 6-year progression of carotid artery atherosclerosis: the Pittsburgh Healthy Heart Project. *Psychosomatic Medicine, 74*(4), 432–439. doi:10.1097/PSY.0b013e3182572599

Katon, W. J., Lin, E. H., Von Korff, M., Ciechanowski, P., Ludman, E. J., Young, B., ... McCulloch, D. (2010). Collaborative care for patients

with depression and chronic illnesses. *New England Journal of Medicine, 363*(27), 2611–2620. doi:10.1056/NEJMoa1003955

Katon, W., Russo, J., Lin, E. H., Schmittdiel, J., Ciechanowski, P., Ludman, E., ... Von Korff, M. (2012). Cost-effectiveness of a multi-condition collaborative care intervention: a randomized controlled trial. *Archives of General Psychiatry, 69*(5), 506–514. doi:10.1001/archgenpsychiatry.2011.1548

Katon, W., Unutzer, J., Wells, K., & Jones, L. (2010). Collaborative depression care: history, evolution and ways to enhance dissemination and sustainability. *General Hospital Psychiatry, 32*(5), 456–464. doi:10.1016/j.genhosppsych.2010.04.001

Kendler, K. S., Thornton, L. M., & Gardner, C. O. (2000). Stressful life events and previous episodes in the etiology of major depression in women: an evaluation of the "kindling" hypothesis. *American Journal of Psychiatry, 157*, 1243–1251. doi:10.1176/appi.ajp.157.8.1243

Kiecolt-Glaser, J. K. (1999). Norman Cousins Memorial Lecture 1998. Stress, personal relationships, and immune function: health implications. *Brain, Behavior, and Immunity, 13*(1), 61–72. doi:10.1006/brbi.1999.0552

Knight, J. M., Kerswill, S. A., Hari, P., Cole, S. W., Logan, B. R., D'Souza, A., ... Rizzo, J. D. (2018). Repurposing existing medications as cancer therapy: design and feasibility of a randomized pilot investigating propranolol administration in patients receiving hematopoietic cell transplantation. *BMC Cancer, 18*(1), 593. doi:10.1186/s12885-018-4509-0

Knight, J. M., Rizzo, J. D., Logan, B. R., Wang, T., Arevalo, J. M., Ma, J., & Cole, S. W. (2016). Low socioeconomic status, adverse gene expression profiles, and clinical outcomes in hematopoietic stem cell transplant recipients. *Clinical Cancer Research, 22*(1), 69–78. doi:10.1158/1078-0432.CCR-15-1344

Koolhaas, J. M., Bartolomucci, A., Buwalda, B., de Boer, S. F., Flugge, G., Korte, S. M., ... Fuchs, E. (2011). Stress revisited: a critical evaluation of the stress concept. *Neuroscience and Biobehavioral Reviews, 35*(5), 1291–1301. doi:10.1016/j.neubiorev.2011.02.003

Kubzansky, L. D., Huffman, J. C., Boehm, J. K., Hernandez, R., Kim, E. S., Koga, H. K., ... Labarthe, D. R. (2018). Positive psychological well-being and cardiovascular disease: JACC Health Promotion

Series. *Journal of the American College of Cardiology, 72*(12), 1382–1396. doi:10.1016/j.jacc.2018.07.042

LaFrance, W. C., Jr., Miller, I. W., Ryan, C. E., Blum, A. S., Solomon, D. A., Kelley, J. E., & Keitner, G. I. (2009). Cognitive behavioral therapy for psychogenic nonepileptic seizures. *Epilepsy & Behavior, 14*(4), 591–596. doi:10.1016/j.yebeh.2009.02.016

Lazarus, R. S. (1984). *Stress, Appraisal, and Coping.* Springer.

Levine, M. E., & Crimmins, E. M. (2014). A comparison of methods for assessing mortality risk. *American Journal of Human Biology, 26*(6), 768–776. doi:10.1002/ajhb.22595

Lewis, T. T., & Van Dyke, M. E. (2018). Discrimination and the health of African Americans: the potential importance of intersectionalities. *Current Directions in Psychological Science, 27*(3), 176–182. doi:10.1177/0963721418770442

Lichtman, J. H., Bigger, J. T., Jr., Blumenthal, J. A., Frasure-Smith, N., Kaufmann, P. G., Lesperance, F., ... American Psychiatric Association (2008). Depression and coronary heart disease: recommendations for screening, referral, and treatment: a science advisory from the American Heart Association Prevention Committee of the Council on Cardiovascular Nursing, Council on Clinical Cardiology, Council on Epidemiology and Prevention, and Interdisciplinary Council on Quality of Care and Outcomes Research: endorsed by the American Psychiatric Association. *Circulation, 118*(17), 1768–1775. doi:10.1161/CIRCULATIONAHA.108.190769

Lichtman, J. H., Froelicher, E. S., Blumenthal, J. A., Carney, R. M., Doering, L. V., Frasure-Smith, N., ... American Heart Association Statistics Committee of the Council on Epidemiology and Prevention and the Council on Cardiovascular and Stroke Nursing (2014). Depression as a risk factor for poor prognosis among patients with acute coronary syndrome: systematic review and recommendations: a scientific statement from the American Heart Association. *Circulation, 129*(12), 1350–1369. doi:10.1161/CIR.0000000000000019

Liu, S. S., & Ziegelstein, R. C. (2010). Depression in patients with heart disease: the case for more trials. *Future Cardiology, 6*(4), 547–556. doi:10.2217/fca.10.18

Loucks, E. B., Schuman-Olivier, Z., Britton, W. B., Fresco, D. M., Desbordes, G., Brewer, J. A., & Fulwiler, C. (2015). Mindfulness and cardiovascular disease risk: state of the evidence, plausible

mechanisms, and theoretical framework. *Current Cardiology Reports, 17*(12), 112. doi:10.1007/s11886-015-0668-7

Madhu, S. V., Aslam, M., Siddiqui, A. A., Goyal, S., & Mishra, B. K. (2020). Association of copeptin with sense of coherence in individuals with varying degrees of glucose intolerance. *Psychosomatic Medicine, 82*(2), 181–186. doi:10.1097/PSY.0000000000000768

Marmot, M. (2015). *The Health Gap.* Bloomsbury.

Mauss, D., Jarczok, M. N., & Fischer, J. E. (2015). A streamlined approach for assessing the Allostatic Load Index in industrial employees. *Stress, 18*(4), 475–483. doi:10.3109/10253890.2015.1040987

Mauss, D., Li, J., Schmidt, B., Angerer, P., & Jarczok, M. N. (2015). Measuring allostatic load in the workforce: a systematic review. *Industrial Health, 53*(1), 5–20. doi:10.2486/indhealth.2014-0122

McCraty, R. (2017). New frontiers in heart rate variability and social coherence research: techniques, technologies, and implications for improving group dynamics and outcomes. *Frontiers in Public Health, 5,* article 267. doi:10.3389/fpubh.2017.00267

McEwen, B. S. (1998). Stress, adaptation, and disease. Allostasis and allostatic load. *Annals of the New York Academy of Sciences, 840,* 33–44. www.ncbi.nlm.nih.gov/pubmed/9629234

(2017a). Allostasis and the epigenetics of brain and body health over the life course: the brain on stress. *JAMA Psychiatry, 74*(6), 551–552. doi:10.1001/jamapsychiatry.2017.0270

(2017b). Neurobiological and systemic effects of chronic stress. *Chronic Stress (Thousand Oaks), 1.* doi:10.1177/2470547017692328

McEwen, B. S., Biron, C. A., Brunson, K. W., Bulloch, K., Chambers, W. H., Dhabhar, F. S., ... Weiss, J. M. (1997). The role of adrenocorticoids as modulators of immune function in health and disease: neural, endocrine and immune interactions. *Brain Research. Brain Research Reviews, 23*(1–2), 79–133. www.ncbi.nlm.nih.gov/pubmed/9063588

Messer, K., Trinidad, D. R., Al-Delaimy, W. K., & Pierce, J. P. (2008). Smoking cessation rates in the United States: a comparison of young adult and older smokers. *American Journal of Public Health, 98*(2), 317–322. doi:10.2105/AJPH.2007.112060

Miller, G. E., Brody, G. H., Yu, T., & Chen, E. (2014). A family-oriented psychosocial intervention reduces inflammation in low-SES African

American youth. *Proceedings of the National Academy of Sciences of the United States of America, 111*(31), 11287–11292. doi:10.1073/pnas.1406578111

Miller, G. E., Cohen, S., & Herbert, T. (1999). Pathways linking major depression and immunity in ambulatory female patients. *Psychosomatic Medicine, 61*, 850–860.

Monroe, S. M. (2008). Modern approaches to conceptualizing and measuring human life stress. *Annual Review of Clinical Psychology, 4*, 33–52. doi:10.1146/annurev.clinpsy.4.022007.141207

Murthy, V. (2017). Work and the loneliness epidemic: reducing isolation at work is good for business. *Harvard Business Review*, September 26.

Nestler, E. J. (2011). Hidden switches in the mind. *Scientific American, 305*(6), 76–83. www.ncbi.nlm.nih.gov/pubmed/22214133

Noble, B., Clark, D., Meldrum, M., ten Have, H., Seymour, J., Winslow, M., & Paz, S. (2005). The measurement of pain, 1945–2000. *Journal of Pain and Symptom Management, 29*(1), 14–21. doi:10.1016/j.jpainsymman.2004.08.007

Norona-Zhou, A. N., Coccia, M., Epel, E., Vieten, C., Adler, N. E., Laraia, B., ... Bush, N. R. (2022). The effects of a prenatal mindfulness intervention on infant autonomic and behavioral reactivity and regulation. *Psychosomatic Medicine, 84*(5), 525–535. doi:10.1097/PSY.0000000000001066

Oken, B. S., Chamine, I., & Wakeland, W. (2015). A systems approach to stress, stressors and resilience in humans. *Behavioural Brain Research, 282*, 144–154. doi:10.1016/j.bbr.2014.12.047

Okutucu, S., Karakulak, U. N., Aytemir, K., & Oto, A. (2011). Heart rate recovery: a practical clinical indicator of abnormal cardiac autonomic function. *Expert Review of Cardiovascular Therapy, 9*(11), 1417–1430. doi:10.1586/erc.11.149

Olfson, M., Gerhard, T., Huang, C., Crystal, S., & Stroup, T. S. (2015). Premature mortality among adults with schizophrenia in the United States. *JAMA Psychiatry, 72*(12), 1172–1181. doi:10.1001/jamapsychiatry.2015.1737

Ornish, D. (2002). Dean Ornish, MD: a conversation with the editor. Interview by William Clifford Roberts, MD. *American Journal of Cardiology, 90*(3), 271–298. www.ncbi.nlm.nih.gov/pubmed/12127615

Ornish, D., Scherwitz, L. W., Doody, R. S., Kesten, D., McLanahan, S. M., Brown, S. E., ... Gotto, A. M., Jr. (1983). Effects of stress management training and dietary changes in treating ischemic heart disease. *JAMA, 249*(1), 54–59. www.ncbi.nlm.nih.gov/pubmed/6336794

Peng, H., Zhu, Y., Strachan, E., Fowler, E., Bacus, T., Roy-Byrne, P., ... Zhao, J. (2018). Childhood trauma, DNA methylation of stress-related genes, and depression: findings from two monozygotic twin studies. *Psychosomatic Medicine, 80*(7), 599–608. doi:10.1097/PSY.0000000000000604

Penninx, B. W. (2017). Depression and cardiovascular disease: epidemiological evidence on their linking mechanisms. *Neuroscience and Biobehavioral Reviews, 74*(Pt B), 277–286. doi:10.1016/j.neubiorev.2016.07.003

Pinker, S. (2018). *Enlightenment Now: The Case for Reason, Science, Humanism, and Progress.* Allen Lane.

Porges, S. W. (2011). *The Polyvagal Theory.* W. W. Norton.

Rifkin, J. (2009). *The Empathic Civilization: The Race to Global Consciousness in a World in Crisis.* Tarcher/Penguin.

Ripoll Gallardo, A., Pacelli, B., Alesina, M., Serrone, D., Iacutone, G., Faggiano, F., ... Allara, E. (2018). Medium- and long-term health effects of earthquakes in high-income countries: a systematic review and meta-analysis. *International Journal of Epidemiology, 47*(4), 1317–1332. doi:10.1093/ije/dyy130

Rossom, R. C., Solberg, L. I., Magnan, S., Crain, A. L., Beck, A., Coleman, K. J., ... Unutzer, J. (2017). Impact of a national collaborative care initiative for patients with depression and diabetes or cardiovascular disease. *General Hospital Psychiatry, 44*, 77–85. doi:10.1016/j.genhosppsych.2016.05.006

Rutters, F., Pilz, S., Koopman, A. D., Rauh, S. P., Te Velde, S. J., Stehouwer, C. D., ... Dekker, J. M. (2014). The association between psychosocial stress and mortality is mediated by lifestyle and chronic diseases: the Hoorn Study. *Social Science and Medicine, 118*, 166–172. doi:10.1016/j.socscimed.2014.08.009

Sapolsky, R. (2004). *Why Zebras Don't Get Ulcers.* Holt Paperbacks.

Sarabia-Cobo, C. M. (2015). Heart coherence: a new tool in the management of stress on professionals and family caregivers of patients with dementia. *Applied Psychophysiology and Biofeedback, 40*(2), 75–83. doi:10.1007/s10484-015-9276-y

Schroder, A., Rehfeld, E., Ornbol, E., Sharpe, M., Licht, R. W., & Fink, P. (2012). Cognitive-behavioural group treatment for a range of functional somatic syndromes: randomised trial. *British Journal of Psychiatry, 200*(6), 499–507. doi:bjp.bp.111.098681 [pii] 10.1192/bjp.bp.111.098681

Schroder, A., Sharpe, M., & Fink, P. (2015). Medically unexplained symptom management. *Lancet Psychiatry, 2*(7), 587–588. doi:10.1016/S2215-0366(15)00233-3

Seeman, T. E., Singer, B. H., Rowe, J. W., Horwitz, R. I., & McEwen, B. S. (1997). Price of adaptation–allostatic load and its health consequences. MacArthur studies of successful aging. *Archives of Internal Medicine, 157*(19), 2259–2268. www.ncbi.nlm.nih.gov/pubmed/9343003

Seligman, M. (2006). *Learned Optimism: How to Change Your Mind and Your Life.* Vintage Books.

Selye, H. (1956). *The Stress of Life.* McGraw-Hill.

Sgoifo, A., Montano, N., Esler, M., & Vaccarino, V. (2017). Stress, behavior and the heart. *Neuroscience and Biobehavioral Reviews, 74*(Pt B), 257–259. doi:10.1016/j.neubiorev.2016.11.003

Shern, D. L., Blanch, A. K., & Steverman, S. M. (2016). Toxic stress, behavioral health, and the next major era in public health. *American Journal of Orthopsychiatry, 86*(2), 109–123. doi:10.1037/ort0000120

Silberman, A., Banthia, R., Estay, I. S., Kemp, C., Studley, J., Hareras, D., & Ornish, D. (2010). The effectiveness and efficacy of an intensive cardiac rehabilitation program in 24 sites. *American Journal of Health Promotion, 24*(4), 260–266. doi:10.4278/ajhp.24.4.arb

Slavich, G. M., & Shields, G. S. (2018). Assessing lifetime stress exposure using the Stress and Adversity Inventory for Adults (Adult STRAIN): an overview and initial validation. *Psychosomatic Medicine, 80*(1), 17–27. doi:10.1097/PSY.0000000000000534

Smith, B. W., Epstein, E. M., Ortiz, J. A., Christopher, P. J., & Tooley, E.M. (2013). The foundations of resilience: what are the critical resources for bouncing back from stress? In S. Prince-Embury & D. Saklofske (eds.), *Resilience in Children, Adolescents, and Adults.* The Springer Series on Human Exceptionality. Springer. doi:10.1007/978-1-4614-4939-3_13

Smith, T. W. (2019). Relationships matter: progress and challenges in research on the health effects of intimate relationships. *Psychosomatic Medicine, 81*(1), 2–6. doi:10.1097/PSY.0000000000000660

Stankiewicz, A. M., Swiergiel, A. H., & Lisowski, P. (2013). Epigenetics of stress adaptations in the brain. *Brain Research Bulletin*, *98*, 76–92. doi:10.1016/j.brainresbull.2013.07.003

Starr, P. (2013). *Remedy and Reaction: The Peculiar American Struggle over Health Care Reform*. Yale University Press.

Stetka, B. (2017). Where's the proof that mindfulness meditation works? *Scientific American*, October 11.

Suls, J., Green, P. A., & Davidson, K. W. (2016). A biobehavioral framework to address the emerging challenge of multimorbidity. *Psychosomatic Medicine*, *78*(3), 281–289. doi:10.1097/PSY.00000000 00000294

Tawakol, A., Ishai, A., Takx, R. A., Figueroa, A. L., Ali, A., Kaiser, Y., ... Pitman, R. K. (2017). Relation between resting amygdalar activity and cardiovascular events: a longitudinal and cohort study. *Lancet*, *389*(10071), 834–845. doi:10.1016/S0140-6736(16)31714-7

Tracey, K. J. (2015). Shock medicine. *Scientific American*, *312*(3), 28–35.

Tyler, M. E., Kaczmarek, K. A., Rust, K. L., Subbotin, A. M., Skinner, K. L., & Danilov, Y. P. (2014). Non-invasive neuromodulation to improve gait in chronic multiple sclerosis: a randomized double blind controlled pilot trial. *Journal of Neuroengineering and Rehabilitation*, *11*, 79. doi:10.1186/1743-0003-11-79

Tyrka, A. R., Price, L. H., Kao, H. T., Porton, B., Marsella, S. A., & Carpenter, L. L. (2010). Childhood maltreatment and telomere shortening: preliminary support for an effect of early stress on cellular aging. *Biological Psychiatry*, *67*(6), 531–534. doi:10.1016/j.biopsych.2009.08.014

Vaccarino, V., Almuwaqqat, Z., Kim, J. H., Hammadah, M., Shah, A. J., Ko, Y. A., ... Quyyumi, A. A. (2021). Association of mental stress-induced myocardial ischemia with cardiovascular events in patients with coronary heart disease. *JAMA*, *326*(18), 1818–1828. doi:10.1001/jama.2021.17649

Vaccarino, V., & Bremner, J. D. (2017). Behavioral, emotional and neurobiological determinants of coronary heart disease risk in women. *Neuroscience and Biobehavioral Reviews*, *74*(Pt B), 297–309. doi:10.1016/j.neubiorev.2016.04.023

Vaccarino, V., Sullivan, S., Hammadah, M., Wilmot, K., Al Mheid, I., Ramadan, R., ... Raggi, P. (2018). Mental stress-induced-myocardial ischemia in young patients with recent myocardial infarction:

sex differences and mechanisms. *Circulation, 137*(8), 794–805. doi:10.1161/CIRCULATIONAHA.117.030849

Van Dam, N. T., van Vugt, M. K., Vago, D. R., Schmalzl, L., Saron, C. D., Olendzki, A., ... Meyer, D. E. (2018). Mind the hype: a critical evaluation and prescriptive agenda for research on mindfulness and meditation. *Perspectives on Psychological Science, 13*(1), 36–61. doi:10.1177/1745691617709589

van der Kolk, B. (2014). *The Body Keeps the Score: Brain, Mind, and Body in the Healing of Trauma*. Penguin.

Vlek, C. (2018). Induced earthquakes from long-term gas extraction in Groningen, the Netherlands: statistical analysis and prognosis for acceptable-risk regulation. *Risk Analysis, 38*(7), 1455–1473. doi:10.1111/risa.12967

Walker, E. R., McGee, R. E., & Druss, B. G. (2015). Mortality in mental disorders and global disease burden implications: a systematic review and meta-analysis. *JAMA Psychiatry, 72*(4), 334–341. doi:10.1001/jamapsychiatry.2014.2502

Wang, Z., Hui, Q., Goldberg, J., Smith, N., Kaseer, B., Murrah, N., ... Sun, Y. V. (2022). Association between posttraumatic stress disorder and epigenetic age acceleration in a sample of twins. *Psychosomatic Medicine, 84*(2), 151–158. doi:10.1097/PSY.0000000000001028

Woolf, S. H., & Schoomaker, H. (2019). Life expectancy and mortality rates in the United States, 1959–2017. *JAMA, 322*(20), 1996–2016. doi:10.1001/jama.2019.16932

Wulsin, L., Herman, J., & Thayer, J. F. (2018). Stress, autonomic imbalance, and the prediction of metabolic risk: a model and a proposal for research. *Neuroscience and Biobehavioral Reviews, 86*, 12–20. doi:10.1016/j.neubiorev.2017.12.010

Wulsin, L. R., Sagui-Henson, S. J., Roos, L. G., Wang, D., Jenkins, B., Cohen, B. E., ... Slavich, G. M. (2022). Stress measurement in primary care: conceptual issues, barriers, resources, and recommendations for study. *Psychosomatic Medicine, 84*(3), 267–275. doi:10.1097/PSY.0000000000001051

Wulsin, L., Vaillant, G., & Wells, V. (1999). A systematic review of the mortality of depression. *Psychosomatic Medicine, 61*, 6–17.

Zannas, A. S., & Chrousos, G. P. (2017). Epigenetic programming by stress and glucocorticoids along the human lifespan. *Molecular Psychiatry, 22*(5), 640–646. doi:10.1038/mp.2017.35

Index

About the Author

Lawson Wulsin, MD, is professor emeritus in the Department of Psychiatry and Behavioral Neuroscience and in the Department of Family and Community Medicine at the University of Cincinnati, where he has worked most of his career, with brief intervals as visiting professor at the University of Nairobi (1995–1996) and the visiting scholar at the National Heart, Lung, and Blood Institute (2003–2004). He served as director of the Primary Care Mental Health Integration Program at the Cincinnati VA Medical Center (2007–17).

His subspecialty is psychosomatic medicine, and his research and teaching have focused on the relationship between depression and heart disease and the process of how stress contributes to physical illnesses.

He is the author of *Treating the Aching Heart: A Guide to Depression, Stress, and Heart Disease* (Vanderbilt University Press, 2007), numerous scientific publications, and, since 2013, a series of essays posted as blogs under the banners "You're on My Mind" and "Deep Dives: Pearls from the Stress Response System" (www .lawsonwulsin.com).

He is the founder in 1995 and former program director of the University of Cincinnati's Family Medicine Psychiatry Residency Program, which trains physicians to be board certified in both disciplines. He is a member and past president of the Association of Medicine and Psychiatry, and he has served in leadership roles in the Academy of Consultation Liaison Psychiatry, the American Psychosomatic Society, and the American Psychiatric Association.

He served on the American Psychiatric Association's DSM5 Task Force.

From 2006 to 2007, he was the contributor to a weekly column, "Mind Matters," in *The Cincinnati Enquirer*. He has participated in TV, radio, and journalism interviews with local and national newscasters, concerning depression, panic disorder, and depression's links to heart disease.

He is the father of four sons and lives in Cincinnati with his wife, Victoria Wells Wulsin, MD, DrPH, who is professor in the Department of Family and Community Medicine and in the Department of Environmental and Public Health Sciences, University of Cincinnati.